HARDY

Novelist and Poet

BY THE SAME AUTHOR

Hawk among the Sparrows
Avalon and Sedgemoor: a portrait of lowland Somerset

Edited and introduced by Desmond Hawkins

Stories, Essays and Poems of D. H. Lawrence
Poetry and Prose of John Donne
The BBC Naturalist Books I and II

HARDY

Novelist and Poet

Desmond Hawkins

'Nay, from the highest point of view, to precisely describe a human being, the focus of a universe, how impossible!'

The Woodlanders

DAVID & CHARLES NEWTON ABBOT LONDON
VANCOUVER
BARNES & NOBLE BOOKS NEW YORK
(a division of Harper & Row Publishers, Inc)

To the Vice-Chancellor and Senate of Bristol University—recalling that just half a century has passed since the university conferred an honorary doctorate on the subject of this book.

ISBN 0 7153 7113 4 (Great Britain)
ISBN 0–06–492752–0 (United States)

This edition first published in 1976
in Great Britain by
David & Charles (Publishers) Limited
Newton Abbot Devon

Published in Canada by
Douglas David & Charles Limited
1875 Welch Street North Vancouver BC

First published in the USA by
Harper & Row Publishers Inc
Barnes & Noble Import Division

Printed in Great Britain by
Latimer Trend & Company Ltd Plymouth

Contents

Illustrations

Foreword

Since the writing of books about Thomas Hardy has become a growth industry, I ought perhaps to justify this addition to the mounting pile. With recycling so much in fashion I could plead that I am now merely replacing an earlier book of mine on Hardy's novels, which would otherwise have been reprinted. This is comforting in terms of the actual felling of trees, wastage of ink and so on, but it puts the matter in rather humbler terms than I intend. I have tried on this occasion to do something more: to bring within a critical and interpretative framework the whole of Hardy's formidable creation in prose and verse, and to associate with it as much biographical and historical material as the reader may need to give depth and context to what I hope will be a comprehensive appraisal.

There are many ways of writing about Hardy and many angles from which an interesting light can be thrown on his work. To the reader who may have his own strongly held preference I should declare at once that I am, by trade and instinct, a literary critic—and not a social historian, a rural economist, a theologian, a political activist or a pedlar of philosophical systems. My aim is therefore to keep the reader as close as possible to Hardy's words; and to examine those words critically as part of the fabric of a literature which belongs inextricably to a particular time and a particular place, and helps to define that time and that place, but which also transcends time and place in the way that poets have the power to do.

In examining a work of such voluminous bulk as Hardy's one must accept that few readers will have a compendious and recent familiarity with the entire subject-matter. It may be reasonable to assume that many who glance over this page will have read one or two of Hardy's novels and some of his poems; but which ones? For each individual the answer is different. I have therefore shaped my commentaries on the novels in such a way that they include enough information about plot and character to be intelligible to those who do not have these basic facts at their fingertips. For those who like additionally to have a brief synopsis and note of the principal characters separately available, an appendix is provided.

Anyone writing about Hardy today must acknowledge how gratefully he climbs on the backs of those scholars whose patient research and critical acumen have accumulated the body of knowledge we now have. I feel a particular debt to Professor Richard L. Purdy whose *Thomas Hardy, a bibliographical study*—so much more than one expects a bibliography to be—has corrected many false notions and set the record straight in innumerable details; his friendly counsel, in conversation and correspondence, is the most welcome of gifts. The debt to American scholarship is indeed considerable: Carl Weber, J. O. Bailey and Harold Orel stand out among those whose publications are indispensable for any serious student of Hardy. The naming of names is always invidious on such occasions but I cannot omit their English counterparts—Frank Pinion, whose *Hardy Companion* is an essential book of reference, and Robert Gittings whose searching exploration of Hardy's early years has helped me to solve some at least of those problems and mysteries that are inseparable from the subject. To them, and to those others whose insights into Hardy's work are reflected in my bibliography, I express my deep gratitude. If I appear to be wearing a garment that they helped to weave they will recognise, I hope, that I do so with a proper modesty.

There is, to change the metaphor, one other well into which we all lower our buckets. Originally published in two individually titled volumes, it is now usually referred to in its single-volume form as *The Life of Thomas Hardy*. Ostensibly the authoress is Hardy's second wife (and widow) Florence Emily Hardy, but it is generally recognised that—apart from the closing chapters—the book was written by Hardy himself and is to be regarded as an autobiography couched in the third person. As such it must be considered capricious, unreliable, at times intentionally misleading, occasionally smug, but in its whole effect a totally fascinating medley of events, asides, ruminations, personalities, 'shop' talk and copious quotations from the notebooks and journals that Hardy kept over so many years. It was prepared in readiness for publication immediately after his death, probably with the intention of discouraging other would-be biographers. I shall refer to it hereafter simply as *The Life*. In the same way I propose to abbreviate some other familiar and frequently cited titles, referring to *Tess*, *Jude* etc for *Tess of the d'Urbervilles*, *Jude the Obscure* etc, though only after giving the title in full initially.

For the freedom to draw on Hardy's published works, by way of illustration and example, I am indebted to the Trustees of the Hardy Estate and Macmillan, London & Basingstoke; for the opportunity to study some of Hardy's correspondence and Emma Hardy's notebooks, and to quote from them, I am indebted to the Trustees of the Thomas Hardy Memorial Collection and to Roger Peers, the Curator of the Dorset County Museum at Dorchester—to whom also I must express my gratitude for help in selecting material for the illustrations, and specifically to the Trustees for permission to reproduce plates 1, 3a, 4a, 4b, 5a, 7a, 7b and 8a. For the other illustrations I offer my grateful acknowledgements to the Royal Opera House Archive, Covent Garden, for plate 2a; to the Dorset County Library for plate 3b; to my friend, John Arlott, for entrusting to me his signed photo of Hardy, plate 5b; and to the *Dorset Evening Echo* for plate 2b.

I also wish to thank Mr Leo d'Erlanger and the archivist of the Royal Opera House, Covent Garden, for information about the

Tess opera and Hardy's early association with the opera house; Mrs Elsa Stannard for bringing to my attention a letter of Hardy's to R. D. Blackmore; Mr M. V. Carey and Mrs Pleydell-Railston for information about Agnes Grove; Mr James Gibson for textual advice; and, as always, the infinitely helpful librarians whose ungrudging assistance and genuine interest are one of the pleasures of an author's life. In this particular instance I think gratefully of the Dorset County Library Service in its various branches and of the library of Southampton University. And for assistance of another kind I express my thanks to Teresa Donovan, who has turned my various handwritten drafts into a coherent typescript.

In conclusion I should mention that some parts of this book have appeared in *The Contemporary Review*, The BBC Third Programme, *The Dorset Evening Echo* and the Thomas Hardy Society Symposium, *Thomas Hardy and the Modern World*. To those concerned I offer the customary acknowledgement.

I

Early Years

The truly great stand upon no middle ledge; they are either famous or unknown

(*Desperate Remedies*)

On 14 July 1909, Thomas Hardy and his first wife, Emma, attended the Royal Opera House, Covent Garden, for the English *première* of *Tess*, an operatic version of Hardy's novel by Frédéric d'Erlanger. For Emmy Destinn, who was to sing the title role created by Rina Giachetti in Naples three years earlier, it was a return to Covent Garden: in 1905 she had introduced *Madame Butterfly* to England. For Hardy, though he had had no hand in the libretto, it was an occasion when the outward and visible signs of the fame that had come to him were displayed with impressive public emphasis. Queen Alexandra was in the royal box and the occasion was clearly one of the main events of the London season. The opera was acclaimed as a success. Further performances were given the following year—the year of Hardy's seventieth birthday and his receipt of the Order of Merit. His place among the foremost writers of his day was proclaimed unequivocally.

For a man as affected as Hardy was by the 'ghosts' of earlier days and the ironies of reminiscence, that glittering evening at Covent Garden must surely have prompted thoughts of an earlier theatrical occasion in which he played some part. On that same stage where Destinn sang *Tess*, Hardy had many years before appeared in person—in a pantomime. The time was December 1866, the piece was *Ali Baba and the Forty*

Thieves, and Hardy's contribution to its success had been limited to a walk-on part as a 'nondescript'—the fortieth thief perhaps.

He was at that time a rather lonely young architectural assistant of twenty-seven, living in digs in London and nurturing literary ambitions which were becoming blighted by a total absence of success or encouragement. His poems had gained him nothing but rejection slips. Baulked in that direction his thoughts turned to playwriting—stimulated no doubt by his theatregoing during the five years he had spent in London. Phelps's Shakespearean productions at Drury Lane particularly appealed to him: he attended every one, with the text open in front of him.

Realising that the theatre demanded specialised literary techniques, Hardy looked for an opportunity to acquire practical experience. Through his architectural work he had come to know a blacksmith who made not only the ecclesiastical ironwork in which Hardy was professionally interested but also the trapdoors for the stage at Covent Garden. It was thanks to the good offices of this craftsman that Hardy was able to mingle with the actors in the pantomime and get the feel of a professional production. No longer pinning his hopes on his ability to rival Browning and Swinburne, Hardy now looked to the theatre as the setting in which fame and fortune would be his.

In the recounting of a period of his life from which so little reliable information has become available, it is undeniably comforting to handle the programme of that 'New Grand Comic Christmas Pantomime' which Gilbert à Beckett had written and for which 'The Machinery' was provided by Mr Sloman who, in Hardy's words, 'made crucifixes and harlequin-traps with equal imperturbability'. The programme itself was perfumed by Rimmel's, whose 'newly invented Arabian perfume' was introduced in the Cavern scene. This was only one of several commercial 'plugs' in true pantomime style: in the final harlequinade a University Boat Race scene brought on the young men, including Hardy presumably, in the 'New Fashions for 1867 by

Samuel Brothers of Ludgate Hill', while they mingled with the ladies of the corps de ballet in a 'grand University Revel'. One way and another, it was quite an evening. It began at seven o'clock with a new comic operetta; at a quarter to eight *Ali Baba* began and continued until past eleven o'clock, terminating with the customary harlequinade. For Hardy it must have been in some ways a startling and liberating experience. It was certainly different from the rural life of his native Dorset.

The kind of play that Hardy was contemplating as the next employment for his hopeful pen had little kinship with the work of Gilbert à Beckett. After two years of reading nothing but poetry Hardy inclined to the idea of a play in blank verse—something which, forty years later, he was to achieve in a sense, if *The Dynasts* can be adequately described as 'a play'. But in these early years in London nothing from Hardy's pen reached the stage and there is no evidence that his experience in *Ali Baba* was put to any use. Nor did he at this time think of trying his hand at novel writing, although his letters to his sister Mary contain recommendations of contemporary novels that she is advised to read. Like many another young provincial, Hardy was stimulated by the wealth of intellectual and aesthetic experience that he found in the capital but was unable to make any personal mark.

Three years after he first came to London Hardy wrote in a note on the occasion of his twenty-fifth birthday: 'Not very cheerful. Feel as if I had lived a long time and done very little.' Two years later, with nothing more to show for his efforts, he returned to Dorset. 'I was a child till I was 16', he wrote many years later, 'a youth till I was 25; a young man till I was 40 or 50.'

At home in Dorset Hardy had a secure and firmly rooted family background. Born on 2 June 1840, at Higher Bockhampton in the parish of Stinsford, near Dorchester, he continued to look on his birthplace as 'home' until he was thirty-four (when he married). His work might lead him to move into lodgings in London or Dorchester or Weymouth, but he always came back to Bockhampton for weekends or holidays or between jobs. It was there he wrote most of his earliest novels; when he came to plan his own permanent home as a married man he chose to be within walking distance of Bockhampton, at Dorchester.

What is now called Hardy's Cottage (owned by the National Trust and open to the public) had been built in 1801 by Hardy's great-grandfather, not for himself but for his son, Thomas—Hardy's grandfather—who died in 1837. In 1840 the cottage was occupied by Hardy's parents, Thomas and Jemima. Here they reared their four children (two girls and two boys) in modest comfort. Although Hardy was to say later that his father 'did not possess the art of enriching himself by business', he was neither a man of straw nor a peasant. By trade a master mason and jobbing builder he owned a dozen cottages, a brickyard, a small freehold farm at Talbothays and some houses adjoining the farm. With his cidermaking and his fiddleplaying he seems to have been a convivial and neighbourly man. There was a tradition of musicmaking in the Hardy family—music for worship and music for dancing. This twin heritage is engrained in Hardy's writing: the country ballads and folk-dance tunes, the hymns and psalms, the haunting patterns and rhythms of the music—in contrasting moods and modes—that accompanied so many youthful hours were a constant source of inspiration to the poet and novelist in later years. Many examples spring to mind: among the poems that lilting ballad that Swinburne admired particularly, *The Dance at the Phoenix*; of the short stories *The Fiddler of the Reels*; among the novels the wild dance in the barn at Chaseborough in *Tess of the d'Urbervilles*, the amiable company of the tranter and his friends in *Under the Greenwood Tree*, and the savagely dramatic use of 'Psalm the Hundred-and-Ninth, to the tune of Wiltshire' by Michael Henchard in *The Mayor of Casterbridge*. Hardy could be describing himself when he writes of Tess:

> that innate love of melody, which she had inherited from her ballad-singing mother, gave the simplest music a power over her which could well-nigh drag her heart out of her bosom.

And Henchard expresses a similar responsiveness when he speaks of the psalm tune 'that would make my blood ebb and flow like the sea'.

Hardy has left an account of his own musicmaking as a boy. He mastered the violin early and by the time he had reached his teens he had skill and assurance enough to play his fiddle at village weddings and farmhouse dances. It was a family rule to accept no payment for these performances, no matter how long they lasted. On one occasion Hardy played second violin to his father's first for six or seven hours at a farmer's house: at three in the morning father and son walked home through a countryside deep in snow—an adventure that the boy liked to recall long afterwards.

No less familiar to him were the liturgy of the church, the music of worship and the language of the Bible. By the time he was fifteen Hardy was teaching in the local Sunday school. As Carl Weber justly remarked: 'It is an understatement to say that Hardy knew the Bible as no other author who has written English novels ever knew it.' To the end of his days—and in spite of his scepticism and unbelief—Hardy was an inveterate churchgoer. In old age he could still describe himself as 'churchy; not in an intellectual sense, but in so far as instincts and emotions ruled'.

The railway did not reach Dorchester until after Hardy's tenth birthday. During his teens the comic songs and fashionable tunes of London began to displace the old folk music, just as 'radical' ideas tended in a more general and accelerating way to unsettle the enshrined stabilities of convention and belief. But the boyhood horizon of Thomas Hardy was bounded by church and Sunday school, country dance and local anecdote, carol and folk song, psalm and story telling, in much the same way as his father's and grandfather's had been. All his life he retained the countryman's liking for the oddities and quirks of gossip, for strange tales and lively conversation. Recalling one of the old fiddlers of his native village he commended him as 'a man who speaks neither truth nor lies, but a sort of Not Proven compound which is very relishable'.

The Hardys took some pride in their Norman origins, tracing themselves back to John le Hardy, a son of a Bailiff of Jersey, who settled near Wareham in the fifteenth century. The rise and decline of family fortunes was a subject that fascinated Hardy and it was probably nourished by his mother. Jemima Hardy had grown up in acute and distressing poverty, conscious that her mother, Elizabeth Hand, had married 'beneath her'. Elizabeth was apparently a well-read woman with a good library, and Jemima grew up to be an avid reader with a keen sense of her descent in the social hierarchy. Hardy, similarly, described himself as a 'bookworm' and was not prepared to be underrated socially. The suggestion that he spoke in dialect and should write only about rustic scenes and characters vexed him greatly. In a conversation with Vere Collins he stressed that he was not brought up to speak the local dialect. 'I know it', he said, 'but it was not spoken at home. My mother only used it when speaking to the cottagers, and my father when speaking to his workmen.' And to those critics who urged him not to attempt scenes of social life but to 'get back to his sheepfolds' he was quick to point out that he spent three or four months every year in London.

By the time he was sixteen Hardy was ready to start his own venture into the larger world. John Hicks, an architect for whom Hardy's father occasionally did building work, suggested that young Thomas should come to him as a premium pupil for three years. Originally in practice in Bristol Hicks now had an office in Dorchester next door to the school conducted by the Rev William Barnes, the Dorset dialect poet. In this office the young Hardy had his first lessons in Gothic restoration work; and sometimes he slipped in next door to consult Barnes on a problem of grammar and incidentally to admire the poet-schoolmaster's mastery of language and his preoccupation with literature. When Hardy eventually moved to London he took with him a copy of Barnes's *Poems of Rural Life* and later did much to win recognition for Barnes's work.

But in 1856 Hardy was busy making new friendships and exploring new ideas in Dorchester. As is so often the case in the small provincial towns of England, there was a coterie of young men engrossed in the sort of intellectual ferment that every now and then throws up an unusually well-equipped and independent mind. The other young men in the architect's office combined with some of the sons of the local clergy and one or two of Barnes's pupils to involve Hardy in vigorous theological and philosophical debate. To keep pace with them he embarked on a most strenuous course of self-education. Before he left home each day for the office he aimed to put in three hours of study, starting at 5 am. He had had a reasonable grounding in Latin at a local grammar school: this he now developed by reading Virgil, Horace and Ovid, and he also began to teach himself Greek. Nothing could be more characteristic than the course of his study of Greek, which was at first addressed to the *Iliad*, but switched to the New Testament when he needed to defend the doctrine of the Church of England in a running argument with a Baptist fellow-pupil in Hicks's office. Not until his doughty and respected antagonist departed to Tasmania did Hardy feel he could relax his guard and return to Homer.

This early dedication to study was no passing enthusiasm of adolescence. If we think of 'self-improvement' as a typically Victorian virtue, Hardy was very much a child of his age. When he worked within walking distance of the National Gallery he reckoned to spend twenty minutes of his lunch hour there each day. He started attending evening classes in French, with the hope of adding a further language to his Greek and Latin. Over many years he was a familiar figure at the British Museum, accumulating a varied knowledge that ranged from the Napoleonic wars to the prosody of Latin hymns. To be busy with books was to him the most natural thing in the world, and perhaps in the end the most rewarding.

His initial departure from Dorchester to London took place in April 1862. He carried with him letters of introduction which brought him into the employment of Arthur Blomfield, an architect who needed a draughtsman with experience in Gothic work. After six months Hardy felt secure enough to throw away the return half of his railway ticket. For five years he worked for Blomfield, mainly in the drawing office at Adelphi Terrace. And in those five years he gradually formed his resolve to make a name for himself, not as an architect but as a writer.

2

London and Weymouth 1862 - 1870

The world does not despise us; it only neglects us
(Hardy's notebook)

The five years Hardy spent in London, from the spring of 1862 to the summer of 1867, have a seminal importance in any consideration of his work; but they are years clouded by a general obscurity in which only an occasional detail can be clearly seen. Apart from some letters to his sister Mary, we have to rely primarily on such bland recollections as he permitted himself to include in *The Life*. He visited the Great Exhibition two or three evenings a week, tried the underground railway, and attended church services at St Mary's, Kilburn, where 'they sing most of the tunes in the Salisbury hymn-book'. Mary visited him and so did a Dorchester friend, Horace Moule, who was to be of special importance to Hardy as a literary adviser and guide in the early stages of his career. One of the sons of the vicar of Fordington (a part of Dorchester), Horace Moule, contributed reviews to *The Saturday Review* and was the first public champion of Hardy's novels. It was through his agency that Leslie Stephen approached Hardy and commissioned *Far from the Madding Crowd* as a serial for *The Cornhill.*

But apart from Moule, Hardy seems to have had few friends in London. Blomfield's office was not the intellectual forum that Hicks's office in Dorchester had been—or perhaps there was a stricter working discipline. If he found enjoyment in feminine companionship it has gone largely unrecorded. In 1865 he apparently thought of bringing a girl down from London for

Christmas but her identity is not known. He went out occasionally with one of his cousins from Puddletown, Martha Sparks, who was in domestic service in London. And he certainly ruminated about women. A notebook entry in June 1865 reads: 'Walked about by moonlight in the evening. Wondered what woman, if any, I should be thinking about in five years' time.'

The prospect that, in five years' time, he might not be thinking about any woman at all was a remote one. More than many writers Hardy was to draw a great part of his literary impulse from a connoisseurship of women, a preoccupation with the feminine world, an unrelenting urge to explore possible modes of relationship with women in an imaginative sense. In the whole body of his work the proportion in which women dominate is notably large. Few novelists have created so many memorable portraits of individual women. Few poets have written so tenderly of the love of women or with such fondness and charm of women's ways. All that is clear enough—but to determine the point where reality ends and fantasy begins is a problem that teases every student of Hardy's writing.

In *The Life* there are one or two slight reminiscences of shy teenage romances that remained inarticulate and unrequited. By early manhood a pervasive mood of respectability comes down like a mist on the chronicling of Hardy's encounters with the opposite sex: no unseemly passion ruffles the smooth surface of the narrative. It is only when one reads the poems that the gaps and evasions in *The Life* begin to show. Hardy himself indicated that there was more of his personal life in a hundred lines of his poetry than in all the novels, referring to 'circumstances not being so veiled in the verse as in the novels'.

But if *The Life* is in this respect an incomplete self-portrait, the collective impression suggested by the poems must also be treated with reserve. In feminine company Hardy could often find in quite a slight incident a sufficient impulse to project the sort of fantasy from which a poem developed. When he needed to do so he could talk himself into a poetic relationship which had very little correlation with anything that occurred in the literal world of 'real life'. Some weightier occasions will emerge later. Here let us consider a not very serious example from his teenage days.

In his account of the young beauties who first excited his admiration he mentions a farmer's daughter, Louisa, for whom he felt something more than the fleeting emotion that prompted him later to commemorate 'Lizbie Browne', that beautiful red-head whose father—like Fancy Day's in *Under the Greenwood Tree*—was a gamekeeper. For Louisa Hardy went through a spell of dumb devotion, unable to engage her in conversation when they met walking in a lane near Stinsford, and then travelling on Sundays to Weymouth to stand and watch her attending church with her fellow-pupils at a boarding school. All that ever passed between them was a shy smile and a 'Good evening'.

In spite of that, Louisa Harding is celebrated in three of Hardy's poems and has an honoured place among what might be called the brides of his imagination—those whom he implies he might have married or with whom he has some kind of tryst after death. In *The Passer-by* he writes in the person of Louisa recalling her romance with 'that youth I loved too true'. In July 1913, only eight months after he had buried his first wife in Stinsford churchyard where Louisa also lay, Hardy wrote 'Louie'—a poem which evokes her 'phantom' beside 'the elect one's'. He was conscious that the two women who in life had been strangers to each other were 'such neighbours now!' And lastly, at the very end of his life, he wrote 'To Louisa in the Lane'—urging her to 'meet me again as at that time/In the hollow of the lane'. When he realises that 'such is a deed you cannot do', he contents himself with the thought that he must wait 'till with flung-off flesh I follow you'.

On the basis of those three poems the incautious reader might well believe that the young Louisa had been so enamoured of Hardy as to think of him as 'My joy, my fate' in circumstances which created a lifelong bond between them. The facts of their very slight acquaintance are clear enough to puncture that particular balloon, but the episode shows how strongly Hardy could draw such characters into the orbit of his inner world on only the slenderest pretext. In more adult circumstances later the plain biographical facts tend to be veiled with an unyielding prudence, and often impenetrably so. We may be grateful that the poems go so far to remedy a shortcoming in *The Life*, but they can all too readily deceive us by distortions of another kind.

In 1865 Hardy was just starting to get to grips with the problems of writing verse. In his own words: 'By 1865 he had begun to write verses, and by 1866 to send his productions to magazines.' Some of his earliest poems bear the address of his lodgings in Westbourne Park Villas. Here, to fit himself for his task, he worked at technical exercises and concentrated all his reading on the classics of English poetry. One of his enterprises was to convert the Book of Ecclesiastes into Spenserian stanzas. He learnt to handle the sonnet form; tried his hand at a dialect poem reminiscent of Barnes in *The Bride-Night Fire*; and had a period of fascination, which he never quite gave up, with heavy Anglo-Saxon alliterations. Nor was he unresponsive to the most up-to-date contemporary work. Swinburne's *Poems and Ballads* had caused a sensation when they appeared in 1866, and Hardy was quick to make his own delighted discovery of them. In 1897 he wrote to Swinburne of 'the buoyant time of thirty years ago, when I used to read your early works walking along the crowded London streets, to my imminent risk of being knocked down'.

In speaking of Hardy's early poems it is important to bear in mind that his first book of verse, *Wessex Poems*, was not published until 1898; hardly any of his poems had appeared separately before that date. Those poems which bear dates in the 1860s had therefore been waiting for thirty years or more and must be assumed to have undergone a measure of revision at some stage. Hardy was the kind of writer who could put aside unfinished work and return to it much later. Even with a completed work he was always liable to give it a final polish and perhaps some important amendment before sending it away to the publisher.

The early poems as we now see them are not necessarily, therefore, to be regarded as untouched examples of what editors were rejecting in 1866. In general the dates that Hardy affixes to his poems need to be treated with some reserve as they may refer to the first roughing-out of a concept which was developed later. Even so it is not unreasonable to believe that one can discern the kind of beginning that Hardy made as a poet in those poems of early date which suggest the awkward and sometimes derivative struggles of an authentic poet feeling his way towards an individual utterance.

Already some of the typical Hardyesque preoccupations are apparent at the outset. 'Hap', of 1866, with its 'purblind Doomsters' and 'Crass Casualty' is a clumsy forerunner in sonnet form of that important and somewhat controversial group of philosophical poems in which Hardy engages in what may conveniently be termed 'God struggles'. The straining vocabulary of 'In Vision I Roamed' is a prelude to Hardy's tireless wrestling with the English language and his readiness to experiment with a phrase like 'orbs of such ostént'. 'Neutral Tones', of 1867, contains a strength of personal emotion that seems to keep suggesting the cryptic undertones and sibylline inner meanings that characterise another great body of his mature work—those poems which crystallise about some private emotional impulse. The core of much of his finest work can be identified in the poems that took shape in Westbourne Park Villas. To make them 'quite worthy of publication', Hardy later claimed that no more was needed than 'the mere change of a few words or the rewriting of a line or two'.

Whatever merits we with hindsight may detect in Hardy's first poems, they earned him no recognition at the time. His interest in the alternative possibilities of the theatre soon died away, and by the summer of 1867 he was disenchanted with a London that had lost its first glamorous novelty and had so little apparent need for the talents of a budding author. While his spirits were at this low ebb he received a request from his old employer, John Hicks, to recommend any suitable young man he might know to act as an assistant in church restoration. Hardy responded promptly. Finding life in London a strain on his health he proposed himself to return to the fresher air of Dorchester and resume his earlier relationship with Hicks. He has left no record of his feelings, but the return to his starting point after five years can have been no cause for rejoicing.

Back in Dorset, and with no particular objective immediately in view, Hardy took stock of his prospects and made a momentous decision. He virtually gave up writing poetry, ignored any temptation to start a blank-verse drama, and began to draft a novel. Through the autumn and winter of 1867/8 this new and unexpected enterprise absorbed his energies. It was to be 'a story with no plot' according to the subtitle, and it would contain some original verses—presumably selected from those written in London. The title Hardy chose for it was *The Poor Man and the Lady*. It was written in the first person 'by the Poor Man'. By the early months of 1868 he was making a fair copy of the finished work and in July he posted his MS to Macmillans. The reply he received from Alexander Macmillan was a rejection of the book as a publishing proposition, but in terms that any unknown beginner could justly consider encouraging. Macmillan expressed the view that 'if this is your first book I think you ought to go on' and John Morley, whose opinion on the MS had been sought by Macmillans, commented: 'If the man is young he has stuff and purpose in him.'

With the hope that some rewriting would make his story acceptable Hardy called on Macmillan in December, but did not succeed in altering Macmillan's decision. The publisher had originally criticised Hardy's 'ignorant misrepresentation' of upper-class characters; in particular he thought Hardy overdid the 'utter heartlessness' of fashionable conversation about the working classes. Evidently this was not the kind of book that influential opinion in London would welcome and Macmillan saw no hope of salvaging the book by tinkering with it. Since Hardy was not prepared to put it aside Macmillan advised him to approach Chapman & Hall, which he did immediately. At first they seemed disinclined to publish the book, but they did not reject it out of hand and Hardy had to consider the possibility of his putting up £20 as a guarantee against a loss. With nothing settled, Chapman asked Hardy to call and see 'the gentleman who read your manuscript'.

By this time, March 1869, Hardy had left Hicks's office in Dorchester and been settled back in London for some weeks. When he called to see Chapman & Hall's reader he found himself in the presence of George Meredith—and in passing it is worth noting the rather remarkable fact that the first two publishers' readers to whom Hardy's work was submitted were men of the eminence of Morley and Meredith. Like Morley, Meredith saw promise in Hardy's work and wanted to publish him. He also echoed the Macmillan view that a raw and unremitting satirical onslaught on society might injure Hardy's future. He urged the young author not to 'nail his colours to the mast' so positively, since he would certainly antagonise the conventional reviewers. Like Macmillan, Meredith urged Hardy to make a fresh start. His more specific advice was to pursue a purely 'artistic' purpose, adopting a complicated and ingenious plot of the kind that had brought Wilkie Collins into vogue.

Hardy was eventually to take Meredith's advice, but before doing so he made one more attempt to find a publisher for *The Poor Man*. He sent the manuscript to Tinsley Brothers. An unnamed friend of his in London acted as a go-between in a brief negotiation with William Tinsley who—like Chapman & Hall—seemed to require financial support from Hardy as a condition of acceptance and on a scale that Hardy was not prepared to consider. He asked for the return of his manuscript and came reluctantly to the conclusion that the combined advice of Macmillan, Morley, Meredith and Tinsley must be heeded. He put aside *The Poor Man* and never allowed anyone else to see it. Eventually he destroyed the manuscript, but not before he had dismantled it and made use of much of what he always regarded with the affection that authors often feel for their first work.

Hardy was an economical man who liked to keep things by him until the right moment came for him to work them up and put them to good use. The rural scenes in *The Poor Man*—notably the Christmas Eve at the tranter's which John Morley had singled out for praise—were fused into a different plot in *Under the Greenwood Tree*. Some of the London satire was probably embedded in *A Pair of Blue Eyes* and *The Hand of Ethelberta*. Descriptive passages found their way into *Desperate Remedies* and the story-line—which had pleased none of the professional readers—made an unhappy appearance in a magazine serialisation in 1878 as *An Indiscretion in the Life of an Heiress*. Hardy never gave it the status of book publication and excluded it from his collected fiction. But as late as 1925 he published a remarkably vivid poem entitled *A Poor Man and a Lady*, with a footnote to indicate that it preserved an episode in the story of *The Poor Man and the Lady*. And in *The Life* he recorded his view that his first published novel, *Desperate Remedies*, was 'quite below the level' of his unpublished first-born.

Early in 1869 Hardy received news in London that his old employer, John Hicks, had died. In April a Weymouth architect, who had bought Hicks's practice, invited Hardy to help him with the completion of Hicks's outstanding church works. This new architect, G. R. Crickmay, was not himself a 'Gothic' man and he evidently wanted Hardy to return to the Dorchester office. By this time Hardy had found an agreeable compromise between his literary ambitions and his architectural work: he moved from one short-term engagement to another as the need arose. His latest sojourn in London had been organised in this freelance manner and enabled him to pursue his negotiations with publishers and generally employ his time as he chose. To Crickmay's invitation Hardy responded by agreeing to spend a fortnight in Dorchester, working on the church drawings that Hicks had left uncompleted.

It soon became apparent that there were several months of employment for Hardy's particular talents; Crickmay accordingly persuaded him to move to Weymouth and settle in lodgings there at 3 Wooperton Street, the home of a Mr Frederick Kennell. Wooperton Street is a pleasant little row of terrace houses, from which in 1869 Hardy had a clear view northward to the Ridgeway. Mr Kennell's neighbour at Number One was the Town Surveyor, George Seaman (who incidentally owed his appointment to the folly of his predecessor, who shortened his career by publicly insulting the Mayor). The accommodation of Hardy next to the Surveyor was possibly due to the pervasive influence of his new employer.

George Rackstrow Crickmay was one of the most prominent citizens of Weymouth at this time; he was manager of the Water Company besides being a busy architect whose local commissions included Weymouth College, the Working Men's Club and St John's Schools 'in the Early English style'. He was also involved in a big development scheme for residential housing promoted by a local landowning MP and 'racing notability', Sir Frederic Johnstone. During the period that Hardy worked for him Crickmay began building the Weymouth and Dorset County Royal Eye Infirmary (which opened in 1872) and was also busy with the Weymouth Royal Hospital, the foundation stone of which was laid on 29 May 1871 'with grand masonic ceremonial'. Small wonder that he needed an extra assistant to cope with the residue of church restoration work taken over from Hicks's office.

Weymouth in summertime was much to Hardy's taste. He liked to swim in the bay in the early morning and when his day's work was done he enjoyed taking a rowingboat out to sea. Life in lodgings at Weymouth was very different from the 'mechanical and monotonous existence' that he had known in his earlier years in London. Now he was stimulated to resume the writing of poetry by the liveliness of the place, with its bands playing and cheerful crowds promenading:

> The boats, the sands, the esplanade,
> The laughing crowd;
> Light-hearted, loud
> Greetings from some not ill-endowed;
>
> The evening sunlit cliffs, the talk,
> Hailings and halts,
> The keen sea-salts,
> The band, the Morgenblätter Waltz.

To the Victorian villagers of Dorset, Weymouth represented the acme of seaside pleasure and entertainment. For all his newly acquired sophistication Hardy must have responded instinctively and predictably to the gay holiday atmosphere. In the autumn the engagement by Crickmay of a new assistant brought an added liveliness into the office. This young man, on whom Hardy said he modelled Edward Springrove in *Desperate Remedies*, persuaded Hardy to join a quadrille class. In *The Life* Hardy described the quadrille class as 'a gay gathering for dances and love-making by adepts of both sexes', and he added that 'a good deal of flirtation went on'. The explicitness of this recollection and the rather raffish Victorian overtones of the phrase 'love-making by adepts of both sexes' are in striking contrast to the normally suffocating prudence of *The Life*; and to assume that any single word in that elaborately contrived *persona* is unconsidered would be most unwise.

Weymouth probably represented a defined and important stage in the more secret life from which, in his poems, Hardy occasionally lifts a corner of the veil. If we draw together the poems that he explicitly associates with the years 1869 and 1870, or with Weymouth, we can hardly escape the conclusion that they have an immediate autobiographical relevance and that their emotional intensity springs from Hardy's relationship with one or more of the young women of his acquaintance. There are exceptions to this generalisation—the fictional narrative of 'The Contretemps' for example—and there is room for debate about the certainty with which this or that poem can be associated with Weymouth, but I believe the weight of the evidence points to this period as one of great emotional turbulence and stress.

It seems reasonable to accept at face value Hardy's own assertion that he was slow to mature, a late developer. All too little is known about the five years he spent in London from 1862 onwards, but there is a sort of negative presumption that no great romance disturbed what was mainly a rather lonely and solitary existence. However, after his return to Dorset (though probably no earlier than 1868) he formed an attachment of some kind with Tryphena Sparks, one of his cousins who lived in nearby Puddletown. With what degree of seriousness they considered themselves to be 'engaged' to each other must be a matter for conjecture, where so little firm evidence is forthcoming. No correspondence between them seems to have survived. Indeed when Tryphena died, in 1890, Hardy wrote 'Not a line of her writing have I' as the first words of a poem entitled 'Thoughts of Phena: at News of her Death'.

The obscurity of this relationship with Tryphena, the lack of contemporary evidence, makes it difficult to prove or disprove the speculations that tend to flourish in such circumstances. There are grounds for believing that the engagement ring Hardy gave to his first wife had originally been intended for a girl who lived in the neighbourhood of Hardy's home, and Hardy is said to have thought afterwards that this somewhat 'second-hand' gift to Emma brought him bad luck. The jilted sweetheart could well have been Tryphena, if only because no better claim has been canvassed. The suggestion that, before they parted, Tryphena had conceived a child of which Hardy was the father and which eventually grew to manhood is one of those engaging elaborations of gossip that appeal to those who are not troubled by the total absence of any of the usual modes of verification. Like the tales of the old fiddler that Hardy described, the story of this child is 'a sort of Not Proven compound which is very relishable'—or not, according to taste. That Hardy could have preserved such a secret inviolate for sixty years is not the least of the improbabilities.

What is certain is that Tryphena went to a teachers' training college in London for two years, completed her course in the autumn of 1871 and in the following January went to Devon as the headmistress of a Plymouth school; married there and had four children before she died. At the time of her death Hardy referred to her in his journal in rather distant and impersonal terms as 'the woman whom I was thinking of—a cousin'. There is no subsequent indication in *The Life* or in the poems that his thoughts returned again to her with sufficient warmth to excite a renewed interest—which is odd when one reflects how assiduously he explored in verse the dramatic or lyrical possibilities of every romantic memory that he could summon. She endures in the one poem and the suggestion that some of the circumstances in *Jude the Obscure* derive from her. Her name is mentioned once more, in somewhat strange circumstances, in *Tess of the d'Urbervilles*. Among the fowls that Mrs d'Urberville treats as pets and has engaged Tess to care for, there are two which are mentioned by name. One is called Strut; the other, Phena. The writing of *Tess* occupied Hardy during 1889 and 1890.

Where her presence should most strongly have left its mark on Hardy's poetry is in that period from the summer of 1869 to the beginning of 1870 when he seems to have had a sudden intense period of verse writing associated with his move to Weymouth. Before that time he had been concentrating on prose in his first novel and had temporarily abandoned poetry: subsequently he went to St Juliot and fell in love with Emma, while Tryphena had embarked on her training course at Stockwell. But there was a period when Hardy and Tryphena were able, or could have been able, to spend time together in Weymouth, dancing together at the quadrille class or elsewhere, boating and walking together and doing the things that the poems describe.

Even so, it is difficult to put such a precise interpretation on the mysterious hints and clues that the poems appear to offer. Some of them seem particularly conscious of the girl's parents being close at hand. 'The Dawn after the Dance' which is set in Weymouth opens with the words 'Here is your parents' dwelling'. In 'Her Father' the girl, coming to a secret rendezvous, warns 'Father is at hand!' The context suggests a busy street in Weymouth. Neither the parents of Tryphena Sparks nor their home seem to be relevant. We can be certain that, in these poems, Hardy is living through a period of more personal and intense emotion than he has yet known, but whether the cause is Tryphena or a Weymouth girl or more than one is something that he concealed in the cryptic and anonymous terms he used.

There are about a dozen poems to which Hardy at some time attached the word 'Weymouth' or the date '1869' or '1870'. Those which can be confidently ascribed to the second half of 1869 at Weymouth include 'At a Seaside Town in 1869', 'Singing Lovers', 'Her Father', 'The Dawn after the Dance' and 'At Waking'. To this group also it is virtually certain that 'On the Esplanade' belongs, and there are others which, with less certainty, I am inclined to add. 'In the Vaulted Way' has been interpreted as a St Juliot poem, but with no great conviction, and might as plausibly be read as a daybreak parting after a Weymouth dance. Robert Gittings has argued persuasively that 'The Place on the Map' describes a Weymouth scene. I agree with him and want additionally to suggest that 'Had You Wept' may refer to the same incident: the imagery of eyes 'which had lost the art of raining' is common to both poems and suggests a kinship between them.

Taken collectively these poems seem to crystallise a period of emotional turbulence far in excess of anything Hardy had felt hitherto. If they are to be read autobiographically—and it is difficult to see them in any other light—they show him in a turmoil of passionate feeling, engrossed in the preoccupations of lovers, experiencing betrayal, reconciliation, rejection, by turns elated and sombre in mood, and hinting at some further tragedy that never quite reveals itself. There are moments too of disillusion and self-disgust (in 'Her Father' and 'At Waking' as two examples) when he admits that he cares only for 'her pink and white' and—if that be discounted—she is a very ordinary specimen 'of earth's poor average kind'. In general the poems speak more eloquently of the pains of love than of its pleasures. It would be reckless to treat them as 'evidence' in either a police court or a casebook sense, but at least they are not inconsistent with the delayed initiation of a repressed but volatile temperament. In retrospect the years before 1869 look like a long, smouldering, incoherent adolescence.

There is one other remarkable fact to be mentioned about these poems. They remained in Hardy's notebooks, unpublished, for forty years. He had already decided, during his time in London, that his verses were unwanted by the editors of the day. At Weymouth he must have felt impelled to write poetry in answer to a private and personal need but with no thought of publication. The literary work that he regarded as practical and capable of success was in prose. The more immediate effect of the move to Weymouth was to give him the impetus and the setting for the first chapters of the new novel he now planned to write in response to Meredith's advice. The plot was to be as intricate and sensational as *The Moonstone* (which Tinsley had published in the previous year, 1868) but Hardy drew his raw material from what lay close to hand—Cytherea Graye, the book's heroine, is established in lodgings at Weymouth with her brother who works in an architect's office. The story begins to move when they take a trip on a pleasure boat across Weymouth

Bay to Lulworth Cove and she meets her brother's new colleague, Edward Springrove.

Between Cytherea and Edward there is a conventional romance in which the man does no more than meet the novelist's routine requirements. But Cytherea is drawn with undeniable freshness and spirit. Within the limits of what is proper conduct for a heroine of the period she displays an emotional responsiveness and a liveliness of sensibility which offer more than a hint of the great feminine characterisations that were to succeed her. Indeed what must strike a modern reader of *Desperate Remedies* most pleasurably is the extent to which Hardy's particular gifts so frequently break through the complicated paraphernalia of the plot with which he had saddled himself. Three features of the book certainly invite comment.

The first is the affectionate attention given to the rustic inhabitants of the village of Carriford. The cidermaking scene at the *Three Tranters Inn* shows already the authentic quality of those swiftly drawn sketches of rural life and character in which Hardy is the supreme master. Did he ever use the economy of a couple of words to more richly humorous effect than in the description of Clerk Crickett as 'a kind of bowdlerized rake'? And we could have leaped ahead into the pages of *Far from the Madding Crowd* or *The Return of the Native* when Gad Weedy offers his reflections on the fact that the Clerk is Mrs Crickett's third husband:

> 'I used to think 'twas your wife's fate not to have a liven husband when I zid 'em die off so,' said Gad.
>
> 'Fate? Bless thy simplicity, so 'twas her fate; but she struggled to have one, and would, and did. Fate's nothing beside a woman's schemen!'
>
> 'I suppose, then, that Fate is a He, like us, and the Lord, and the rest o' 'em up above there,' said Gad, lifting his eyes to the sky.

Next to be mentioned is the generation of a narrative momentum. Throughout all his work Hardy lies open to the criticism that he uses far-fetched coincidences, improbable eavesdroppings and other clumsy contrivances to manipulate his characters into dramatic situations, but there is no denying his sheer storytelling force. As he comes towards the end of one phase of the action he is already leaning forward towards the next in the compelling way that makes his readers follow. It is an art that is heightened by serial writing and more particularly by the plot of complex ingenuity which takes its rhythm from cliffhanger to cliffhanger. To that extent *Desperate Remedies* was a valuably testing trial for Hardy's first public endeavour.

Towards the end it is sometimes difficult to discern any more of a motive than a desire to simplify the author's task, but for most of the way he shows an unflagging zest for one twist after another in his compound of murder and mystery. And it was a gratifying stroke of inventiveness which enabled him to introduce a poem as the decisive clue from which the dénouement proceeds. Nor is this the only reminder of the author's commitment as a poet. In his first description of Edward Springrove he speaks of him in terms that might be applied to himself: 'He's a thorough bookworm—despises the pap-and-daisy school of verse—knows Shakespeare to the very dregs of the footnotes. Indeed, he's a poet himself in a small way.' And in the 1912 Preface he mentions that he 'dissolved' into the prose of *Desperate Remedies* some of the early poems that he had been unable to publish.

The most remarkable feature of the book, however, in its implications for his later novels is the relationship between the heroine, Cytherea, and the formidable and wealthy Miss Aldclyffe with whom she seeks employment. The early stages of their encounter have a sensual directness that seems to come from unguarded springs of character over which Hardy has only an imperfect control. The initial interview in a Budmouth hotel is drawn in terms of unspoken physical flirtation: 'Both the women showed off themselves to advantage as they walked forward in the orange light.' And Miss Aldclyffe muses explicitly to herself,

> It is almost worth while to be bored with instructing her in order to have a creature who could glide round my luxurious indolent body in that manner, and look at me in that way—I warrant how light her fingers are upon one's head and neck.

At this point Miss Aldclyffe has not the least inkling of what she later discovers, that Cytherea is the daughter of the man she once wanted to marry. Having engaged the girl as her lady's maid and immediately plunged into a tempestuous scene with her (during which the link between them is disclosed), she goes later to Cytherea's bedroom and pleads: 'Let me come in, darling . . . I came to ask you to come down into my bed, but it is snugger here.'

Cytherea recognises that 'it was now mistress and maid no longer; woman and woman only'. In the scene that follows Hardy lays an emphasis on what he declares to be the maternal nature of Miss Aldclyffe's passionate behaviour:

> The instant they were in bed Miss Aldclyffe freed herself from the last remnant of restraint. She flung her arms round the young girl, and pressed her gently to her heart. 'Now kiss me,' she said. '*You seem as if you were my own, own child.*'

The italics are mine and I add them to draw attention to that final sentence. Were it omitted, the total effect would be unmistakably lesbian and Hardy would be, to that extent, misrepresented. But the scene does not stop there, with a maternal kiss. Miss Aldclyffe begins to demand of Cytherea: 'Why can't you kiss me as I can kiss you?' and she then asks jealously if Cytherea has ever been kissed by a man. When Cytherea refuses to deny that she has, Miss Aldclyffe's emotional turbulence reaches an extraordinary intensity.

> 'Cytherea, try to love me more than you love him—do. I love you more sincerely than any man can. Do, Cythie: don't let any man stand between us. O, I can't bear that! . . . I thought I had at last found an artless woman who had not been sullied by a man's lips. . . . You can hardly find a girl whose heart has not been *had*—is not an old thing half worn out by some He or another! . . . I—an old fool—have been sipping at

your mouth as if it were honey, because I fancied no wasting lover knew the spot. But a minute ago, and you seemed to me like a fresh spring meadow—now you seem a dusty highway.'

In his examination of Miss Aldclyffe's relationship with Cytherea, in *Thomas Hardy: the Novels and Stories*, Albert J. Guerard comments: 'The extreme frankness and clumsiness of this scene is the strongest evidence that Hardy had no idea what he was writing about, however unerringly the subconscious worked.' This puts the matter in extreme terms, but Hardy seems to justify them with his comically prim little summing-up: 'This vehement imperious affection was in one sense soothing, but yet it was not of the kind that Cytherea's instincts desired.'

In a novice's novel this wildly passionate nightscene is a remarkable piece of writing. Put in the perspective of Hardy's total work as we can now see it, it falls into place as an example of his special genius for a kind of emotional writing in which some hidden force within a character seems to take possession of the writer and impel him to adventure beyond the limits of his conscious creation. In the last resort glib labels like 'maternal' or 'lesbian' are equally inadequate to describe the full implication of Hardy's imaginative penetration of the subconscious levels of human feeling. What in *Desperate Remedies* may seem grotesquely wild and uncontrolled will later become a primary element in the masterpieces of his maturity.

Hardy wasted no time in completing his version of what he believed the literary world required. He can scarcely have put pen to paper much before October, but he had a fair copy made of nearly the whole of it in time to submit it to a publisher in the first week of the following March. Surprisingly he did not invite Meredith's judgment, which might have been expected to approve the new style, but sent the manuscript to Macmillan's. Alexander Macmillan rejected it out of hand, whereupon Hardy still ignored Meredith's expressed interest and approached Tinsley.

The response from Tinsley was businesslike. He sent Hardy

the reader's report, indicated the alterations that Hardy should make, and quoted the sum of money that he required Hardy to put up as a guarantee against loss on eventual sales. By the end of the year a contract was completed. Hardy provided £75 towards the printing costs (of which about £60 was later refunded). Tinsley declared he had 'no doubt the book is clever' and in March 1871 it duly appeared in three anonymous volumes. The literary career of Thomas Hardy, which was to extend over another fifty-seven years, had begun.

3

A Cornish Romance 1870 - 1872

No prelude did I there perceive
To a drama at all,
Or foreshadow what fortune might weave
From beginnings so small.

(*At the Word 'Farewell'*)

The final manuscript of *Desperate Remedies* that Tinsley sent to the printers was not, as the earlier version had been, in the handwriting of Thomas Hardy. It was a fair copy transcribed by Emma Lavinia Gifford, an exact contemporary of Hardy's who lived with her married sister at St Juliot in Cornwall, where her brother-in-law was the rector. She and Hardy had met for the first time in March, two days after he had sent *Desperate Remedies* to Macmillan. Crickmay had apparently become worried about the long delay in dealing with some unfinished matter of Hicks's concerning the church at St Juliot. During his lifetime Hicks had failed to initiate any positive action over the restoration work that the rector of St Juliot wanted to see started and since Hicks's death the St Juliot file had only gathered more dust. Crickmay therefore asked Hardy to make the journey to Cornwall for a preliminary survey of what was required.

As there was sickness in the house it was Emma who received the young architect and played hostess to him. In later years she was to draw from Henry Moule the comment: 'Poor woman, she is phenomenally plain!' but at thirty she still had much of the radiance and bloom of youth. Moreover she was a high-spirited vivacious character, with a robust vitality that evidently excited

Hardy. The week he spent at St Juliot was decisive for both of them. When the time came to return to Weymouth and Hardy went into the rectory garden to take his leave of Emma:

> Even then the scale might have been turned
> Against love by a feather,
> —But crimson one cheek of hers burned
> When we came in together.

Thus began a romance which, in the later intensity of its bitterness and the tenderness of its devotion, must always puzzle and fascinate Hardy's readers. Five months after his first visit Hardy returned to St Juliot and over four years his courtship of Emma followed roughly this pattern of a couple of visits each year to St Juliot, where he stayed for a week or two, with an exchange of letters to sustain their relationship in the interval between those memorable days when together they explored the surrounding countryside, with Emma sometimes on horseback—an aspect of her personality that Hardy particularly admired.

The years of courtship were years of professional uncertainty for Hardy as he wavered between architecture and authorship. As a draughtsman he worked sometimes at Weymouth for Crickmay and sometimes he found temporary employment in London. He seemingly experienced no difficulty in earning money when he wanted to do so, and it was for different reasons at different times that he divided his year between Bockhampton, Weymouth, London and St Juliot. In London he visited museums and art galleries, spent some time with Horace Moule and kept in touch with the literary world. At home at Bockhampton he could find a congenial atmosphere for writing. At Weymouth he supervised the plans for the restoration work at St Juliot, which in turn justified another visit to Emma.

The reception of *Desperate Remedies* gave little practical encouragement, although *The Athenaeum* spoke of it as 'a powerful novel' and *The Morning Post* hailed it as 'an eminent success'. It was dismissed by *The Spectator* in contemptuous terms for 'daring to suppose that an unmarried lady owning an estate could have an illegitimate child'. After remarking that the author was wise to conceal his identity and thus not to 'disgrace the family name' *The Spectator* reviewer added, with a touch of vindictive humour, that 'the law is hardly just which prevents Tinsley Brothers from concealing their participation also'. The damage done by *The Spectator* might have been offset by a favourable review—probably written by Horace Moule—in *The Saturday Review*, but it appeared too late to influence sales.

Hardy's sensitivity to criticism is well exemplified by the fact that the wound inflicted by *The Spectator* had not healed when, nearly half a century later, *The Life* was drafted. The hostile notice was carefully reproduced, to be dismissed disdainfully with the assurance that 'it does not seem to have worried Hardy much or at any rate for long'. Yet a few lines later we read: 'He remembered, for long years after, how he had read this review . . . The bitterness of that moment was never forgotten.' It evidently rankled without abatement, just as the later criticism of *Tess* and *Jude* was to rankle and become the cause—or the pretext—for the ending of Hardy's career as a novelist.

In the summer of 1871 Hardy was writing *Under the Greenwood Tree* which he submitted to Macmillan's in August with a reminder that they had already seen some of the rural material in 'a tale submitted a long time ago (which never saw the light).' Alexander Macmillan thought the public would find the tale 'very slight and rather unexciting'. Although he expressed a readiness to reconsider the book six months later, Hardy took his general response to be a rejection and as this was the third manuscript to be returned by Macmillan's he decided to trouble them no further. Instead he wrote to Tinsley. He told Tinsley that he had 'nearly finished a little rural story, but owing to the representation of critic-friends who were taken with D.R. [ie *Desperate Remedies*], I have relinquished that and have proceeded a little way with another, the essence of which is plot, *without crime*—but on the plan of D.R.'

The plain fact is that Hardy was in a state of deep uncertainty. He could not decide whether he might thrive as a novelist sufficiently well to abandon architecture and, if so, whether it would be by way of 'Rural Paintings of the Dutch School' (as he described *Under the Greenwood Tree*) or 'plots without crime, on the plan of *Desperate Remedies*'. He needed a wise counsellor as much as he needed an unqualified success—and he lacked both.

At the end of 1871 he had on hand the manuscript of *Under the Greenwood Tree* and part of the first draft of the 'plot without crime' which later became *A Pair of Blue Eyes*. He had also an unsettled account with Tinsley over the costs of *Desperate Remedies* about which Tinsley had written 'I am almost afraid you will not get all the money back you paid'. Hardy therefore pressed Tinsley to render an account and mentioned that he had delayed completion of his new work until he had a clear idea of how his first novel had done financially. Tinsley, when he eventually settled up, possibly felt that the result was not so bad as he expected: for the first time he showed an interest in Hardy's 'little rural story', of which he had been told five months earlier. Hardy immediately promised to call at Tinsley's office in a few days. When doing so he presumably took the manuscript of *Under the Greenwood Tree* with him as Tinsley's next letter said: 'If you are my way any day I will tell you what I think of *Under the Greenwood Tree*.' A week later he had offered, and Hardy had accepted, £30 for the copyright. In a matter of weeks the book was published.

Nothing could be in sharper contrast with the melodrama of *Desperate Remedies* than this gentle comedy precipitated by the intention of a newly arrived vicar, Parson Maybold, to disband the church musicians—the Mellstock Quire—and to replace them with an organ played by the new schoolmistress, Fancy Day. This was a theme close to Hardy's own youthful experience and he drew his portraits of the Dewy family and their fellow-musicians from direct recollections of local worthies. Sketched without condescension or burlesque, these quizzical, ironical humorists of the Dorset countryside are among his happiest creations. They capture the spirit and the idiom of village life with an intimacy that no other writer can match. The scene in which the Quire finally confronts the vicar is one of the finest sustained passages of comic writing in the English language.

Interweaving the conflict between old and new forms of church music is a fairly conventional romance between the schoolmistress, Fancy, and Dick, the son of Reuben Dewy, the tranter and spokesman for the Quire. What is here worth noting is that, in the vicissitudes that lead up to their marriage, Hardy begins to touch on a theme that is to preoccupy him later—the theme of candour and deceit. In order to make Dick jealous, Fancy 'confesses' to a make-believe flirtation with a local farmer, Mr Shiner. She does not, however, mention a serious and briefly accepted proposal of marriage from Parson Maybold for whom she had very nearly forsaken Dick. The book ends, not in the idyllic way that some critics have implied, but with an astringent irony when Dick tells his bride that the reason why they are so happy is because 'there is such full confidence between us'. He is thinking of her apparent (but false) candour over Mr Shiner and adds: 'We'll have no secrets from each other, darling, will we ever?—no secret at all.' To this Fancy replies: 'None from today,' but as she does so she is thinking of Parson Maybold, of—these are the words that close the book—'a secret she would never tell'. In those words is the germ of *A Pair of Blue Eyes* and later of *Tess*.

With *Under the Greenwood Tree* now launched in the wake of *Desperate Remedies* Tinsley was ready to take Hardy seriously as a writer with a future. He had printed '1000 rather good bills for railways and street hoardings so that your works will be well before the public'; and he was eager to read as much of Hardy's new story as was ready, since he needed a serial to start in the autumn in *Tinsley's Magazine*.

In view of the important part William Tinsley played in Hardy's earliest ventures it is worth pausing here to consider the odd and inaccurate version that appears in *The Life*, where Hardy gives the impression that he met Tinsley by accident in the Strand and, when Tinsley urged him to produce another book, Hardy said he was now concentrating on architecture and had to be persuaded by Tinsley to dig out the manuscript of *Under the Greenwood Tree*. The fact that they had kept in touch by a desultory but steady and continuing correspondence over the preceding months is overlooked. The calendar of Hardy-Tinsley letters in R. L. Purdy's invaluable bibliographical study, *Thomas Hardy*, makes it clear that no accidental meeting in the street was required to bring author and publisher together.

But what is more surprising than the slightly romantic intervention of chance (a device always dear to Hardy) is the portrayal of Tinsley. When one reflects on the many occasions when Hardy's ability with dialogue and description might have enlivened the pages of *The Life*, it is surprising that Tinsley is singled out for such lavish treatment. In recalling the conversation in the Strand Hardy gives us a *verbatim* Tinsley in stage-cockney, with 'wot' for 'what' and 'wos' for 'was'. Just why Hardy chose to work up this strange little lampoon amid the normally restrained and dignified prose of *The Life* is not easy to understand. He may have read, and been offended by, something that Tinsley wrote in the memoirs he published shortly before his death, though he spoke not unkindly of him in 1921 to Vere Collins, saying nothing worse of him than that 'He was a shrewd chap when dealing with young authors' and recalling that in his later years of poverty Tinsley had asked Hardy to help him to obtain a Civil List grant.

During 1872 Hardy was a not unfamiliar caller at Tinsley's office in a sidestreet off the Strand. In one of his letters to Tinsley he used the phrase 'when I last called', and the growing relationship between them was undoubtedly important to the young author. The favourable reception accorded to *Under the Greenwood Tree* must have strengthened Hardy's belief in his ability to transfer his efforts successfully from architecture to novel writing. For the first time he found himself in the position of writing a story which was sold in advance when he accepted Tinsley's commission to provide a serial immediately. This was to be the story with a Cornish setting, begun the previous summer and provisionally entitled *A Winning Tongue Had He*. Hardy now set to work in earnest on it and when he sailed from London Bridge to Cornwall in August he was able to show Emma a contract for £200 for this new story, in the creation of which she was an important factor.

Renamed *A Pair of Blue Eyes*, the story began its serialisation in the September issue of *Tinsley's Magazine*. As in *Desperate Remedies* the central characters include a young architect and Hardy draws freely on his own immediate experience. In particular the book embodies his excited discovery of the romantic Cornish landscape and the first ardours of 'being in love' with Emma. It lacks the charm and the endearing homeliness of *Under the Greenwood Tree*, but for compensation it shows Hardy beginning to subdue the feverish theatricalities of *Desperate Remedies* to the accent of tragedy that was to sound through his later novels; it also commences the serious exploration of that 'immortal puzzle' to which Hardy referred in the preface to *The Woodlanders* with the words 'given the man and woman, how to find a basis for their sexual relation'.

Elfride in *A Pair of Blue Eyes* is a genteel prototype of Tess as surely as Henry Knight is a spiritual cousin of Angel Clare; and in the wild bundle of far-fetched improbabilities which is Mrs Jethway, Hardy first sketched the ballad-like finger of fate, the silent accuser, the shadow of retribution, which glides through his masterpieces. Here she is the first really recalcitrant sign of the problems that await a poet who intends to contain tragedies of Elizabethan intensity within the conventions of realistic prose. One feels that Mrs Jethway must have been inadvertently dropped on the roadside by a theatre company touring Cornwall with *The Duchess of Malfi*. It is interesting to recall that Coventry Patmore, writing to Hardy as a total stranger, expressed the view that *A Pair of Blue Eyes* was not a conception for prose. He 'regretted at almost every page that such unequalled beauty and power should not have assured themselves the immortality which would have been impressed upon them by the form of verse'.

Be that as it may, Hardy was never to be drawn to the extended narrative-poem which had been developed so vigorously and successfully in the first half of the nineteenth century. Without losing sight of what Patmore meant, it is worth stressing the close affinity of *A Pair of Blue Eyes* with the sternly unpoetic prose of Jane Austen, particularly with *Emma*. Both books are addressed to the theme of deceit—self-deceit no less than the deception of others, and Hardy's Henry Knight shows more than a passing resemblance to Jane Austen's Mr Knightley.

In *A Pair of Blue Eyes* Elfride sets off a train of disappointments and regrets by what seem to be harmless deceits. From mistaken kindness to a local farmer, Felix Jethway, she deceives him into believing that she loves him. When she disabuses him, he carries on the deceit by allowing his mother to believe that Elfride has jilted him and from this innocuous beginning Mrs Jethway's implacable hatred of Elfride develops. Similarly, when the young architect, Stephen Smith, comes to discuss the restoration of the local church with Elfride's father (who is the rector) another web of deceit begins to spin. Stephen conceals his lowly parentage in order to persuade Elfride to elope with him. When the elopement collapses in a hasty withdrawal Elfride deceives her father and also her next suitor, Henry Knight, by suppressing uncomfortable facts. And when Stephen Smith returns and chances to meet Elfride with Knight, to whom she is now engaged, he falls in with the general air of deception and—from generous motives—does not permit his own previous engagement to Elfride to become known to Knight.

So, though Elfride has committed no sin or unpardonable act of folly even, she is caught in the toils of deception from a general concern with the keeping up of appearances. Her lover, Henry Knight, becomes step by step a hostile inquisitor as her sad little pretences fall under his scrutiny. 'Her natural honesty', we read, 'invited her to confide in Knight, and trust to his generosity for forgiveness: she knew also that as mere policy it would be better to tell him early if he was to be told at all . . . But she put it off. The intense fear which accompanies intense love in young women was too strong.'

While she hesitates Knight inexorably raises the stakes. 'Elfride,' he says, 'there is one thing I do love to see in a woman—that is, a soul truthful and clear as heaven's light. I could put up with anything if I had that.' How closely he echoes Mr Knightley's sentiments as he expressed them to Emma:

> 'Mystery—Finesse—how they pervert the understanding! My Emma, does not everything serve to prove more and more the beauty of truth and sincerity in all our dealings with each other?'

Indeed the whole protracted battle of wits between Elfride and Knight shows Hardy to have an uncommonly sensitive touch in the kind of writing at which Jane Austen excelled—the creation of a vivacious dialogue on the surface of which are reflected undercurrents in the depths of feeling below. And when they sit down to play, literally, a game of chess it is peculiarly symbolic of their whole relationship.

With the final crumbling of Elfride's defences and the departure abroad of both Knight and Stephen Smith the prospect of a romantic love is ruled out. Elfride marries the widowed Lord Luxellian, with whose young children she is already on affectionate terms. Shortly however, she dies and the train which carries her coffin from London to Cornwall is also, by a grisly coincidence, the one chosen by both Henry Knight and Stephen Smith for what each believes to be a journey of reconciliation with the Elfride they have since learnt they should never have surrendered. The dénouement at their journey's end closes the book on an unexpected note of black comedy.

Proofs of the first instalment were posted to Hardy at the Bodmin home of Emma's father. The visit had become necessary in view of the likelihood of Emma's marriage to the young man who now presented himself for paternal scrutiny. Mr Gifford was a solicitor who no longer practised his profession and was subject to bouts of alcoholism. He seems to have been obsessed with the more snobbish and sterile details of class-consciousness—a characteristic that he unfortunately transmitted to his daughter—and he is said to have called Hardy a 'base churl'.

The episode must have cast a cloud over the remainder of Hardy's stay in Cornwall but he should otherwise have been in good spirits as the year waned. In October Tinsley wrote to say: 'I am longing to read the third portion of *Blue Eyes* for I *shall* lose my reputation as a judge of good fiction if you don't do great things.' Hardy was beginning to feel confident that he could now reject employment in architectural work and rely on his pen for financial support. In December he received an unexpected approach from another 'judge of good fiction' and a more discerning one than Tinsley. This was Leslie Stephen, the editor of the *Cornhill Magazine*, who had been told by Horace Moule that Hardy was the anonymous author of *Under the Greenwood Tree*. After some appropriate compliments Stephen asked to see anything that Hardy could offer as suitable for serialisation in the *Cornhill*. It was a flattering invitation, but before Hardy could make an effective response he had to complete the writing of *A Pair of Blue Eyes*. However, as soon as he could do so he sketched for Stephen the outline of 'a pastoral tale . . . in which the chief characters would be a woman-farmer, a shepherd, and a sergeant in the Dragoon Guards'. And he had already thought of a good title for it: *Far from the Madding Crowd*.

4

A Wife and a Profession 1873 - 1875

. . . a new light among novelists
(*The Spectator, 3 January 1874*)

In 1873 Hardy spent Christmas with Emma at St Juliot—the last Christmas they were to spend in this way as a courting couple. If the prospects for their marriage were discussed and Hardy's financial circumstances affected the timing, Emma must have been pleased to hear the latest news of the new serial in the *Cornhill* and the encouraging interest of Leslie Stephen. At the age of thirty-three, with three novels to his credit but small monetary reward from them, Hardy was now on the verge of the substantial and clinching success that he needed. To Leslie Stephen he confided: 'Perhaps I may have higher aims some day, and be a great stickler for the proper artistic balance of the completed work, but for the present circumstances lead me to wish merely to be considered a good hand at a serial.' His determination to give up architecture while taking on the responsibility of marriage was indeed a circumstance in which he needed to be sure that he could make a living by writing serials. In the words of *The Life*: 'Having now to live by the pen . . . he had to consider popularity.'

With the Christmas holiday over he made his way to the railway station at Plymouth. It was there, on New Year's Eve, that his eye was caught by the January number of *The Cornhill*, containing the first instalment of *Far from the Madding Crowd*. It must have seemed apt that such a moment should occur in the city where his betrothed was born: 'In a room by the Hoe, like the bud of a flower.'

And yet, as he worked on the later instalments, there was something ominous in a comment of Emma's that he copied into his notebook from one of her letters: 'Your novel seems sometimes like a child all your own and none of me.' It was certainly a very different kind of story from the Cornish romance of *A Pair of Blue Eyes* in which Emma could so easily recognise her touches of inspiration. It belonged squarely in Dorset.

Of the six major novels on which Hardy's enduring reputation as a novelist is mainly based *Far from the Madding Crowd* was the first and certainly not the least. In several ways it must be reckoned as the foundation on which his later achievements were built. First and foremost it sealed his commitment to 'Wessex' as the theatre of his imagination. It was in the pages of *Far from the Madding Crowd* that the name of the old Saxon Kingdom began to exchange its historical and antiquarian associations for the new meaning that Hardy has given it.

The book also reveals for the first time Hardy's readiness to tackle tragedy in the grand manner. Looking back at the three stories he had published it would seem that his talent lay in romantic comedy with some satirical touches, the more vehement emotions being diverted into melodramatic unrealities and in that way defused. So far the love he had written about was the love of romantic courtship: real enough in its pains and its ardours but softened with illusions and stopping short of irretrievable catastrophe. *Far from the Madding Crowd* by contrast is about marriage and adultery and death in terms as stark as life can show. One has only to put Bathsheba Everdene, the heroine of *Far from the Madding Crowd*, beside her three predecessors, Cytherea, Fancy and Elfride, to recognise the tremendous advance that Hardy had made. Like them she starts as a pretty girl in a romantic situation; unlike them she is tested to the limits of her endurance by the blows of harsh and credible events that expose her folly and proclaim her courage to the full.

If one other quality of the book is to be singled out here as a distinctive feature it must be the whole *mise-en-scène*, the Wessex countryside itself, which is celebrated with a richness of detail and a springing vitality that add warmth and intimacy to every scene. The whole procession of the farming year at Weatherbury, the customs and speech of the countryside, the motions of life in all its forms—these constitute a tremendous and resonant background for the drama of the central characters. As the story moves from climax to climax it gains an unforced realism from its unfolding context of farm and field and market place in the changing rhythms of the seasons. And it is of course this portrayal of a 'landscape with figures' which became a prime characteristic of Hardy's novels.

Bathsheba herself is a fine creation—more assertive than Tess, not so wild as Eustacia (in *The Return of the Native*) and altogether warmer and more positive than Grace (in *The Woodlanders*). She is perhaps the most normal and natural and instantly likeable of Hardy's heroines. 'There was,' he writes, 'a light air and manner about her now, by which she seemed to imply that the desirability of her existence could not be questioned; and this rather saucy assumption failed in being offensive, because a beholder felt it to be, upon the whole, true.' He comments later 'her philosophy was her conduct, and she seldom thought practicable what she did not practise'.

Her vulnerable point, on which the whole action hinges, is her 'insensibility to the possibly great issues of little beginnings'. It is a theme which much engaged Hardy, this recognition of the landslides of disaster that can spring from a momentary impulse. In *The Return of the Native*, for example, the whole climactic sequence of tragic events is triggered by Eustacia's failure to open her door and welcome her mother-in-law. In the case of Bathsheba there are two such moments which epitomise what T. S. Eliot called:

> The awful daring of a moment's surrender
> Which an age of prudence can never retract.

The first is when, in darkness, she encounters Sergeant Troy and her dress is caught in his spur. She allows herself to be drawn into a bewitching conversation and finds she is no match for his silver-tongued flattery. Though she intends to snub him she cannot resist his compliments. Her vanity betrays her, until: 'Her tone and mien signified beyond mistake that the seed which was to lift the foundation had taken root in the chink: the remainder was a mere question of time.'

The second is when, as a girlish prank, she sends an anonymous valentine to her sober-sided neighbour, Farmer Boldwood, without pausing to think of the effect on this repressed and melancholy man and the possibility that he may discover her authorship (which he does). He assumes the valentine to be seriously intended and the intensity of his submerged, inner life is suddenly released, revealing an emotional violence that had been belied by his dull exterior: 'His equilibrium disturbed, he was in extremity at once. If an emotion possessed him at all, it ruled him . . . though it was possible to form guesses concerning his wild capabilities from old flood marks faintly visible, he had never been seen at the high tides which caused them.'

Competing with these two men for Bathsheba there is a third, Gabriel Oak. He is a rising young sheep farmer who is ruined when his flock is driven over a precipice by a dog he had neglected to control. He becomes a shepherd employed by Bathsheba, whose personal fortunes have risen by the inheritance of a farm at Weatherbury from her uncle at the same time that Gabriel's fell—and consequently his hope of marrying her is abandoned. The story therefore develops round Bathsheba's changing relations with the three men: Boldwood, to whom she owes an obligation because of her folly with the valentine; Troy, who fascinates her with his panache and a sort of demon-lover quality which promises to satisfy her need to be mastered; and the staunch undemanding Gabriel Oak, who protects her interests as best he can.

Oak is first in the field and he represents the moderate middle-of-the-road unemphatic qualities that have a kinship with his native landscape. Morally he is the counterpart of Norcombe Hill where he grazes his flocks, and which Hardy describes as 'an ordinary specimen of those smoothly-outlined protuberances of the globe which may remain undisturbed on some great day of confusion, when far grander heights and dizzy granite precipices topple down'. Troy and Boldwood are the men who suggest vistas of grander heights and dizzy precipices; Oak is described as occupying morally 'that vast middle space of Laodicean neutrality which lay between the Communion people of the parish and the drunken section . . . he was a man whose moral colour was a kind of pepper-and-salt mixture'.

To Bathsheba, in the spirited pride of her youth, this pepper-and-salt diffidence is unexciting. 'It wouldn't do, Mr Oak,' she says when he proposes marriage in his more prosperous days. 'I want somebody to tame me; I am too independent; and you would never be able to, I know.'

It is Sergeant Troy who establishes a symbolical mastery over her, in one of Hardy's most brilliantly inventive scenes—the display of swordsmanship in which Troy dazzles, unnerves and fascinates Bathsheba. Combining the grace of a ballet with the dexterity and daring of a circus knife-throwing act, this demonstration of the swordsman's art is as much a mating display as any in the animal kingdom. As the soldier faces the woman and his blade flashes in the light, each movement becomes part of a deepening and compelling ritual. It is a *tour de force* of its kind, without a rival until the sheaf-gathering scene in D. H. Lawrence's *The Rainbow*, forty years later.

When Troy's sword is finally sheathed in its scabbard he kisses Bathsheba and she feels 'like one who has sinned a great sin'. In this she is akin to other Hardy characters, to Grace Melbury in *The Woodlanders*, for example, and Sue Bridehead in *Jude*. 'Diana was the goddess whom Bathsheba instinctively adored,' Hardy writes. Until that moment with Troy 'it had been a glory to her to know that her lips had been touched by no man's on earth'. She is thus an embodiment of the feminine archetype of purity and chastity that Henry Knight was seeking in *A Pair of Blue Eyes*, that Angel Clare thought he had found in Tess, and that Hardy was repeatedly drawn to explore in his writings. Her 'sin' can perhaps be best described as her abasement before a pleasure-seeking man interested only in conquest: she has surrendered to the gratification of being mastered. As Matthew Moon observes sagely in a harvest-field discussion among the labourers, 'maids rather like your man of sin'.

For Troy the coin has another side. 'In setting a gin I have caught myself,' he says—words that Alec d'Urberville might echo. Though he marries Bathsheba he cannot change his image of her as 'the proud girl who had always looked down upon him'. In these terms he can, as a husband, humiliate her: he is incapable of loving her. His affection and his tenderness, such as they are, are committed elsewhere, to one of Bathsheba's workpeople—the humble and artless Fanny Robin. At one time Troy had intended to marry Fanny; ironically it was he who was left waiting at the altar because she, characteristically and almost inevitably, went to the wrong church. Like Gabriel Oak, Fanny had to pay a savage price for a moment's inattention. Pregnant with Troy's child, she drifted away from Weatherbury.

In comparison with Hardy's major feminine portraits Fanny is little more than a conventionally stylised version of the betrayed and forlorn maid of balladry. But when she returns to Casterbridge workhouse to die in childbirth and in so doing to haunt and destroy Bathsheba's marriage, she excites Hardy's compassion to produce some of the most powerful passages he had yet written. As her strength fails during her journey a large dog pulls her along. By degrees the relationship between them transcends reality and takes on an epic quality, until at last Fanny collapses at the workhouse door. When she is carried over the threshold she enquires about the dog: 'Where is he gone? He helped me.' And the man replies: 'I stoned him away.'

When Fanny dies next day Hardy comments: 'The one feat alone—that of dying—by which a mean condition could be resolved into a grand one, Fanny had achieved.' Because her corpse is the responsibility of the parish of Weatherbury Bathsheba sends one of her workmen, Joseph Poorgrass, to fetch the coffin, loading it on to his waggon from the workhouse morgue-door which 'seemed to advertise itself as a species of Traitor's Gate translated to another sphere'. And so the coffin is lodged overnight in Bathsheba's farmhouse after a delay at the *Buck's Head*, where Poorgrass chances to meet two boon companions, Jan Coggan and Mark Clark, and engages with them in one of their most hilarious conversations. That night, unable to restrain herself, Bathsheba opens the coffin. It contains, beside Fanny, a stillborn child.

The scene that follows, when Troy enters the room unawares, is not one to be paraphrased: it must be read in full. Suffice to say here that Troy subsequently disappears and is believed to have drowned. By degrees Boldwood revives his claim to Bathsheba and gives a Christmas party to make public the renewed understanding between them, with the hope that they may marry when Troy's death is well established. But Troy is alive still, has returned to Weatherbury and interrupts the party to command Bathsheba to accompany him. Boldwood, goaded to madness, shoots him.

Nothing remains but for Hardy to engineer the happy ending that was required of him by editors and publishers. The loyal and useful Oak is now free to resume his wooing of Bathsheba. If their final union is an unexciting climax to the events that have preceded it, at least there are Joseph Poorgrass, Jan Coggan, Mark Clark and the rest of the rustics to round off the story with a flourish—and incidentally to demonstrate their great value to Hardy for just such contingencies.

Despite the happy ending the burden of the story is clear enough. With every turn of the plot Hardy is emphasising the massive consequences of seemingly trivial actions. If Gabriel had shut the dog indoors, if Fanny had gone to the right church, if Troy's spur had not caught in Bathsheba's dress, if Bathsheba had sent her playful valentine to almost any man except the volcanic Boldwood—the examples multiply of petty follies that a merciful God might readily forgive, but that Blind Chance launches inexorably towards a crushing retribution. Here, in his fourth novel, Hardy had plainly enunciated with a wealth of graphic detail one of the great themes that preoccupied him throughout his career. At the core of his compassion there is this contention that human actions too often have disproportionate consequences: that, by implication, Divine punishment is disproportionate to human sin.

The immediate importance of *Far from the Madding Crowd* at the time of its publication lay in its revelation of a fresh, original and massive talent emerging into full mastery. Far away now were the days of the *Spectator*'s savage derision for *Desperate Remedies*. Reviewing the first instalment, which appeared anonymously, the *Spectator* poured balm on the old wound with the perceptive words: 'If *Far from the Madding Crowd* is not written by George Eliot, then there is a new light among novelists.' This delighted and amused Leslie Stephen who commented in a letter to Hardy that 'the gentle *Spectator* thinks you must be George Eliot because you know the names of the stars'.

The comparison with George Eliot must have pleased Hardy since he regarded her as a 'great thinker—one of the greatest living'. But he was quite clear about the difference between them in that genre which Merryn Williams, in *Thomas Hardy and Rural England*, has defined as 'country writing'. In Hardy's view George Eliot had 'never touched the life of the fields'. In reflecting on the distinctive nature of rustic humour he described George Eliot's work as 'evidencing a woman's wit cast in country dialogue rather than real country humour'. For him the real thing, the genuine article, was 'rather of the Shakespeare and Fielding sort'.

This is particularly interesting as a commentary on Hardy's own work. It is a reminder that he could easily overcome those barriers of class and sex which prevented other writers from mingling easily in the life of the fields and observing at first hand the unconstrained humour 'of the Shakespeare and Fielding sort' that flowed from the likes of Jan Coggan and Joseph Poorgrass. His approach was free from the condescension which stereotyped such farmworkers as 'Hodge', the oaf in a smock. In his advice to the illustrator of *Far from the Madding Crowd* Hardy expressed the hope that 'the rustics, although *quaint*, may be made to appear intelligent, and not boorish at all'. It is worth noting here incidentally that Hardy himself refers to them as 'rustics'. In discussing his novels critics find it convenient to refer comprehensively to the 'rustic chorus'—an unhappy phrase if it suggests a patronising approach, but a serviceable one taken in the same spirit in which Hardy used the word.

Hardy finished writing the story in July 1874. On 17 September at St Peter's, Paddington, he and Emma were married by an uncle of Emma's, Canon Hamilton Gifford of Worcester (who later became Archdeacon of London). The choice of a London church for the occasion is surprising when the claims of St Juliot seem undeniable. It was the bride's home, after all—and she had hardly ever seen Hardy outside the ambience of St Juliot. The church there had been the cause of their meeting; the rector and his wife had been Hardy's hosts whenever he visited Emma and they continued to be on friendly terms with Hardy after the wedding. Emma was a devout churchwoman for whom the sacrament of marriage would have a profound significance. She and Hardy both seemed to take a highly romantic view of the love that had drawn them together in the idyllic setting of the Cornish coast. What could be more natural, more seemly and more agreeable than that she should be married in the church that he had helped to restore, and as the bride from the rectory where his rare visits had been so eventful and—in Emma's words—'highly delightful'.

Was it the sternness of family disapproval that made Emma consent to a ceremony at such a distance from her kindred and her homeland? It is often stressed that the Victorian class system was a formidable barrier, separating the Giffords who were 'professional' people from the Hardys who were not. No doubt Emma's father still considered she was marrying beneath her, but it is at least possible that Gifford opposition to the marriage could have been relenting by 1874. Emma's age had reached the sobering milestone of thirty-four years and she was certainly not besieged by suitors, while Hardy had just shown with his fourth novel that fame and fortune were no empty dream. The Giffords may understandably have wished that Emma had done better for herself, but some of them perhaps realised that she might have done worse.

Whatever the reason, St Juliot was disregarded; at the church in Paddington Emma met her bridegroom in the company of her uncle, Canon Gifford, and one of her brothers whose role was to deputise for the head of the family and formally give away the bride. The only other person present was Miss L. A. Williams. She was the daughter of Hardy's landlady and signed the register as a witness. She may or may not have been invited: she could hardly be prevented from coming.

There is of course nothing unusual in a quiet wedding. If either partner takes an unconventional view of marriage as a tedious minor formality, then it is nobody's business to carp at the lack of ceremony, the absence of wedding guests and so on. But when all that is conceded there are some odd features in what a casual bystander might have been pardoned for assuming to be a shotgun wedding. There was no best man or groomsman. None of Hardy's London friends attended. From the bride's and groom's complement of parents, brothers and sisters, not one journeyed up from the Westcountry. For such romantic and churchy people it was a surprisingly drab and perfunctory occasion. One is left to wonder what the bride thought of this muted ceremony. In her 'Recollections' written many years later, she recalled that her wedding-day was 'a perfect September day—not brilliant sunshine, but wearing a soft, sunny luminousness; just as it should be'. She allowed herself no further comment.

To Hardy's attitude there are one or two clues worth noticing.

In 'Intra Sepulchrum', a poem published in 1922, he imagines himself after death discussing with Emma their life together: significantly he recalls that, with her, he

> Played at believing in gods
> And observing the ordinances,
> I for your sake in impossible codes
> Right ready to acquiesce.

That he had decided, as early as 1874, that marriage was the 'impossible code' he later judged it to be is unlikely, but he can perhaps be fairly described as in the rebellious and transitional stage of Edward Springrove in *Desperate Remedies* who observed that Miss Aldclyffe 'like a good many others in her position, had plainly not realised that a son of her tenant and inferior could have become an educated man, who had learnt . . . to view society from a Bohemian standpoint'.

If we consider the young men with whom Hardy associated in London and Dorchester and Weymouth—draughtsmen, clerks, articled pupils, bright and intelligent newcomers to the fringes of professional or semi-professional life but in many cases with no commitment to the established order and often beset with personal insecurities—we can readily allow that the intellectual ferment in which they found themselves fostered the sort of alignment which enabled them to view society 'from a Bohemian standpoint', with a consequent scepticism about class and religion as the two main pillars of Victorian society.

As an educated man, one who knew almost by heart works like John Stuart Mill's 'On Liberty', Hardy was rapidly emancipating himself from preoccupations with class and convention. To offset the disapproval of the Giffords he could assert his conviction that 'a person who socially is nothing is thought less of by people who are not much than by those who are a great deal'. It may not be fanciful to suggest that he came to the wedding as a deliberately solitary figure, a true 'Bohemian' who was neither leaving one class nor joining another but was indifferent to both as regimental devices. His business was with Emma, solely, and in a matter-of-fact spirit which only later acquired the sheen and patina of unalloyed romance. St Peter's, Paddington, was convenient: that sufficed. The married couple travelled at once to Brighton and Hardy pencilled a note to his brother, Henry, asking him to tell 'all at home' that the wedding had taken place and that the details of it would appear in an advertisement-notice in the *Dorset Chronicle*.

Starting her honeymoon at Brighton, Emma prepared to record her impressions in a new notebook. 'Sea rough,' she wrote, 'Tom bathed.' Mainly she concentrated her attention on the Aquarium, studying the seals and turtles and observing that all fish close their eyes while sleeping. In the streets she was much taken with the goat carriages, one of which she sketched, and she was amused by a 'fat baby boy holding the reins importantly'.

They stayed in Brighton for several days and seemingly attended church service twice on the Sunday, as Emma noted: 'Evening. St Peter's crowded but not so much as in the morning.' She was also struck by the atmosphere of a Sunday in Brighton: 'like a Parisian Sunday, all enjoyment and gaiety and bands of music and excursionists'. Perhaps Paris was in her mind because, as Hardy had written to his brother, they were moving on from Brighton to France 'for materials for my next story'.

Two months later, when *Far from the Madding Crowd* was published in book form, the author was living at Surbiton. Those of us who also have lived at Surbiton must always find this a very relishable paradox. It is however more than that. It symbolises a great division and tension in Hardy, an enduring disquiet about his own relationships to Wessex on the one hand and to 'Society' on the other.

He has left us an idyllic and perhaps romanticised picture of himself during the writing of *Far from the Madding Crowd*, when he rambled through the countryside surrounding Bockhampton and picked up large dead leaves or white chips of wood left by the woodcutters on which to write notes as they came suddenly into his mind. But if one side of his nature wanted to identify as closely as possible with the grass-roots of his being, to be supremely the deep Wessex countryman, the other side listened respectfully to the authoritative voice of Lady Ritchie, who was not only Leslie Stephen's sister-in-law but Thackeray's daughter and who assured Hardy that 'a novelist must necessarily like Society'.

The reason that Hardy was living in Surbiton was apparently the same one that had made him steer the honeymoon through Rouen and Paris. His next novel was already firm enough in outline to ensure that the Wessex element would be subordinate to the Society one. Hardy therefore wanted a base in or near London. In the following spring he moved Emma from Surbiton to a part of London familiar to him from his bachelor days, Westbourne Grove.

Having secured such a successful story for the *Cornhill*, Leslie Stephen was quick to invite Hardy to follow it up with another. Tinsley meanwhile would have liked a successor to *A Pair of Blue Eyes* and apparently invited one. When Hardy had broken the news to him that *Far from the Madding Crowd* was already promised to 'a friend', Tinsley complained of a breach of courtesy. As he had published Hardy's first three stories he felt that Hardy might have told him of the intention to go elsewhere with his fourth.

Their association was never renewed and in 1878 Tinsley's career as a publisher ended in bankruptcy. His parting comments on *Far from the Madding Crowd* were shrewd and, in view of his disappointment, not ungenerous. He spoke of the book as 'brim full of genius', prophesied that Hardy would make a great name as a writer of fiction, and concluded: 'I think your genius truer than Dickens's ever was, but you want a monitor more than the great Novelist ever did.'

The monitor Hardy now had was Leslie Stephen, whom R. L. Purdy describes as 'the finest critic Hardy encountered in his career as a novelist'. Their friendship was an important influence on Hardy and Stephen's critical attention to literary detail was undoubtedly helpful. His sub-editing skill and his feeling for shape and length improved Hardy's manuscripts. His practical comments helped to professionalise Hardy. But when all that is conceded it must be said he seems not to have recognised the real point of Hardy's genius; his moral timidity—however much it may be extenuated tactically—denied Hardy the discriminating support that he must at times have needed sorely. Their association had scarcely begun before Stephen was writing—

> Troy's seduction of the young woman will require to be treated in a gingerly fashion . . . I mean that the thing must be stated but that the words must be careful—excuse this wretched shred of concession to popular stupidity; but I am a slave.

Stephen, in his bowdlerising moments, liked to insist that he objected as an editor, not as a critic, and therefore 'in the interest of a stupid public, not from my own taste'. Perhaps he comforted himself by so dividing his judgment. Less comforting is the fact that, having acquired *The Hand of Ethelberta* for the *Cornhill*, he managed to lose *The Return of the Native* because, according to Hardy, 'he feared that the relations between Eustacia, Wildeve and Thomasin might develop into something "dangerous" for a family magazinc'. He therefore refused to commit himself to serialisation until he could see the entire story completed; Hardy consequently made other arrangements.

Hardy seems to have embarked on *The Hand of Ethelberta* from two motives: a desire to write the kind of novel that would display his capacities as a professional novelist taking the *beau monde* as subject matter, and a determination to avoid being typecast as a regional writer specialising in rustic scenes and characters. Perhaps it was a gesture to Emma's ladylike preoccupations or to Leslie Stephen's fastidious taste. If so, it was largely wasted on Emma who thought the story had 'too much about servants in it'.

Looking back on it a hundred years after it was written it is easy enough to dismiss the book as a fiasco. The plot is ludicrous and the style reflects a deep and potentially crippling uncertainty of purpose. As if unable to settle down, Hardy's talents fly off tangentially in conflicting directions at each turn of the story. Like a coquette trying on hats he offers us a variety of personations. There is Hardy the satirist in the comic theatre tradition that, from Ben Jonson to Sheridan, gave burlesqued names to the characters it lampooned: Neigh, Ladywell, and Mrs Menlove are Hardy's additions to that long ancestry. There is Hardy, the smart coiner of sophisticated epigrams a generation before Oscar Wilde patented the process, as for example 'that gentle order of society which has no worldly sorrow except when its jewellery gets stolen', or 'forgetting my existence as much as if he had vowed in church to love and cherish me for life'.

There is Hardy the thinker and man of learning, playfully kicking around references to Utilitarianism and Benthamism; and there is Hardy the inner voice of Wessex, filling his opening pages with some of his richest passages of rustic speech.

But there is something else, too, which gives a semblance of coherence to these dissociated elements. There is the pervading spirit that first impelled Hardy to write *The Poor Man and the Lady* and which prompted Macmillan's opinion that it 'meant mischief'. Hardy's own description of that lost first work was that it tended to be 'socialistic, not to say revolutionary'. It is worth looking more closely at Ethelberta herself to discover how much she embodies that earlier attitude, if only in a cryptic and comic fashion.

In his preface of 1895 Hardy admitted that 'a high degree of probability was not attempted in the arrangement of the incidents'. It would indeed be otiose to summarise here every twist and turn of the story and it is sufficient to outline Ethelberta's intentions and actions. She is the daughter of a butler whose name, taken from a village near Weymouth, identifies the family with Wessex. Ethelberta herself has been a governess, but a marriage above her station and subsequent widowhood results in her living with her mother-in-law, Lady Petherwin, on condition that she does not publicly recognise her own family. Privately and secretly, however, Ethelberta resolves to alleviate the poverty of her parents and their numerous brood. She publishes a book of poems, 'not exactly virginibus puerisque', and wins a measure of fame which she develops in public recitals as a storyteller. In his earlier days in London Hardy had attended some of Dickens's readings at the Hanover Square Rooms and would have visualised Ethelberta performing in similar fashion. When Lady Petherwin dies, bequeathing her London house to Ethelberta but no money with it, the Chickerel family unite in a plan to maintain Ethelberta's social position by masquerading as her servants and entertaining paying guests from abroad.

In passing it must be said that any 'poverty' endured by the Chickerels would have occurred a decade earlier. With her father in regular employment as a butler, a sister working as a pupil teacher, two brothers in demand as skilled tradesmen and another brother ready for work, Ethelberta's anxiety for the wellbeing of the remainder does more credit to her heart than her head. Nevertheless she launches her one-woman crusade into the upper levels of social and intellectual London with a vigorous drive from below and from without. She is the champion of the lower orders of Wessex, taking on the élite of the capital at their own game and with her tongue in her cheek. It is not too far-fetched to say that she has taken the chip off the shoulder of the young author of *The Poor Man and the Lady* and now wears it herself with a startling insouciance and boldness.

Supremely it is the characterisation of Ethelberta alone which holds together this brittle and erratic story. She epitomises those tensions and conflicting aims which seem to have been most important to Hardy at this time. He wanted to demonstrate his ability to handle the London scene with assurance. He still saw the novel as a vehicle for radical satire. Like her he was concerned with loyalty to 'class and kin'. A familiar gauntlet is thrown down when a minor character declares that 'mediocrity stamped

"London" fetches more than talent marked "provincial" '. And it is Ethelberta who brings to a head Hardy's dissatisfaction with the prevailing customs of romantic fiction.

Always available among Ethelberta's suitors is the sensitive young provincial musician, Christopher Julian, who is set up at the outset as the conventional partner for the happy ending that such a serial predicates. But Hardy develops Ethelberta along suffragette or Women's Lib lines, preserving her femininity but giving her a man's career structure and prudential considerations. In Victorian terms she is an anti-heroine, rejecting romance for the goals that men pursue—power, public acclaim, the ability to make financial provision for her family and to consolidate a wise alliance by marriage. Events carry her from 'soft and playful Romanticism to distorted Benthamism', and Hardy poses the question: 'Was the moral incline upward or down?'

In the conclusion of the story he is at his most provocative. The romantic young musician is denied Ethelberta and assigned to her younger sister, Picotee. Courtship for Ethelberta becomes a romping farce with three suitors, Neigh, Ladywell and the wicked old Wessex landowner, Lord Mountclere, all pursuing her to France and proposing simultaneously. She chooses Mountclere, expels his French mistress and lives—well, not happily ever after, perhaps, but comfortably and agreeably ever after. She soon assumes the master's role as boss of the Mountclere estates and runs them in a businesslike and successful way. Once again she is shown to be out-manning the male world.

All in all, this stands as probably Hardy's most bizarre performance. In it he purged his anti-romantic satirical impulse by giving full rein to it and exploring its limits. There were to be echoes later, in *Two on a Tower* for example, but Hardy never really returned to the style of *Ethelberta.* Nevertheless, in his gallery of feminine portraits hers is one that is not to be passed by lightly or dismissed with indifference.

For the sake of verisimilitude in the settings of his stories Hardy liked to live as close as possible to the scenes he was describing. After the winter at Surbiton he wrote to his new publisher, George Smith of Smith & Elder: 'We are coming to Town for three months on account of Ethelberta, some London scenes occurring in her chequered career which I want to do as vigorously as possible—having already visited Rouen and Paris with the same object.' After the three months at Westbourne Grove the Hardys went househunting in Dorset, took a steamboat from Bournemouth to Swanage and found lodgings there with an invalided sea captain. 'I am a countryman again,' Hardy wrote to R. D. Blackmore. Ethelberta similarly travelled to 'Knollsea', giving Hardy the opportunity to include in the book a charming picture of Victorian Swanage 'lying snug within two headlands as between a finger and thumb'. *The Hand of Ethelberta* may rank low among Hardy's writings but his account of the wives of Swanage is too good to overlook.

> Some wives of the village, it is true, had learned to let lodgings, and others to keep shops. The doors of these latter places were formed of an upper hatch, usually kept open, and a lower hatch, with a bell attached, usually kept shut. Whenever a stranger went in, he would hear a whispering of astonishment from a back room, after which a woman came forward, looking suspiciously at him as an intruder, and advancing slowly enough to allow her mouth to get clear of the meal she was partaking of. Meanwhile the people in the back room would stop their knives and forks in absorbed curiosity as to the reason of the stranger's entry, who by this time feels ashamed of his unwarrantable intrusion into this hermit's cell, and thinks he must take his hat off. The woman is quite alarmed at seeing that he is not one of the fifteen native women and children who patronise her, and nervously puts her hand to the side of her face, which she carries slanting. The visitor finds himself saying what he wants in an apologetic tone, when the woman tells him that they did keep that article once, but do not now; that nobody does, and probably never will again; and as he turns away she looks relieved that the dilemma of having to provide for a stranger has passed off with no worse mishap than disappointing him.

Hardy made another use of the months in London. On the sixtieth anniversary of the Battle of Waterloo he and Emma visited Chelsea Hospital and chatted to some of Wellington's veterans. At the same time Hardy entered in his notebook these significant words: 'Mem: A Ballad of the Hundred Days. Then another of Moscow. Others of earlier campaigns—forming altogether an Iliad of Europe from 1789 to 1815.'

With *The Hand of Ethelberta* completed there was no need to remain in Swanage so they made a second visit to the Continent. Among the places they visited was Waterloo. On their return to England they again spent Waterloo Day at Chelsea Hospital. Twelve years were to pass before Hardy began to sketch his plans for *The Dynasts*: twenty or more before the work really started to take shape. When he was not obliged to write immediately in response to a commission—as with his serials—Hardy liked to germinate slowly. His interest in the Napoleonic wars was a life-long interest. As a boy he had found in a cupboard some old illustrated numbers of a periodical called *A History of the Wars* to which his grandfather—a volunteer at the time of Napoleon's feared invasion of England—had subscribed. These had quickened an interest which did not come to full realisation until Hardy was in his sixties. In his own words he was 'quick to bloom; late to ripen'.

5

The Native Returns 1876 - 1878

Lifelong to be
Seemed the fair colour of the time
(*The Musical Box*)

In the first two years of their marriage the Hardys had lived in four different places and twice crossed the Channel to explore France and the Low Countries. It was now time to settle down to a more stable home-life. In July 1876, therefore, they moved into a house overlooking the river Stour at Sturminster Newton. 'Riverside Villa' or 'Rivercliff' as it was sometimes called was a 'dusky house that stood apart'. The proximity of the river was a decided attraction as Hardy liked to take out a rowingboat for his relaxation. Swimming and rowing were favourite outdoor pursuits of his, from his Weymouth days.

With a housemaid living in, Thomas and Emma embarked on a quiet and pleasantly conventional life, much like that of any young middle-class couple in their first home. At Christmas they visited Hardy's parents. Looking back long afterwards on the two years spent at Sturminster and picturing in memory Emma

'White-muslined, waiting there
In the porch with high-expectant heart'

Hardy spoke of their time together then as 'this best of life'.

At Sturminster Hardy was well placed to extend and deepen his knowledge of Dorset. The little market town on the Stour is a gateway to the Vale of Blackmoor. The adjacent villages include Marnhull which, as 'Marlott', was to be the birthplace and home of Tess. The steep escarpment along the southern edge of Blackmoor Vale is crowned with those peaks which resound like a litany through Hardy's writings—Bulbarrow, Nettlecombe Tout, Dogbury, High Stoy and Bubb Down. He and Emma both enjoyed walking, exploring the countryside, sketching and making notes: doubtless Hardy received and probably recorded many new impressions which were to be crystallised later in his novels and stories of Wessex. But the immediate subject for his pen was the landscape further south, the scene of his childhood and youth, 'the vast tract of unenclosed wild known as Egdon Heath'. The book that engaged his working hours during the two happy years at Sturminster Newton was *The Return of the Native.*

This, the second of his six major novels, carries his sense of the dramatic qualities of a landscape to a pitch that he never exceeded. The barren austerity of Egdon Heath, with its inherent paganism and its outcropping acts of witchcraft, releases a presence of such formidable power that it encompasses those who inhabit it and imparts to their lives a bias with which they must contend. The original unity of the east Dorset heathlands was already being broken up by enclosure and agriculture in Hardy's time, and over the past 150 years the acreage of what he named collectively 'Egdon' has shrunk from 75,000 acres to 25,000, but in *The Return of the Native* he emphasised its pristine essence as the archetype of 'those wild regions of obscurity which are vaguely felt to be compassing us about in midnight dreams of flight and disaster'. Under the play of Hardy's poetic imagination the Heath transcends its inanimate character and acquires human attributes: 'As with some persons who have long lived apart, solitude seemed to look out of its countenance. It had a lonely face, suggesting tragical possibilities.'

The native who returns to Egdon is Clym Yeobright, only son of a widowed mother. He has been living in Paris, engaged in some undefined branch of the diamond trade. During his absence his mother's only companion has been her orphaned niece, Thomasin, whom Mrs Yeobright would like Clym to marry in due course. Two other men present themselves as possible husbands for Thomasin: one is Damon Wildeve, an engineer who has abandoned his profession and become the landlord of the local inn; the other is Diggory Venn who travels about the district selling reddle, a red ochre in which at that time sheep were dipped. Of both men Mrs Yeobright disapproves. She disapproves also of Eustacia Vye, a spirited girl of nineteen who lives on the Heath with her grandfather. When Clym asks his mother who Miss Vye is, she answers: 'A proud girl from Budmouth. One not much to my liking.'

The story follows the changing relationships between these six characters. At the outset Eustacia and Wildeve have a curious and secret hot-and-cold romance which terminates when Wildeve marries Thomasin, while Eustacia sets her cap at Clym. She dreams of the day when, as Clym's wife and as 'the mistress of some pretty establishment, however small, near a Parisian boulevard, she would be passing her days on the skirts at least of the gay world'. But Clym renounces all that Paris and the diamond trade symbolise. He is, by Hardy's definition, a newly evolving sort of man. 'In Clym Yeobright's face', he writes, 'could be dimly seen the typical countenance of the future.' Clym is indeed what we should now recognise as a drop-out, a recruit to the 'alternative' society. He wants to settle down on Egdon as a teacher of the underprivileged.

> Yeobright loved his kind. He had a conviction that the want of most men was knowledge of a sort which brings wisdom rather than affluence. He wished to raise the class at the expense of individuals rather than individuals at the expense of the class.

There could be no greater contrast to such a character than Eustacia Vye, the most sensational and volcanic of Hardy's heroines. Never did he use more startlingly exuberant phrases than in his description of this exotic creature for whom Egdon was a prison.

> Eustacia Vye was the raw material of a divinity . . . She had the passions

> and instincts which make a model goddess, that is, those which make not quite a model woman . . . Her presence brought memories of such things as Bourbon roses, rubies, and tropical midnights; her moods recalled lotus-eaters and the march in 'Athalie'; her motions, the ebb and flow of the sea . . .

And so on. Her pagan eyes are 'full of nocturnal mysteries', her soul is 'flame-like', and her prayer is: 'Send me great love from somewhere, else I shall die.' More shrewdly Hardy observes: 'She seemed to long for the abstraction called passionate love more than for any particular lover'; and he adds that 'Her loneliness deepened her desire. On Egdon, coldest and meanest kisses were at famine prices; and where was a mouth matching hers to be found?'

Her marriage with Clym is doomed from the outset. Her belief that she can persuade him to return to Paris is a pathetic delusion. His determination to qualify as a teacher by intensive study is frustrated by failing eyesight. And there is always danger in the two unsatisfied figures that prowl around the borders of their married life—the possessive, grudging mother and the ex-lover Wildeve, disenchanted with his own marriage to the mild and commonplace Thomasin.

Mrs Yeobright's relationship with Clym is defined plainly enough when she hears that he has given to Eustacia a burial urn from a local barrow excavation instead of taking it home to her, as he first intended:

> When Clym came home . . . his mother said, in a curious tone, 'The urn you had meant for me you gave away.'
>
> Yeobright made no reply; the current of her feeling was too pronounced to admit it.

Later, when he returns to his mother's house after kissing Eustacia:

> The light which shone forth on him from the window revealed that his face was flushed and his eye bright. What it did not show was something which lingered upon his lips like a seal set there. The abiding presence of

> this impress was so real that he hardly dared to enter the house, for it seemed as if his mother might say, 'What red spot is that glowing upon your mouth so vividly?'

Mrs Yeobright's attitude to her future daughter-in-law is unequivocal. She condemns her as 'lazy and dissatisfied' and as a 'hussy', and asserts bluntly, 'I have never heard that she is of any use to herself or to other people.' To extenuate her vindictiveness she protests to Clym, 'all I wish to do is to save you from sorrow', but he is nonetheless shaken by the merciless character of her hostility.

The threat from Wildeve is altogether subtler, more erratic, more fitful. Hardy defines the man thus:

> To be yearning for the difficult, to be weary of that offered; to care for the remote, to dislike the near; it was Wildeve's nature always. This is the true mark of the man of sentiment . . . He might have been called the Rousseau of Egdon.

This desultory ladykiller, pulled into Eustacia's orbit and yet no match for her, remains an errant hazard in her course. Even when they have gone their separate ways, there remains a bond of a kind between them.

And so the climax is reached, in one of those satires of circumstance at which Hardy excels. To the humble cottage where Clym and Eustacia are living in near poverty Mrs Yeobright comes on a pilgrimage of reconciliation, and Wildeve also and separately comes in no underhand way but as the husband of Clym's cousin. It is a fatal coincidence. Clym, exhausted from his labours as a furzecutter—which he has become—is sleeping. Eustacia, fearing the interpretation that Mrs Yeobright may put on Wildeve's presence, is concerned to smuggle him away and assumes that Clym will awake and welcome his mother when she knocks. But Clym sleeps on. Mrs Yeobright, having seen enough to believe that Eustacia refuses to admit her, turns back rebuffed. The long walk in the heat of the day exhausts her: she sinks down, is bitten by an adder and dies what must be described as a symbolically venomous death, bequeathing to others her description of herself as 'a broken-hearted woman cast off by her son'.

The impact of Mrs Yeobright's death, or rather of its apparent cause, drives Clym and Eustacia apart in mutual recrimination and bitterness of spirit. Her instinct is to fly from the Heath which, in its barrenness, has so impoverished her hopes of feeling 'all the beating and pulsing that is going on in the great arteries of the world'. Once again she uses the old signal of a lighted bonfire that brings Wildeve to her. He is to help her escape, though no longer as her lover. 'He's not *great* enough for me to give myself to', she says. 'To break my marriage vow for him—it is too poor a luxury!'

Her plan ends in disaster. As in *Far from the Madding Crowd* the central characters are drawn together in a night-time convergence at the point where sudden death provides its stark solution. Eustacia stumbles into a weirpool and is drowned. Wildeve dies trying to save her. Nothing remains but to tidy up the loose ends in the accepted way. The mysterious and menacing figure of the reddleman washes the redness from his skin, becomes a respectable dairy farmer and persuades the widowed Thomasin to make a fresh start as Mrs Diggory Venn. Clym becomes an itinerant preacher with an ethical but non-theological message for those who care to listen. And to this somewhat muted fanfare of happiness Hardy added later an astonishing footnote:

> . . . the original conception of the story did not design a marriage between Thomasin and Venn. He was to have retained his isolated and weird character to the last, and to have disappeared mysteriously from the heath, nobody knowing whither—Thomasin remaining a widow. But certain circumstances of serial publication led to a change of intent.
>
> Readers can therefore choose between the endings, and those with an austere artistic code can assume the more consistent conclusion to be the true one.

It is an oddity of our literature that a novel of this stature should be left by its creator in such an unresolved condition.

Hardy gradually became adept at the preparation of his MSS in alternative versions, providing a toned-down and bowdlerised form for serialisation, and he might have been expected to restore the 'more consistent conclusion' at some later date when he was preparing a new edition of *The Native*. But here he was content to invite his readers to 'correct the misrelation' as he did similarly in *The Distracted Preacher* and again over a lesser detail in *The Withered Arm*.

The reddleman, marrying Thomasin or no, remains one of Hardy's most numinous and original characters, rich in symbolical plausibilities, liable to appear at any moment and intervene in the action before once more disappearing into the darkness and the shadows of the Heath. It is he most of all who embodies the very spirit of Egdon in his outlandish nomad life. The nightscene where he gambles with Wildeve by the light of some hurriedly gathered glow-worms is one of the best known passages in the book but there are many which give a comparable richness of context to the central framework of the action: the bonfires lighting the darkness 'like wounds in a black hide', the Christmas mummers bringing Eustacia to her first meeting with Clym, the wild dance at the village gipsying, the forces of witchcraft and superstition that suddenly break through. Hardy drew very fully on the folk world of his childhood to furnish an ambience that remains uniquely his.

Like some evil cauldron Egdon brews its pungent vapours and wraithlike mists in which people become confused and lost. If *A Pair of Blue Eyes* is about deception, *The Return of the Native* is about misunderstandings and misconceptions. Eustacia clings to the impossible belief that Clym will after all resume his Parisian career; Clym, no less blindly, considers her to be an ideal school matron; Mrs Yeobright thinks her olive branch has been flung back in her face. Furthermore, to these all-too-human misconceptions is added a sort of cosmic malevolence. Clym's letter of reconciliation just fails to reach Eustacia in time. Mrs Yeobright's peacemaking visit comes at an inopportune moment.

Clym's eyesight fails when he starts to study. At every turn the best of intentions come up against some frustrating circumstance.

Nevertheless the seeds of disaster are in their characters from the outset. If Wildeve is, as Hardy says, 'the Rousseau of Egdon', Eustacia is the Heath's Emma Bovary—or perhaps more precisely its Caroline Lamb, looking for some impossibly tempestuous Byron to transport her from the nullity of hated Egdon to Paris at least. Clym is no less confused, always dreaming of what he is going to do but doomed like Eustacia to wander in a world of fantasies—though fantasies of a different kind. Both of them are hopelessly alienated from the realities of their situation. And Mrs Yeobright, grim, obstinate, inflexible, swift to disapprove, a petty woman in a stiflingly small world, is bound to take an overdose of umbrage sooner or later. The issues that precipitate the overthrow of the main characters may seem to be of less gravity and power, at least in the language of 'real life', than in Hardy's other major tragedies: it is his particular achievement in this book to build them up so relentlessly and inevitably to a climax of awesome magnitude.

In making his arrangements for the serial publication of *The Return of the Native* Hardy had to look for some alternative to *The Cornhill*, in consequence of Leslie Stephen's nervous disengagement. He seems to have had no high opinion of the magazine which in the event published it: he spoke scornfully of 'publication in (of all places) *Belgravia*'. This periodical was owned by Chatto & Windus, who at about the same time acquired *Under the Greenwood Tree* from Tinsley in the course of his bankruptcy. The takeover of Tinsley's assets may have stimulated an interest in Hardy's latest work, or the decision by *Belgravia*'s editor may have been coincidental; in either case the association with Chatto's was transient and once again it was Smith, Elder who handled book publication.

As he came towards the end of *The Return of the Native* Hardy decided that he needed professionally to be in London. He has not left on record any reason for the decision, which was to end what he later described as 'our happiest time'. The old restlessness to get away from the claustrophobic provincialism of Wessex and demonstrate his literary sophistication may have been one cause. Another, which is sometimes overlooked or under-rated, could be his need for the research facilities that he found at the British Museum, where he spent over many years a substantial part of his time in London. The rupture of his valuable connection with Leslie Stephen and *The Cornhill* must have augmented any unsettled feeling and reminded him of the importance, for a professional author, of being 'in the swim' with editors and critics and publishers; with the literary world of London, in other words.

In March 1878 the Hardys moved therefore from Sturminster Newton to a house in the London suburb of Upper Tooting, which they had rented for three years. In his notebook Hardy wrote the sad words 'End of the Sturminster Newton idyll'. And perhaps he recalled, or read again, a note of a few months earlier which adds an undertone of poignancy to this time of his happiness with Emma. Their maid, Jane, had apparently been receiving a secret lover at night after the Hardys had retired. As Hardy later found out, she had oiled the hinges and slid back the bolt of the back door so that the man could enter silently. These details, incidentally, seem to have stayed in Hardy's mind and been transmuted into the poem 'I Say I'll Seek Her':

> The creaking hinge is oiled,
> I have unbarred the backway,
> But you tread not the trackway
> And shall the thing be spoiled?

The young man who sought the Hardys' housemaid was not quiet enough on one occasion, the illicit visits were discovered and poor Jane fled on the instant in shame and dismay. There the matter seemingly ended, with Hardy noting rather primly: 'The further career of this young woman is not recorded, except as to one trifling detail.' The nature of the 'trifling detail' is left undisclosed at that point, but a page later *The Life* quotes a note-book entry made two months after the girl's departure: 'We hear that Jane, our late servant, is soon to have a baby. Yet never a sign of one is there for us.'

One is left to wonder what subtle shades of irony were blended in Hardy's choice of that single word 'trifling'. Of the four Hardy children he was the only one who married and he was to die childless. The first seeds of later sorrow were perhaps sown already at the end of the 'two-years idyll' but Hardy always regarded the stay at Sturminster Newton as a kind of Eden from which he and Emma were excluded by their departure and to which they could never be readmitted. 'Such beginning was all,' he wrote. 'Nothing came after.' In bitterness of heart he passed this terrible final judgment:

A preface without any book,
A trumpet uplipped, but no call;
That seems it now.

6

The Professional Author 1878 - 1885

Primed for new scenes with designs smart and tall
(*A Two-Years Idyll*)

The three years that Hardy spent in the London suburban house near Wandsworth Common did a great deal to determine the kind of man and the kind of writer he was ultimately to be. When he made the move from Dorset he was within a couple of years of his fortieth birthday—a mature age for even a late developer. As the author of half-a-dozen novels he could count himself a recognised and established writer of whom great things must now be expected. He had clearly come to London for the express purpose of consolidating and enhancing his reputation.

He was soon dining around, meeting publishers and literary celebrities. At one table he sat down in the company of Matthew Arnold, Henry James and Richard Jefferies, and as such occasions followed one another it must have seemed that only Tom Cobley was missing. One of his first actions was to join the Savile Club. In his own words he 'by degrees fell into line as a London man again'.

Here it is perhaps worth recalling that he had previously lived in London for five years (1862–7) and returned to London intermittently—sometimes for several months at a stretch—during the years 1869–74. Since his marriage he had spent a winter at Surbiton and some further months at Westbourne Grove. It is no exaggeration to say that, of the first twenty years of his adult life, about half was spent in London. He was keen to stress that he 'knew every street and alley west of St Paul's like a born Londoner, which he was often supposed to be'.

There can be little doubt that in one phase of his nature Hardy relished the ambivalence which enabled him to be, by turns, the London clubman and the man of Wessex. When he paid a visit home to call on William Barnes at Came Rectory it was in the afterglow of a visit to Henry Irving's closing night at the Lyceum, where Hardy 'went to his dressing-room, found him naked to the waist; champagne in tumblers'.

The first big question to be resolved was the kind of story that was to follow *The Return of the Native*. Should it stay among the sheepfolds of Wessex, should it be another work of ingenious plot involving the upper classes, or should it break new ground altogether? And, whatever the decision, would it restore the old relationship with *The Cornhill*? Conversations began with Leslie Stephen and Hardy prepared for him an outline of what was to become *The Trumpet-Major*. The idea had novelty and yet it was a thoroughly logical combination of Hardy's passion for the Napoleonic period and his feeling for Wessex characters and scenes. One might have expected Stephen to grasp it at once as a bold and original theme which would presumably have the additional advantage of posing no moral danger to the family audience that he guarded so scrupulously.

But something went wrong. *The Trumpet-Major* did not appear in *The Cornhill*. Although Hardy and Stephen remained on friendly terms their professional association was never renewed. The story was serialised in *Good Words*, a Scottish periodical edited with a prudish care that made Stephen seem positively reckless. Hardy was asked to avoid swearwords and to transfer to a Saturday a lovers' meeting that he had placed on a Sunday afternoon (to the outrage of Sabbatarian feeling, no doubt). 'In both requests I readily acquiesced,' he recalled, 'as I restored my own readings when the novel came out as a book.'

It was to become a normal practice with Hardy to prepare his MSS with built-in bowdlerisations indicated in inks of different colours, so that his intended text could be swiftly restored for book publication. He seems to have accepted the wide division between what was permissible in book form but unacceptable to magazine editors. At the climax of his career, when *Tess of the d'Urbervilles* and *Jude the Obscure* were subjects of violent controversy, he came to feel that the pressures of the censorious made the task of a serious novelist impossible, but in the meantime he was prepared to shrug his shoulders and make the best of an unpropitious system.

The Trumpet-Major has always had its champions, perhaps because the book is suffused with a sweetness of sentiment and an ingenuousness that set it apart from almost everything else of Hardy's. The noble rivalry between the two sons of Miller Loveday for the hand of Anne Garland is conducted according to the conventional rules of light romantic fiction. John Loveday, the Trumpet-Major, is perpetually strong, silent and selfless to such a degree that one almost expects him to have leafy branches instead of arms. Of the other characters Festus Merriman is a strange pastiche of the Smollett-Fielding-Dickens tradition of boisterous comedy: technically it is an interesting exploratory attempt by Hardy to go right outside the effective range of his genius and wisely he never repeated the experiment.

The opening chapters have a vivacity and sureness of touch which tend to flag when the creaking machinery of the plot becomes more insistent. If one retains an affection for this undemanding potboiler it is because of the attractive writing on subsidiary topics—the little 'Dutch paintings' in the *Greenwood Tree* manner. The precious moments come when Hardy turns aside from his story to sketch a streetscene, to discourse on the properties of beer or cider, to celebrate the glories of an old-fashioned kitchen in every detail of its utensils and victuals and culinary customs.

These diversions are a reminder of how much is owed to Hardy by that Westcountry tradition of 'kitchen-comedy' that is associated with such later authors as Eden Philpotts, Walter Raymond, Charles Lee and Jan Stewer. It is this endearing quality which has preserved *The Trumpet-Major* from the neglect into which some of Hardy's earlier novels have fallen, but it would be difficult to claim that, in the portrayal of human emotion and character, it is of any more consequence than the libretto of *Merrie England.* Perhaps it still awaits its true destiny, as the basis of a modern 'musical'.

With *The Trumpet-Major* completed Hardy felt free to make one or two journeys. France beckoned once more; with Emma he sailed to Boulogne and made a tour of Normandy which was to provide material for his next novel, *A Laodicean.* This was commissioned by the American publishers, Harper & Brothers: it was the first occasion that he had written directly for an American firm, although his novels had been in some demand in the United States since as early as 1873 when *Under the Greenwood Tree* first introduced him to American readers. Serialisation of *A Laodicean* was arranged also in Australia, by the *Sydney Mail.*

Unfortunately at the very moment when it would have been most difficult to cancel or postpone the serialisation Hardy was afflicted with a serious and protracted illness. Suffering from an internal haemorrhage he was confined to his bed for six months; for part of the time he had to lie with the lower part of his body upraised. Much of the book was dictated to Emma in these trying and painful circumstances and it is perhaps not surprising that Hardy's friendliest critics have never found it easy to summon much enthusiasm for this, the third and last of his 'novels of ingenuity'.

Hardy himself looked back on the book as being one to please 'that large and happy section of the reading public which has not yet reached ripeness of years; those to whom marriage is the pilgrim's Eternal City, and not a milestone on the way'. It can be taken therefore as a romance, having something in common with *A Pair of Blue Eyes*; but where *Blue Eyes* was a plot without crime, *A Laodicean* is entwined in the ingenuities of a crime-plot and, moreover, one of undeniable mediocrity. Yet there are elements in the story that deserve a happier fate.

The central character, Paula Power, is the daughter of a railway contractor who lives in the castle that her father bought when the impoverished de Stancy family gave it up. Charlotte de Stancy becomes a close friend of Paula, and the heir to the de Stancy title—Charlotte's brother—is a suitor for Paula's hand. So too is George Somerset who, like Stephen Smith in *A Pair of Blue Eyes* and Edward Springrove in *Desperate Remedies*, is an architect. But Somerset explicitly embodies the spirit of modernity: physically he adumbrates 'the future human type'. He and Paula represent the new force that came to challenge old traditions in Victorian England. Paula Power—referred to by one of the characters as 'Miss Steam-Power'—has installed in the castle an electric telegraph which symbolises the new technocracy that is displacing the old supremacy of noble pedigrees, and the architectural restoration of de Stancy castle is the opportunity for Somerset to show his skill.

The confrontation of ancient and modern in social class has a correlation in religion. The Power family is nonconformist—Baptist to be precise. The arguments about Paedo-Baptism that enlivened the days Hardy spent in Mr Hicks's office in Dorchester in the 1860s are put to good use in *A Laodicean* as Paula's devotion to the family faith begins to waver and she is accused of being lukewarm in her beliefs. In defence of her laodicean nature she describes herself as 'one of that body to whom lukewarmth is not an accident but a provisional necessity, till they see a little more clearly'. In short, she puts herself among the agnostics.

But for all her modernity Paula has what she calls a '*prédilection d'artiste*' for the romantic mediaevalism that is enshrined in de Stancy castle. She asks Somerset: 'Do you think it a thing more to be proud of that one's father should have made a great tunnel and railway like that, than that one's remote ancestors should have built a great castle like this?'

And when she and Somerset are looking at the de Stancy monuments Paula says:

> 'I don't wish I was like one of them: I wish I *was* one of them'.
> 'What—you wish you were a de Stancy?'
> 'Yes. It is very dreadful to be denounced as a barbarian. I want to be romantic and historical.'

It is as the Defender of the new Faith of Technocracy that Somerset launches his counter-attack:

> 'Have you forgotten that other nobility—the nobility of talent and enterprise?'
> 'No. But I wish I had a well-known line of ancestors.'
> 'You have. Archimedes, Newcomen, Watt, Telford, Stephenson, these are your father's direct ancestors.'

Rivalry between two men for the favours of a young woman is a stock theme on which Hardy devised many variations. In *A Laodicean* he feints at first with a minor rivalry of a strictly professional kind between Somerset and another architect, Havill, for Paula's patronage in connection with the restoration of the castle. When Havill fades out of the story the real rival appears, Captain de Stancy: it is he who, when his father dies, can offer Paula the romantic and historical position of Lady de Stancy.

In the tournament of courtship that follows, de Stancy's offer of pedigree, title and established tradition is shown to be a false love, calculating and self-seeking in motive and deceitful in method. The true lover is the man of the future who represents the new aristocracy of science and agnostic humanism, George Somerset. But unfortunately this interesting design for the story is subordinated to the dismal plotting of de Stancy's illegitimate son, William Dare. This 'boy-man', as Hardy calls him, uses all his satanic guile to bring about the marriage of his impecunious father with the wealthy Paula. 'I labour under the misfortune of having an illegitimate father to provide for', is his one humorous observation in an otherwise unrelieved tedium of humdrum villainy.

The slow progress of a tour through western Europe keeps the story moving gently, while Dare's stratagems create the sort of suspense that serials require; but the quality of Paula's exchanges with her suitors deteriorates sadly. If the dialogue between Elfride and Mr Knight in *A Pair of Blue Eyes* prompts comparisons with Jane Austen, the stilted exchanges between Paula and de Stancy come closer to the style of Amanda Ros.

By the spring of 1881 Hardy was on the way to a full recovery from his illness, and the pressure of delivering the instalments of *A Laodicean* began to relax as the final episode came in sight. He took stock of his latest spell of London life and came to the conclusion that it 'tended to force mechanical and ordinary productions from his pen, concerning ordinary society-life and habits'. It would certainly be understandable if he looked back nostalgically to the two-year idyll in Dorset during which *The Return of the Native* had been written: the very title must have prompted his next step. By midsummer, 1881, the Hardys had rented a house in Wimborne. The native had returned once more—and for the last time. Though Hardy frequently visited London and other places his home-base henceforward was to be in Dorset.

Wimborne in the 1880s was much as it is today, a small and compact market town clustered about its dominating Minster. Like the Hardys' earlier Dorset home at Sturminster Newton, it lies in the valley of the Stour at the point where that river is joined by its tributary, the Allen, which flows down from Cranborne Chase. The Minster's famous clock is described in Hardy's poem 'Copying Architecture in an old Minster', though it seems likely that the poem was written at an earlier period. When Hardy was actively improving his knowledge of architecture in Dorchester he may well have visited Wimborne to sketch the Minster. What does certainly belong to the year 1882, however, is 'The Levelled Churchyard', an amusing treatment of the idea presented solemnly in the other poem, of the dead in the Minster churchyard engaging in conversation. The presentation of the same idea in two contrasting styles is an occasional feature of Hardy's poetry. For example, 'The Memorial Brass' is a light, slight, gay little version of what in 'The Inscription' becomes a sombre, portentous and laboured narrative.

So it is in the two Minster poems. In 'Copying Architecture in an old Minster' the poet imagines that the clock summons the ghosts from the adjacent graves to what he calls 'a parle'. Heavy with titles and history they prove to be a melancholy company. In 'The Levelled Churchyard', by contrast, the dead complain in lively and humorous terms that the graves have been tidied up so ruthlessly that

> 'We late-lamented, resting here,
> Are mixed to human jam.'

Hardy exploits the comic possibilities of this situation with evident relish. Some roaring drunkard acquires a headstone with a text intended for 'Teetotal Tommy' and the indignant protests of the departed reach their climax with

> 'Here's not a modest maiden elf
> But dreads the final Trumpet,
> Lest half of her should rise herself,
> And half some sturdy Strumpet.'

Hardy is so frequently dismissed as humourless that it is pleasant to dwell on examples to the contrary. His humour is customarily dry with a bias towards irony and black comedy, and it is a far from insignificant element in his make-up. It found inspiration at Wimborne among the living as well as the dead, according to a note he made in 1882 about some play readings that he attended locally.

Apparently a group of neighbours met to read Shakespeare aloud and Hardy jotted down some swift thumbnail sketches of them. There was the wealthy Mrs B 'impassive and grand in her unintelligence, like a Carthaginian statue'. There was the host 'omnivorous of parts—absorbing other people's besides his own'. Encouraged by praise of his powers as a reader, he told Hardy,

'Oh, yes; I've given it a great deal of study—thrown myself into the life of the character, you know; thought of what my supposed parents were, and my early life.' Best of all is the General, reading with gingerly caution after confessing to Hardy that he 'blurted out one of Shakespeare's improprieties last time before he was aware, and is in fear and trembling lest he may do it again'.

The sure touch of the practised novelist is easy to recognise there and it is with the novelist rather than the poet that Wimborne is mainly associated. His principal occupation in the autumn of 1881 was the preparation of *A Laodicean* for book publication, after which he started work on *Two on a Tower*, setting his story in the vicinity of Wimborne (or 'Warborne' as he re-named it).

Among Hardy's lesser novels, which tend to be discarded by all except the more omnivorous of students, *Two on a Tower* competes closely with *A Pair of Blue Eyes* as being most likely to justify a revival of interest. In it several aspects of Hardy's skill as a novelist are well displayed. The theme is a bold one and it is handled resourcefully. The heroine, Viviette, is one of Hardy's most attractive women—older and more sophisticated than most of his heroines but with a warm-hearted impulsiveness that maturity has not quenched. Her young lover, Swithin St Cleeve, is an original piece of character drawing with his devoted pursuit of astronomy. The minor figures are animated, the rural scenes are full of colour, and the theme—the Tyranny of Convention—is very much to Hardy's taste. To his first readers it must have seemed in some respects more 'subversive' than anything he had yet written.

The tower to which the two lovers are drawn is a family monument on the estate of Viviette's husband, Sir Blount Constantine. Swithin uses it as his observatory and Viviette, Lady Constantine, becomes his patroness and confidante. Their difference in age (she is perhaps thirty, he ten years or more younger) reinforces their difference in social class to what should conventionally be an insuperable barrier. But there are two powerful forces threatening the values of convention—the one is intellectual (Swithin's astronomy), the other is sexual, and Hardy epitomises them in a couple of sentences:

> In the presence of the immensities that his young mind had, as it were, brought down from above to hers, they became unconsciously equal. There was, moreover, an inborn liking in Lady Constantine to dwell less on her permanent position as a county lady than on her passing emotions as a woman.

Though presented in cool and discreet tones it is nevertheless a situation which has much in common with that explored later and more sensationally by Lady Chatterley and Mellors. It offers a 'reformed' morality in conflict with conventional values. Viviette's husband has used her with cruelty and then disappeared in darkest Africa: she is therefore, like Connie Chatterley, a frustrated half-widow, effectively husbandless but not bereaved. In a 'natural' morality, freed from convention, Swithin would be her proper mate. In Victorian times, however, he must first become famous (to compensate for his low origin) and she must be free to marry him. It is around these two points that Hardy moves his plot.

First there comes news that Sir Blount has died in Africa and Viviette feels able to make a secret marriage with Swithin (whose eventual fame will later sanctify the marriage socially). She is then confronted with two new circumstances. The first is that the date of Sir Blount's death was misreported and did not occur until *after* her second marriage, which is therefore void. The second is that the simple remedy of a fresh and correctly legal ceremony with Swithin is now threatened by a condition of a legacy which will finance his astronomical research provided he does not marry until he is twenty-five. Splendid woman that she is, she sends Swithin off to remote parts of the Southern hemisphere to profit by his legacy, to win fame as an astronomer and some years later to return and complete the interrupted marriage rites with her.

It is a noble solution but it is flawed by one disastrous miscalculation. She had not considered that, after Swithin's departure and when communication with him was impossible, she might find herself to be carrying his child. For a short while they had sincerely believed their marriage to be valid; she is in fact pregnant. By the rules of the game she must marry quickly. Her brother, Louis, has already been pressing her to marry again for position and wealth by accepting the proposal of the pompous Bishop of Melchester, and this she now does. The Bishop conveys the good news to Louis: 'She was quite passive at last, and agreed to anything I proposed—such is the persuasive force of trained logical reasoning! A good and wise woman, she perceived what a true shelter from sadness was offered in this, and was not the one to despise Heaven's gift.'

Believing that he is consoling Viviette's widowhood the Bishop is in reality sanctifying her impending motherhood. He duly fathers Swithin's child—a 'satire of circumstance' indeed—and soon after dies.

Justifying her action in accepting 'Heaven's gift' Viviette wrote later to Swithin: 'I would have sacrificed my single self to honesty, but I was not alone concerned. What woman has a right to blight a coming life to preserve her personal integrity?' And Hardy comments, 'convention was forcing her hand . . . and to what will not convention compel her weaker victims, in extremes?'

As in *A Pair of Blue Eyes*, Hardy is asking questions about candour and deceit, about pretence and honesty, about integrity and expediency. He is pushing his novel writing into new zones of moral consciousness. Here particularly he is engaged in the sort of special pleading for 'a pure woman' in her conflict with convention which foreshadows another aspect of *Tess*. The love of Viviette for Swithin is a natural and faultless love but it brings her to the kind of blameless disaster that society inflicts in the name of morality. A less scrupulous woman would have solved these problems quite comfortably and without committing any crime, but she would have flouted the conventions of her time. Viviette was not prepared to do that.

It is significant that when Hardy stops tormenting Elfride and Ethelberta and Viviette he gives each of them a black-comedy wedding to an Establishment figure, a member of the House of Lords, a pillar of Church or State. In his later and greater stories he eschewed satirical comedy for a fully developed climax of tragic force and character in the resolution of his dramas. But before he was ready to commit himself to the grand manner of *The Mayor of Casterbridge* and *Tess* and *Jude* he evidently saw himself as a satirist in his handling of issues of class and morality, and of this earlier method *Two on a Tower* is as good an example as any.

The first half of the book is purposeful, eloquent and varied. The rustic episodes are lively and memorable, the sustained meditation on the night sky and inter-stellar space is extremely powerful, and the lesser characters provide some engaging moments. One recalls with pleasure the parson, Mr Torkingham, speaking in 'the strenuously sanguine tones of a man who got his living by discovering a bright side in things where it was not very perceptible to other people'. And there is Tabitha Lark who, having studied music with some success in London, belongs to 'the phalanx of Wonderful Women who had resolved to eclipse masculine genius altogether, and humiliate the brutal sex to the dust'. In the final scene, when Viviette dies in the arms of Swithin on the tower, the unconvincingly romantic ending is given a grimly ironic twist by the words: 'Nobody appeared in sight but Tabitha Lark, who was skirting the field with a bounding tread.' The next chapter of Swithin's life, one feels, has opened.

Two on a Tower ran as a serial during 1882 in *The Atlantic Monthly* and appeared in a three-volume edition in the autumn. After a holiday in Paris Hardy produced a hastily written story, *The Romantic Adventures of a Milkmaid*, which he was able to send to the editor of *The Graphic* in February 1883. Because of its poor quality Hardy intended to exclude it from his collected works, though he was eventually compelled to include it in the 1913 volume entitled *A Changed Man* in order to frustrate pirated reprints of the story in America. It is symptomatic of his tendency at this period to drive himself into excessive production. He seemed determined to push his career along at a faster rate than his talent could support. The London season of 1883 saw Hardy enjoying his fame and listing the celebrities who liked to make his acquaintance, but behind the smiling face of success lay the thought that, in the five years since *The Return of the Native*, he had written nothing of a comparable standard.

When the season ended the Hardys returned to Wimborne and again planned to move. This time their destination was Dorchester which, in Hardy's words, was to be 'their country-headquarters for the rest of their lives'. The emphasis on *country*-headquarters is important: over the next two decades it was their normal practice to spend several months in London during the spring and early summer.

But it was the home soil of Dorchester—the native heath of 'Egdon'—that increasingly drew down the roots of Thomas Hardy into a permanent settlement. By the end of 1883 he was planting Austrian pines on the land at Max Gate where the building of his new house had just commenced: those pines of which he was later to write:

> I set every tree in my June time,
> And now they obscure the sky.

For most of half a century, until his death, this was to be the workshop from which issued three of his greatest novels, *The Woodlanders*, *Tess of the d'Urbervilles* and *Jude the Obscure*, all eight volumes of his poetry, the whole of *The Dynasts*, and much lesser work besides; and it is as a workshop that Max Gate is best considered. It does no great credit to Hardy the architect and as a home it was to witness the progressively bitter deterioration of his marriage, to the point where husband and wife found little pleasure in each other's company and the domestic atmosphere was at times so strained as to excite the comment of visitors.

Today the house belongs to the National Trust but is in private occupation and therefore not open to the public. With the passage of years it has mellowed in ways that dispel some of the less attractive features on which its critics habitually commented. The house itself shows the sort of craftsmanship that the present generation can hardly fail to envy, and the more open aspect of the garden nowadays dispels the old claustrophobic sense of being, in Hardy's words, 'at the bottom of a dark green well of trees'; and pines, at that. To modern eyes it is neither so hard in outline, nor so sombre in atmosphere, as it seems to have been in the 'twenties.

The master of Max Gate, at the time he built it, was a vigorous dark-haired bearded man in his mid-forties, slightly built and on the short side—barely five and a half feet tall. He shaved off the beard soon afterwards but retained a moustache for the rest of his life. In later years the powerfully domed head on the seemingly frail body gave him a gnomelike appearance which is strikingly suggested by Eric Kennington's statue in Dorchester: it somehow comes as no surprise to learn that the subject of the statue disliked being touched by anyone, even in an impulsively friendly way. He also considered it unlucky to be weighed, and in fact never permitted it.

Dorchester's prominence in Hardy's life can scarcely be overstated. As county town and market town it dominated the little rural communities of Stinsford and Bockhampton, only a couple of miles away, in which Hardy grew up. It was the scene of his prentice years as an architect and when he finally settled there he was virtually certain to make it the setting for a novel, especially as he always liked to draw on his immediate surroundings. In 1884 at Shire Place Hall, where he lived while he was supervising the building of Max Gate, Hardy began to write the story which he described as 'more particularly a study of one man's deeds and character than, perhaps, any other of those included in my Exhibition of Wessex life'. The man was, of course, Michael

Henchard who in his hour of glory, and before retribution overtook him, became *The Mayor of Casterbridge*.

Shire Place Hall itself is introduced into the novel as the home of one of the characters and the streets, alleys, buildings and inns of Casterbridge are drawn with a vividness and wealth of detail that could spring only from a close and prolonged intimacy with the Roman-planned town—'as compact as a box of dominoes' in Hardy's apt phrase. The press and bustle of an agricultural market town, the greater social contrasts between high and low than were found in the villages of Wessex, the provincialism of taste and fashion, all are presented with absolute certainty of touch and an occasional sly glint of humour. The two styles of feminine fashion in Casterbridge, for example, are neatly satirised as 'the simple and the mistaken'.

The characterisation of Henchard marks a new departure in Hardy's work. Hitherto the men he has drawn sympathetically have been educated and decorous young professional men or reserved and rather inarticulate young countrymen. In neither group would the more prominent features include an aggressive and hot-tempered virility. The Mayor of Casterbridge, by contrast, is a burly middle-aged man, well over six feet tall, raw and tough in manner, superstitious, moody and—in his anger—savage and unrestrained. He is, in short, the odd man out.

Another innovation was the extent to which the portrayal of Henchard becomes a solo performance dwarfing everything else. It might perhaps be argued that Bathsheba fell not far short of rivalling Henchard in this respect, a point that possibly influenced Hardy to write in his preface of 'one *man's* deeds and character'. Of the earlier men who are able to hold the centre of the stage Henry Knight, Sergeant Troy and Clym Yeobright do not make an effective entry until a quarter of the story has been told. Henchard dominates *The Mayor* from the first page to the last. In all major respects he *is* the book and in this he establishes the new structure that Hardy employed in his two final masterpieces,

Tess and *Jude*—the subordination of everything else to the one obsessive preoccupation with the display of a single soul in its totality.

The Mayor of Casterbridge opens with what is in effect a prologue—an incident in which a drunken man sells his wife at a fair. 'Sales' of this kind are a part of Wessex folk history, as is the skimmington or 'skimmity ride' which occurs later in the book and was a kind of communal satire in which crude effigies or 'guys' accompanied by a clamour of 'rough music' made a public parade of the misdeeds of an unchaste woman. Hardy liked to introduce these old customs and folk memories into his novels, partly for their intrinsic 'quaintness' and to add local colour; but here he gives them a major and devastating significance at the heart of the action.

The man who auctions his wife and baby daughter to a sailor is a journeyman haytrusser, Michael Henchard. He is drunk, on smuggled rum sold by a woman who dispenses a gruel-like drink called 'furmity' in a tent on the fairground. The following day, sober and alone, Henchard vows to touch no alcohol for twenty-one years and goes in search of his wife and child, but fails to find them.

The story proper now opens, twenty years later. Henchard has kept his vow of sobriety, has prospered in business as a hay and corn merchant, and is the Mayor of Casterbridge. He has lived a celibate life, except that—during a period of illness when visiting the island of Jersey—he in some degree compromised a local girl, Lucetta, and would be both obliged and willing to marry her if he were quite free to do so. But it is at this point that his long-lost wife, Susan, appears in Casterbridge with her grown-up daughter, Elizabeth-Jane. The sailor, Newson, who 'bought' Susan from Henchard has apparently been lost at sea and Susan has come increasingly to feel that her only legal husband is still Henchard. Preserving an outward appearance of being distant relatives by marriage, Henchard and Susan live apart for long enough to act through the passage of a courtship which leads to a wedding ceremony (re-enacting their original one) and their reunion in an atmosphere of respectability.

Also arriving at Casterbridge at this time, and staying at the same inn as Elizabeth-Jane and her mother, is a young Scotsman, Donald Farfrae, en route to Bristol whence he intends to emigrate. Farfrae has great personal charm and evident signs of ability and drive in business. Elizabeth-Jane is attracted to him romantically. Henchard, meeting Farfrae by chance, takes to the young Scot with a characteristically impulsive and overwhelming warmth of enthusiasm and persuades him to remain in Casterbridge as the manager of Henchard's business, in place of the man—Jopp—to whom the post had almost been given, and whose disappointment turns to bitterness and enmity.

These are the essential elements in Henchard's story—Farfrae, who is to be the chief figure in his business and public life, and the three women, Susan, Elizabeth-Jane and Lucetta, about whom his domestic emotions and sentiments crystallise, in varying degrees at different times. Yet the compartments are not so neat and watertight as that may suggest, for with Henchard every activity can be emotionally charged: his relationship with Farfrae has the possessiveness, the jealousy, the ebullient affection and the confiding intimacy of a love affair, to the extent that he can later say in all sincerity: 'God is my witness that no man ever loved another as I did thee.'

Farfrae's role, as Hardy presents him, is to be the antithesis of Henchard. Physically and emotionally they are opposites. In business methods and ideas Henchard is old-fashioned and the Scotsman is the progressive innovator. Henchard 'used to reckon his sacks by chalk strokes all in a row like garden-palings, measure his ricks by stretching with his arms, weigh his trusses by a lift, judge his hay by a "chaw", and settle the price with a curse'. Farfrae is a ledgerman, an accountant, a champion of new machines like the recently introduced seed drill. The future is with him, but Hardy notes regretfully that 'the rugged picturesqueness of the old method disappeared with its inconveniences'.

Between the two men, the autocratic boss and the high-powered manager, a clash is inevitable. Their latent rivalry remains dormant through the first 'honeymoon' period of their association and then drives them apart as Henchard becomes increasingly jealous of Farfrae's success. Farfrae starts in business on his own account as a direct competitor and what had begun as a quarrel develops in Henchard's mind to a feud of mounting bitterness.

Nor is it only a feud between rivals in trade. Farfrae comes to represent the traditional challenge of the new and the young to the whole established authority of the dominant male. Like a young buck menacing the ruling stag he threatens every aspect of the old herdmaster's kingdom and will, if unchecked, expel him from it. The death of Susan opens up a new vulnerability in Henchard and the commercial and social struggle with Farfrae becomes an overtly sexual rivalry as well.

By removing Susan, who had tended to neutralise the more volcanic side of Henchard's nature, Hardy now exposes him to two exciting but dangerous manoeuvres. The first is to tell Elizabeth-Jane the truth about her mother's earlier marriage to himself and the episode of the sale—from which she has so far been shielded—and thus to convince her that she is not his step-daughter but his true and only child. The second is to make a tardy amends to Lucetta by marrying her, since he is now free to do so. He takes the first step promptly and could evidently find a considerable delight in the new role of indulgent father-widower, proud of his attractive daughter and consoled by her loving presence. However, he makes the fatal mistake of reading a letter that Susan had left for him with the injunction that it was not to be opened until Elizabeth-Jane's weddingday. From it he learns that the baby he fathered soon died after Susan parted from him and she gave the same name of Elizabeth-Jane to a second baby whose father was of course the sailor, Newson. In consequence the poor girl who has just come to accept Henchard as her father finds him turning suddenly cold and indifferent to her.

Plate 1 Hardy in 1903: a chalk drawing by William Rothenstein presented to the Dorset County Museum by Hannen Swaffer

Plate 2 (left) Emmy Destinn in the title role in d'Erlanger's opera *Tess* at Covent Garden

(right) Wooperton Street, Weymouth. At number three – the darker frontage – Hardy began his professional career as a novelist

With Lucetta similarly there are complications that Henchard had not foreseen. She comes to live in Casterbridge, it is true, with the intention of marrying him; but she is now a wealthy woman as a result of a legacy from her aunt, Templeman, whose name she has adopted. She is to that extent in a more independent mood than Henchard expects: no longer need she allow herself to be taken for granted or made to hurry. All too soon her eye is taken by the effortless charm of Farfrae.

It is at this point that the general air of foreboding which surrounds Henchard—'this man of moods, glooms and superstitions'—develops a tragic momentum of mounting force. Another figure from the past confronts him, in the person of the old furmity-woman in whose tent Henchard auctioned his wife. Brought before the Casterbridge magistrates on a minor charge she recognises Henchard on the bench and denounces him as unfit to sit in judgment. Alarmed by this scandalous insight into Henchard's previous marriage and frightened by the threat of blackmail by him, Lucetta secretly marries Farfrae. The downward spiral of Henchard's misfortunes accelerates. Bankrupt in business, estranged from Elizabeth-Jane, deprived of Lucetta, obliged to watch Farfrae rise in public esteem until it is he who becomes Mayor, Henchard lapses into an impotent obscurity.

Yet there can be no forgetting that 'there was still the same unruly volcanic stuff beneath the rind of Michael Henchard as when he had sold his wife'. Now, twenty-one years later, the vow of sobriety he had made at Weydon Fair was fulfilled and he was released from his oath. The news passed quickly round Casterbridge—'Michael Henchard have busted out drinking after taking nothing for twenty-one years!' With this change, an ugly violence enters his feud with Farfrae, culminating in a murderous assault during which Henchard checks himself only at the last minute from killing the Scotsman.

Hardy's command of changing scales and perspectives is beautifully exemplified here. The man-to-man encounter in physical combat is a secret, private affair, engineered by Henchard who lures Farfrae to the top floor of a granary and challenges him with the words: 'There's the door, forty foot above ground. One of us two puts the other out by that door—the master stays inside.' But at the same time the public, social explosion which is to consummate their feud is on the point of being detonated by the more disreputable citizenry who have got hold of Lucetta's letters to Henchard and are preparing to march through the streets in a 'skimmington'—leading a donkey on which are seated recognisable effigies of Lucetta and Henchard 'back to back, their elbows tied to one another's'. Standing at her window to watch the spectacle Lucetta collapses, shocked, and dies.

Henchard too dies a kind of death, in his own way. He realises the extent of his loneliness, surviving merely as an object of contempt or pity. 'Susan, Farfrae, Lucetta, Elizabeth—all had gone from him, one after one, either by his fault or by his misfortune.' He wanders down to the riverside, to a pool 'he was intending to make his death-bed'. As he prepares for suicide he sees a floating body which turns out to be '*himself* . . . his actual double'. The cause of this miraculous appearance, which deflects him from self-destruction, lies in the disposal by the skimmity gang of the two effigies, which they threw hurriedly into the river. It was the effigy of Henchard which drifted down to Ten Hatches Hole and there confronted him.

For a time Henchard is comforted by Elizabeth-Jane, who takes pity on him, but of her too he is to be finally deprived. Farfrae is again beginning to court her, as in those early days before Lucetta came to Casterbridge; her true father, Newson, has recrossed the Atlantic in which, despite rumour, he was not drowned and must sooner or later expose Henchard's lie about the girl's parentage. Bowed down and beaten by successive blows the old warrior knows that his last possession—his 'daughter', so called—must be taken from him, and he utters his final cry of desolation: 'I, an outcast, an encumberer of the ground, wanted by nobody, and despised by all, live on against my will.'

To find an agreeably romantic conclusion to such a story is like seeking a happy ending to *The Tragedy of King Lear* or the *Book of Job*. But the needs of his time had to be served, and on this occasion Hardy found an ingenious solution. Profiting perhaps from his unsatisfactory experience with the last stages of *The Return of the Native* he now inverted his two final episodes, putting the marriage of Farfrae and Elizabeth-Jane before Henchard's death scene, whereas in other circumstances—for example, the marriage of Bathsheba and Gabriel Oak—the mandatory wedding bells would not have rung until tragedy had left the stage. But now, in a closely integrated finale, Henchard appears uninvited at the wedding, is reproved by Elizabeth-Jane for his deception of her and for trying to prevent Newson from finding her, and walks out of Casterbridge accompanied only by poor timid Abel Whittle who at one time worked for Henchard and lived in terror of him. Most movingly it is the simple rustic speech of Whittle that paints the final scene:

> 'I followed en over Grey's Bridge, and he turned and zeed me, and said, "You go back!" But I followed, and he turned again, and said, "Do you hear, sir? Go back!" But I zeed that he was low, and I followed on still. Then 'a said, "Whittle, what do ye follow me for when I've told ye to go back all these times?" And I said, "Because, sir, I see things be bad with 'ee, and ye wer kind-like to mother if ye were rough to me, and I would fain be kind-like to you". Then he walked on, and I followed; and he never complained at me no more.'

And so the dying Henchard writes down the ultimate bitterness of his Will, witnessed by the illiterate Whittle who preserves it without being able to read those terrifying sentences which end with: 'that no murners walk behind me at my funeral. & that no flours be planted on my grave. & that no man remember me.'

'A Samson shorn' indeed, in Hardy's phrase! This is very much the point of the book—that Henchard is all we mean by the words 'a big man', who stands in self-reliance and without special pleading or extenuation. He dwarfs the morality of his context, he has darknesses upon darknesses within him that can be explored only by the light of Hardy's compassion. His is not a case to be argued, like Tess's; nor a privation to be pitied, like Jude's or Clym's. In the human landscape he rears up with the grandeur of a pinnacle that has within it some geological fault which must lead at last to erosion and collapse. It is this image of rocklike defiance that endures in the words with which he walks out of Casterbridge and parts from Elizabeth-Jane after Newson's return: 'I—Cain—go alone as I deserve—an outcast and a vagabond. But my punishment is *not* greater than I can bear.'

7

The State of Marriage Examined 1885 - 1890

I am a woman, and you are a man. I cannot speak more plainly
(*The Woodlanders*)

The last page of *The Mayor of Casterbridge* was written on 17 April 1885, a couple of months before the Hardys started moving furniture into Max Gate, which was now ready for occupation. Hardy lamented that he had been frequently interrupted in the writing of each part and he was worried that 'his aiming to get an incident into almost every week's part had caused him to add events to the narrative somewhat too freely'. For once he was not writing under the pressure of a serialisation which had begun before the book was completed. The first instalment of *The Mayor* appeared in *The Graphic* on 2 January 1886, and simultaneously in the United States in *Harper's Weekly*. Book publication followed in May, though with some lack of enthusiasm in the publisher, whose reader expressed the view that 'the lack of gentry among the characters made it uninteresting'.

Meanwhile Hardy's next story was already contracted. In 1884, during the writing of *The Mayor*, he promised Macmillans that they should serialise his subsequent novel in their magazine. A woodland story had begun to form in Hardy's mind as early as 1874, and it was perhaps this initial germ of an idea that started to develop during 1885. In November of that year he noted: 'Have gone back to my original plot for *The Woodlanders* after all.' The following spring he and Emma moved to London as usual for the season and Hardy resumed his familiar routine of lunching and dining with the famous, attending concerts, Parliamentary debates and theatres, and reading in the British Museum.

During those weeks in London Hardy may reasonably have felt well satisfied with his immediate circumstances. *The Mayor of Casterbridge* had begun its serialisation in January, *The Woodlanders* was to start appearing in May. In the clubs and drawing-rooms of London he was a recognised 'lion', and back in Dorchester the new house was settling down after its first winter. After a decade and a half of rather intermittent and erratic success he had now established himself in his true and abiding character. There is a ring of confidence in the note with which he began this year of 1886: 'My art is to intensify the expression of things . . . so that the heart and inner meaning is made vividly visible'—a claim that the two serials firmly substantiated.

At the end of July he returned to Max Gate and resumed work on *The Woodlanders* which continued to occupy him throughout the winter. When he re-read the book twenty-five years later he pronounced it '*as a story*, the best of all'. Certainly, a good case could be made for regarding it as the most professional example of the characteristic Hardy novel. It exploits a particular Wessex landscape, the woodlands and orchards of north Dorset. It incorporates good examples of the folk customs and traditional practices that Hardy liked to introduce into his stories. It articulates a sufficiently elaborate plot with less of the implausibilities, eavesdroppings and overstrained coincidences that mar Hardy's fiction. Technically it achieves a much firmer integration of the rustic characters in the main course of the action and it serves, in a satisfactorily unobtrusive way, as a context where Hardy can explore two topics which greatly preoccupied him—the relationship between social classes and the relationship between the sexes inside and outside wedlock. The story has a total validity as a story while at the same time it makes some important moral statements in areas of social ambiguity—something which, at its best, the Novel is well fitted to do in the hands of a writer of Hardy's stature.

The fulcrum of *The Woodlanders* is the character of George

Melbury, a timber merchant who, as the local employer, has a paternal role among the woodland villagers. There is an understanding that his daughter Grace will marry Giles Winterborne, a sturdy yeoman type from the same mould as Gabriel Oak (in *Madding Crowd*), whom he also resembles in being later disqualified as a suitor by financial disaster. Where Gabriel's loss was of his flock of sheep, Giles's is of the cottages he had held under that life-hold system which is a recurring theme with Hardy. Even without that misfortune, however, Giles's suitability to be Grace's husband is in doubt because he is an uneducated stay-at-home woodlander whereas she has been sent away from the village by her ambitious father to acquire an expensive education. In short she has become a 'lady' and is therefore, in the opinion of her class-conscious father, too good for the likes of Giles.

In similar circumstances Oak does no more than remain in a satellite orbit round Bathsheba, but Hardy handles Giles more inventively by adding a secondary relationship with one of the most appealing peasant girls he ever drew, Marty South. She works with Giles in the woodlands, planting trees, and 'alone, of all the women in Hintock and the world, had approximated to Winterborne's level of intelligent intercourse with Nature. In that respect she formed his true complement in the other sex.' 'In that respect'—but without any sexual expression. In Marty's own words to Grace after Giles's death: 'In all our outdoor days and years together, ma'am, the one thing he never spoke of to me was love; nor I to him.'

With Mr Melbury, as with Grace, there is an ambivalence on the class issue. Melbury wants to guarantee public respect for his daughter's accomplishments, and at the same time is uneasy about dishonouring the understanding with Giles. Grace, an essentially hybrid personality, can break off a speech of affected intellectualism and proclaim her true identification with 'dear old Hintock, and the people in it'. What tips the scale, in addition to Giles's financial disaster, is the arrival of a young doctor of gentle birth, Edred Fitzpiers, and the evident interest aroused in him by Grace. The effect of the county family name of Fitzpiers on George Melbury is predictable:

> That touching faith in members of long-established families as such, irrespective of their personal condition or character, which is still found among old-fashioned people in the rural districts, reached its full perfection in Melbury.

Fitzpiers can have Grace for the asking, if he can overcome his reluctance to marry into such a humble family. Like Wildeve in *The Return of the Native* he is a 'man of sentiment', preferring 'the ideal world to the real'. An intellectual dilettante, he is more interested in metaphysical speculation than in medical practice. 'In the course of a year', Hardy writes, 'his mind was accustomed to pass in a grand solar sweep throughout the zodiac of the intellectual heaven.' Over Grace he exercises a certain fascination 'or even more, an almost psychic influence, as it is called'. She has a premonition that 'she could not resist him'.

His desire to possess Grace overwhelms any prudential consideration and he enters into marriage with the intention of settling permanently at a sufficient distance from Hintock and the Melburys. His views on the gulf that separates the gentry from the toiling masses are soon made totally clear. On their way back from the honeymoon he says to Grace: 'I do honestly confess to you that I feel as if I belonged to a different species from the people who are working in that yard.'

His views on love, licit and illicit, are not the subject of a correspondingly honest confession which is just as well for Grace's peace of mind. Fitzpiers is in fact a 'subtilist in emotions' who can love more than one woman at once. He is already involved with a robustly carnal village girl, Suke Damson, who gave herself to him readily enough on Midsummer Night during the traditional revels in which the local maidens go into the woods and seek to learn the names of their future husbands by casting spells. A more serious entanglement develops when Fitzpiers meets the wealthy and mysterious widow, Felice Charmond, and recognises in her a transient sweetheart of his youth. Now in the '*édition définitive* of her beauty' at the age of thirty Mrs Charmond is restless and dangerously impulsive, a creature of 'strange, smouldering, erratic passions, kept down like a stifled conflagration, but bursting out now here, now there'.

Hers is an uneven portrayal and there are moments when she is in danger of degenerating into a novelettish *femme fatale*, but by sheer imaginative drive Hardy lifts her to remarkable heights. As with Eustacia, he throws aside all literary caution in terms that he has earlier defined thus: 'It often happens that in situations of unrestraint, where there is no thought of the eye of criticism, real feeling glides into a mode of manifestation not easily distinguishable from rodomontade.'

It is in this mode that the secret liaison between Fitzpiers and Mrs Charmond gathers in intensity. 'O! Why,' she cries, 'were we given hungry hearts and wild desires if we have to live in a world like this?' And she rails against 'the terrible insistencies of society—how severe they are, and cold, and inexorable—ghastly towards those who are made of wax and not of stone'. Both of them try to retain some measure of control, or at least an outward appearance of propriety, but there is no escape from the chaos of passionate confusion into which they drift: 'Determination to go in this direction, and headlong plunges in that; dignified safeguards, undignified collapses; not a single rash step by deliberate intention, and all against judgment.'

Knowledge of her husband's infidelity does not arouse in Grace that 'feline wildness which it was her moral duty to experience'. Unlike Bathsheba or Eustacia or Viviette, hers is a passive and acquiescent nature. She admits 'I am quiet because my sadness is not of a nature to stir me into action' and when Melbury reproaches her with being 'very tame and let-alone' she replies simply: 'I am what I feel, father.'

There is however an immediate consequence of the disillusion that now possesses the Melburys. The issue of class begins to lose its significance and Grace embarks by degrees on a retreat from her acquired style of cultured gentility to become again eventually 'the crude country girl' of her origins. Melbury is soon engaged in reviving Giles's hopes by describing this change in Grace: 'She told me only this day that she hates refinements and such like. All that my trouble and money bought for her in that way is thrown away upon her quite. She'd fain be like Marty South—think o' that!'

For the rest of the book Hardy concentrates on differences and nuances of sexual *mores* rather than of class, though the two spheres of human behaviour cannot be distinctly separable. In his 1895 Preface to *The Woodlanders* he wrote:

> In the present novel, as in one or two others of this series which involve the question of matrimonial divergence, the immortal puzzle—given the man and woman, how to find a basis for their sexual relation—is left where it stood; and it is tacitly assumed for the purposes of the story that no doubt of the depravity of the erratic heart who feels some second person to be better suited to his or her tastes than the one with whom he has contracted to live, enters the head of reader or writer for a moment. From the point of view of marriage as a distinct covenant or undertaking . . . this assumption is, of course, logical. Yet no thinking person supposes that on the broader ground of how to afford the greatest happiness to the units of human society during their brief transit through this sorry world, there is no more to be said on this covenant; and it is certainly not supposed by the writer of these pages.

In his probing of the conventional view of sexual relations Hardy draws Grace into three remarkable climactic scenes where the shockwaves of some seismic emotion shift the foundations of her belief and conduct. The first is when Mrs Charmond chances upon her in the woods and pretends that the flirtation with Fitzpiers is a light matter which Grace can afford to dismiss as a passing folly. Grace is not to be bluffed so easily and detects a stronger emotion in Mrs Charmond than her 'nothing but playful friendship—nothing!' But at this stage Grace's imagination can go no further than the indiscretions of a sentimental flirtation, in which eyes and lips are the sole instruments of wickedness. She shares the barely credible innocence of her father to whom 'in the simple life he had led it had scarcely occurred . . . that after marriage a man might be faithless'.

Mrs Charmond and Grace therefore fence with each other in their woodland meeting without getting to the heart of the matter and they part, disturbed but with their defences intact. They then both lose their way in the obscurity and darkness of the woods, and it is two rather cold, weary and frightened women who meet again in their wanderings and huddle together to keep warm as they rest. Now the mood changes: 'They did what neither had dreamed of doing beforehand—clasped each other closely. Mrs Charmond's furs consoled Grace's cold face; and each one's body, as she breathed, alternately heaved against that of her companion.'

It is this physical closeness and intimacy which precipitates the breakdown of Mrs Charmond's reserve. She embraces Grace 'more and more tightly' and her breathing grows 'deeper and more spasmodic, as though uncontrollable feelings were germinating'. She proceeds to confess the extent of her involvement with Fitzpiers and warns Grace: 'I *cannot* give him up until he chooses to give up me!'

The full significance of this is lost on Grace who believes that Mrs Charmond, as 'the superior in station and in every way', must have the power to dismiss Fitzpiers if she chooses. Driven to desperation by such ingenuousness Mrs Charmond exclaims: 'Must I tell verbatim, you simple child?' and whispers a few words in Grace's ear. The effect is shattering.

> Grace started roughly away from the shelter of the furs, and sprang to her feet.
>
> 'O, my great God!' she exclaimed, thunderstruck at a revelation transcending her utmost suspicion. 'He's had you! Can it be—can it be!'

The rough, blunt, vulgar explicitness of 'had' in this context is surely extraordinary in a reputable novelist of the period. Spoken in a play, instead of being printed in a novel, it could well have achieved the same kind of notoriety as Eliza Dolittle's 'bloody'. Hardy is normally constant in his avoidance of any direct reference to erotic sexual acts, preferring always to suggest and infer rather than to state, as indeed he does here in having Mrs Charmond whisper words that we are not permitted to 'hear'. Grace's crude outburst is therefore all the more startling. Of its rightness, though, there can be little doubt. It throws Grace back into an instinctive folk idiom as a measure of her shock 'at a revelation transcending her utmost suspicion'; and if the word is a true index of the stunning impact of reality on Grace, it must also reverberate explosively in Mrs Charmond's finely textured world of refined sentiment, exposing its carnal foundations.

The second of the three scenes comes when exaggerated rumours suggest that Fitzpiers may have been fatally injured when thrown from his horse. While Grace prepares his bedroom to receive the wounded man Mrs Charmond and Suke Damson both arrive and virtually invade the Melbury household in their frenzied anxiety. To them Grace says, 'You shall know all I know. Indeed, you have a perfect right to go into his bedroom; who can have a better than either of you?' The situation is bordering on the farcical when she leads the way to the empty bedroom with the words: 'Wives all, let's enter together!'

At that point, in a way that is so characteristic of him, Hardy modulates sensitively from 'the wife's regulation terms of virtuous sarcasm' to the sudden compassionate insight that overwhelms Grace when 'the tears which his possibly critical situation could not bring to her eyes surged over at the contemplation of these fellow-women whose relations with him were as close as her own without its conventionality'.

It is this 'conventionality' of marriage that Hardy now proceeds to test and examine. A new divorce law is thought to offer Grace the freedom to think of a second marriage, with the faithful Giles supplanting Fitzpiers who has meanwhile fled to Europe with Mrs Charmond. When this hope of legal freedom is dashed and a seemingly penitent Fitzpiers returns, Grace leaves home to seek temporary asylum with a school friend. Inevitably she breaks her journey at the log cabin in the woods where Giles has been living since he lost his home. Here she remains for several nights while Giles—impeccably chivalrous—withdraws into 'a wretched little shelter of the roughest kind, formed of four hurdles thatched with brake-fern'. As it is apparently the monsoon season in Wessex Giles is persistently soaked and literally catches his death of cold.

To modern readers this episode must seem grotesque and contrived, with Giles heroically saying 'You can give me my supper through the window,' and Grace's unhelpful pity: ' "I don't like to treat you so hardly", she murmured with deep regret in her words as she heard the rain.' And when she reflects that 'To all this weather Giles must be more or less exposed; how much, she did not know', one is tempted to add that she certainly didn't bother to find out. But for all its implausibilities and its quaint air of Victorian prudery the scene develops a powerful climax. As her dilemma deepens Grace defines it to Giles in these words: 'I am a woman, and you are a man. I cannot speak more plainly. I yearn to let you in, but—you know what is in my mind, because you know me so well.'

Assailed thus by doubts her belief in the 'conventionality' of marriage crumbles when she comprehends the mortal danger to which she has exposed Giles. She calls to him: 'Don't you want to come in? Are you not wet? *Come to me, dearest! I don't mind what they say or what they think of us any more.*'

The italics are Hardy's. They emphasise the importance he attached to this moment as a turning point in Grace's story. For Giles, poor man, there could be no real prospect of his doing anything but die, which he promptly does. And for Hardy, with his central theme now resolved, there remains only the necessary task of winding down to a suitably acceptable ending. Fitzpiers is presented as remorseful and ready to make amends. He even vies with Grace in a general flight from intellectualism, promising to give up his 'strange studies' and burn his 'philosophical literature'. The arcadian simplicity of the woodland folk begins to disclose elements of a philistine puritanism.

Resourceful to the end Hardy introduces a mantrap as the device which precipitates Grace's total reconciliation with Fitzpiers and—as in *Madding Crowd*—he envelops the 'happy' ending in a wonderful display of rustic humour and sentiment. The pontifications of Farmer Cawtree on matrimony, and John Upjohn on the several climates of courtship, are an unalloyed delight. They are also a wry pendant to the bucolic lustiness of Suke, the womanising of Fitzpiers, the romantic *amours* of Mrs Charmond, the technical infidelity of Grace—those varied attempts by Hardy's characters 'to find a basis for their sexual relation'.

The Woodlanders was published on 15 March 1887, by which time Hardy and Emma had crossed the Channel and were on their way to Italy, where Hardy looked with an architect's eye at Milan Cathedral and St Mark's, Venice, and, as a fellow-poet visited the graves of Shelley and Keats. The Italian visit evidently stimulated Hardy's poetic impulse: the little group of 'Poems of Pilgrimage' included in *Poems of the Past and the Present* has its origins in this short break from the labours of fiction writing. In the main the 1880s were years when Hardy's versemaking skills found little opportunity. This was the decade which consolidated his reputation as a writer of prose—of novels primarily, but also of short stories. By 1890 more than half of his lifetime's output of short stories had been written. Some of them incorporated experiences and episodes which, at another time, might have been crystallised in verse.

In 1888, for example, on a July night in Kensington at one o'clock in the morning Hardy got out of bed and stood at the window watching the never-ending procession of market carts passing along Phillimore Place on their way to Covent Garden. In his notebook he recorded this impression: 'Chains rattle, and each cart cracks under its weighty pyramid of vegetables.' The incident is one of those tiny droplets of momentary vision from which Hardy might well have distilled a poem. Instead he worked it up into a beautifully evocative nightscene in an otherwise not very distinguished story, 'The Son's Veto', where the widowed mother is roused from her bed to watch

> . . . waggon after waggon, bearing green bastions of cabbages nodding to their fall, yet never falling, walls of baskets enclosing masses of beans and peas, pyramids of snow-white turnips, swaying howdahs of mixed produce—creeping along behind aged night-horses, who seemed ever patiently wondering between their hollow coughs why they had always to work at that still hour when all other sentient creatures were privileged to rest. Wrapped in a cloak it was soothing to watch and sympathise with them when depression and nervousness hindered sleep.

It was in 1888, incidentally, that Hardy's first collection of stories appeared, under the title *Wessex Tales.* Although they must always be overshadowed by the novels, the best of Hardy's short stories would have made a respectable reputation for a lesser man. Of the *Wessex Tales* there is formidable dramatic power in two—'The Three Strangers' and 'The Withered Arm', both of which have been dramatised in various forms. J. M. Barrie soon saw the potential of 'The Three Strangers': at his suggestion it was adapted for the stage and produced in London at Terry's Theatre in 1893.

Another of the tales, 'The Distracted Preacher', gives a lively picture of smuggling on the Wessex coast and embodies the sort of popular anecdotes that Hardy would have heard in his early days. In a different vein 'Fellow-Townsmen' and 'Interlopers at the Knap' show Hardy working in finer textures and drawing out psychological implications with a quiet subtlety.

To have this first collection of short stories available for publication was fortunate as Hardy had no new novel in prospect to follow up the success of *The Woodlanders.* It was *The Woodlanders*, more than any previous novel, which really made Hardy's position secure. *The Return of the Native* had been received with no great enthusiasm by the critics, had not sold well and was remaindered after four years. *The Mayor of Casterbridge* had a critical success but sold only 613 copies of its English edition. It was left for *The Woodlanders* to combine a favourable reception with a strong public demand; ironically this was the first Hardy book to carry the Macmillan imprint, which he had sought as his original aim nineteen years earlier.

A far cry indeed from the rejected manuscript of *The Poor Man and the Lady*. Now there was an eager demand for anything he wrote and he responded with a variety of projects that occupied him fully over the next four years. Two more volumes of stories were largely written or completed at this time—*A Group of Noble Dames*, which appeared in book form in 1891 and *Life's Little Ironies*, which belong individually to the period 1888–93 and were collected in 1894. A minor novel, *The Well-Beloved*, was commissioned in 1890 and delivered for serialisation in 1892. He was also finding time to write a few poems—and not merely an occasional piece like the lines he wrote for Ada Rehan to speak at one of Lady Jeune's charity performances at the Lyceum, but also poems that rank among his best, such as 'Thoughts of Phena' and 'In a Eweleaze near Weatherbury'. On top of all this *Tess of the d'Urbervilles* began to take shape in 1888 and was completed in 1891.

By correlating Hardy's own notes with the additional material in Professor Purdy's bibliography it is possible to form a good impression of the author at work at this period. In September 1888 he spent some time in the vicinity of Evershot, walking in country that had strong family connections. Visiting Woolcombe he recalled that it once belonged to the senior branch of the Hardys, as did several villages or hamlets thereabouts. Walking on to the crest of Bubb Down he looked eastwards to High Stoy and across the great expanse of the Vale of Blackmoor to distant Shaftesbury on its hilltop. In his journal he wrote two simple definitions:

> 'The Valley of the Great Dairies'—Froom
> 'The Valley of the Little Dairies'—Blackmoor

Plate 3 (above) Beeny Cliff: a pencil sketch by Hardy during his second visit to St Juliot, with a memorable comment made by Emma Gifford; *(below)* the County Gaol at Dorchester, painted in 1796 by W. Upham. This was a powerful element in the personal landscape of Hardy's youth

Plate 4 Two illustrations for *Far from the Madding Crowd* by Helen Paterson or – as she signed herself after her marriage – Helen Allingham: *(above)* Bathsheba and Troy with Fanny Robin's coffin; *(below)* Troy swept out to sea off Lulwind Cove

He noted that the Vale of Blackmoor was 'almost entirely green', and added: 'The decline and fall of the Hardys much in evidence hereabout.' He recalled when young seeing one of these declining relatives 'walking beside a horse and common spring trap, and my mother pointing him out to me and saying he represented what was once the leading branch of the family. So we go down, down, down.'

For us, contemplating that image of the seedy individual with his horse and trap, another name springs to mind at once. It is Tess's father, poor drunken 'Sir' John Durbyfield. The green Vale of the Little Dairies is her childhood home where 'the fields are never brown and the springs never dry'; the Valley of the Great Dairies is the setting of Talbothays Farm in the valley of the river Froom, where Tess and Angel Clare met and fell in love. The walk that Hardy took on that September day in 1888 from Evershot to Bubb Down seems to have germinated his next novel, and arguably his greatest, *Tess of the d'Urbervilles.*

Another note made by Hardy in the following spring suggests the inner, moral drama of Tess—not the social decline of her family but the consequences of her sexual 'ruin' by Alec d'Urberville: 'That which, socially, is a great tragedy, may be in Nature no alarming circumstance.'

But in between these notes Hardy jotted down a quite different strand of thought: 'The story of a face which goes through three generations or more, would make a fine novel or poem of the passage of Time. The differences in personality to be ignored.' The poem entitled 'Heredity' may have sprung from this note: more closely related to it is the strange story which found its final form as *The Well-Beloved.* It is the slightest and probably least valued of Hardy's novels and—put beside *Tess*—it looks a mere oddity, but the fortunes of the two stories were in some ways entwined. Taken together they illustrate very clearly the increasing dilemma that bedevilled Hardy's relations with editors, publishers, critics and public opinion generally.

The word *Beloved* as part of a book title was originally intended for *Tess*. As *Too Late Beloved* or *Too late, Beloved!* the story of a girl called variously Love, Cis, Sue and Rose-mary, with alternative surnames of Woodrow and Troublefield, was undertaken by Hardy for serialisation by a Lancashire firm which specialised in syndication and had already bought three of his short stories. It was the intention of this firm, Tillotson's of Bolton, to start publishing the new story before the end of 1889, and in September 1889 Hardy sent them about half of what we now know as *Tess of the d'Urbervilles*. It was at once evident to Tillotson's that the story was quite unsuitable for them, without massive alterations. The contract was therefore cancelled by mutual consent.

In its place Hardy accepted a fresh commission to supply 'something light'. With the unfinished *Tess* on his hands he could not start this new project until the end of 1891 but he promised to deliver the MS by the end of March 1892. He assured Tillotson's later that: 'There is not a word or scene in the tale which can offend the most fastidious taste.'

This inoffensive piece, 'written entirely with a view to serial publication', made its bow originally as *The Pursuit of the Well-Beloved*. Not until Hardy had virtually ended his career as a novelist with the publication of *Jude the Obscure* did he consider book publication for his lightweight serial. Under the shortened title of *The Well-Beloved*, with an altered ending and extensive revision, it was published in March 1897—more than a year after *Jude* and as a very odd pendant to his work as a novelist.

The Well-Beloved is the most fanciful and implausible of all Hardy's stories. He himself described it as aiming to communicate an interest of an 'ideal or subjective nature', to which 'verisimilitude in the sequence of events' was subordinated. The main thread of the story is the relationship of a sculptor, Jocelyn Pierston, to Avice Caro—like him a native of the Isle of Slingers (ie Portland)—and subsequently to her daughter and grand-daughter. To all three generations Pierston proposes marriage and at the third attempt he very nearly succeeds in wedding the grand-daughter. It is a weird story to serve as the basis for what

Hardy intended to be a popular romantic serial and his readers must have found it hard to credit. And yet, as if to prove that truth can compete with the wildest fiction, a similar courtship was reported in Hardy's lifetime. In 1873 a French nobleman married the grand-daughter of the girl he had courted unsuccessfully forty-one years earlier. So curious a match may have come to Hardy's notice though I can find no evidence for such a conjecture. However, he tells us that he sketched the story originally many years before its publication, when he was 'comparatively a young man'; if he read a report of the Baron's marriage at the time he would in fact have been thirty-three.

The point of the story for Hardy, nevertheless, was not its oddity or its originality but the weight of philosophical idea that it could carry. The character of Pierston is a study of the fickleness and the idealism of men. In one sense he is, in Hardy's words, 'the Wandering Jew of the love-world', a womaniser easily and capriciously attracted from one 'beloved' to the next. But in another sense he is a man infatuated with an ideal of womanhood, an unattainable goddess, whom he keeps discovering fleetingly and imperfectly in one woman after another. Shelley's words, 'One shape of many names', were chosen by Hardy as the book's epigraph and he emphasised in a letter that it was his interest in the Platonic Idea that prompted the story.

So it is that, when the young Pierston returns from London to his native isle and is greeted affectionately by a boyhood sweetheart, Avice the First, he swiftly sees her as probably the next 'abode' of that 'migratory, elusive idealisation he called his Love who, ever since his boyhood, had flitted from human shell to human shell an indefinite number of times'. His instant proposal of marriage leads to a very prim and circumspect treatment of what Hardy considers to be a special custom of the isle and refers to as the 'formal ratification' of a betrothal. Not until much later in the story does he explain more bluntly that what he is describing is not an exchange of documents but a prenuptial union demonstrating the couple's fertility.

Pierston and Avice are both too sophisticated in their various ways to take the tradition seriously. He now belongs to smart London society even though 'his urbanism sat upon him only as a garment', and she has been taught 'to forget all the experiences of her ancestors' and to replace the local vernacular by 'a governess-tongue of no country at all'. She therefore does not accompany him in the traditional way on the long farewell walk to the nearest railway station, a privation swiftly compensated for him by the chance companionship of Marcia Bencomb, the 'Junoesque' daughter of a local quarry owner.

Marcia is in flight from the paternal home after a family quarrel. Together, she and Pierston are drenched in a rainstorm and go to a hotel to dry out overnight and already, as he sits drying her steaming garments, 'the spirit, emanation, idealism, which called itself his Love was flitting stealthily from some remoter figure to the near one in the chamber overhead'. Before they were halfway to London next day 'the Beloved was again embodied; she filled every fibre and curve of this woman's form'. By the time they reach London, where Marcia intends to stay with an aunt, his mind is made up. ' "My queenly darling!" he burst out; "instead of going to your aunt's will you come and marry me?" '

The startling suddenness of this proposal leads to an exchange that must be quoted in full:

> 'Will you ever be a Royal Academician?' she asked musingly, her excitement having calmed down.
>
> 'I hope to be—I *will* be, if you will be my wife.'
>
> His companion looked at him long.
>
> 'Think what a short way out of your difficulty this would be', he continued. 'No bother about aunts, no fetching home by an angry father.'
>
> It seemed to decide her. She yielded to his embrace.

As so often happens with Hardy's characters, there is a muddle over the wedding arrangements. Marcia's quarrel with her father is patched up and she returns to her island home unmarried, after 'two or three days' resultless passion'. For Pierston the search for the Beloved goes on. 'He never knew where she would next be, whither she would lead him, having herself instant access to all ranks and classes, to every abode of men . . . He loved the masquerading creature wherever he found her, whether with blue eyes, black eyes, or brown.'

In high society he finds a 'New Incarnation' of the Beloved in the widow, Nichola Pine-Avon. As he is now over forty Pierston 'dared not make unmeaning love with the careless selfishness of a younger man'. However he visits the widow 'with expectations of having a highly emotional time, at least'. Then he learns that Avice Caro is dead, and the restlessness of his emotional life begins to oppress him. He realises that in Avice's nature, as in his own, 'was some mysterious ingredient sucked from the isle; otherwise a racial instinct necessary to the absolute union of a pair'.

The need for this 'ground-quality' of a common folk heritage becomes the dominant force in Pierston's life. He returns to the Isle and tries to marry Avice's daughter. They develop a cordial but ultimately frustrating relationship as she is already married, unhappily, to an absent husband. A reconciliation is effected by Pierston's agency and in due course Avice the Third grows up to a nubile condition. Avice the Second sends for Pierston in a spirit of wholly unconvincing determination to have as her son-in-law the man who did not quite make it as her father or husband. Avice the Third displays the utmost docility and complaisance until the night before the wedding when, on a momentary impulse, she elopes with Marcia Bencomb's stepson. Avice the Second, suffering from mortification of the spirit and *angina pectoris* promptly dies and Pierston, that 'native of natives', at last marries the other island-love of his youth, the long forgotten Marcia.

As a novel, *The Well-Beloved* undoubtedly merits the derision it invariably receives. The plotting of the story is clumsy and perfunctory, the writing undistinguished and at times ludicrous. Even so, this weird fantasia on the fickleness of man throws some ıportant light on matters that need to be examined in a ntext later. That it occupied Hardy's mind during the .hen his thoughts were also concentrated on *Tess* and *ɹude* makes it one of the oddities of literary history.

This, then, was the stopgap provided for Tillotson's when the *Tess* contract was cancelled. Now let us return to Tess herself, in her quest for a publisher. In *The Life* Hardy records that he had 'three requests, if not more, on his list' for a serial. But of course they wanted something bland enough to leave the placidity of their readers unruffled. If Hardy chose to write about a village maiden 'betrayed' he already knew, from his experience with Suke Damson in *The Woodlanders*, that editorial advice would be to 'let the frailty be construed mild' (in the delightful phrase that Mowbray Morris, the editor of *Macmillans Magazine*, had used in respect of Suke Damson's behaviour in *The Woodlanders*); and 'mild' is not the word for the consequences of Tess's 'frailty'.

Seen through the eyes of a Victorian magazine editor the targets at which Hardy was now aiming made a formidable list. In *Tess* he attacked the double standard of morality, which rated fornication as a peccadillo in men but a wickedness in women, with unmarried parenthood as a woman's ultimate disgrace. He questioned the validity of an unconsummated marriage in opposition to an illicit union. He probed the terms on which Christian burial could be allowed or withheld. He exposed some of the moral and economic pressures to which the humble and lowly were subjected by the ruling class. And by adding to the title of the story the provocative sub-title 'A Pure Woman' Hardy was challenging, whether deliberately or not, some of the most cherished and unquestioned moral assumptions of his time.

After Edward Arnold had rejected *Tess* for *Murray's Magazine* Hardy turned again to Mowbray Morris. After all, Morris had printed *The Woodlanders* with no more serious opposition than a request 'not to bring the fair Miss Suke to too open shame'. His response now was prompt and unequivocal. *Tess* was not for him. Accordingly the year 1889 ended with Hardy, at the height of his fame, contemplating three rejections of his latest work on the grounds of its 'improper explicitness'. He was tempted to forgo serial publication and publish in volume form only, but felt he could not afford this way out of his dilemma.

The course he adopted was one that he believed to be 'unprecedented in the annals of fiction'. Instead of submitting his MS intact and risking another rejection he set to work to bowdlerise it to what he judged to be the level of emasculation that an editor would tolerate. Some sections, removed completely, were to be published separately as self-contained episodes. Rewritten or suppressed passages were to be restored when he was permitted to 'piece the trunk and limbs of the novel together, and print it complete' in the subsequent volume publication. Meanwhile, after these acts of literary 'surgery' in inks of different colour, the disinfected serial version was offered to *The Graphic* and accepted.

For the moment Hardy's troubles seemed to be over, but he had also to deliver to *The Graphic* half a dozen of the stories in his *Group of Noble Dames*. With these, as with the MS of *Tess*, the editor, Arthur Locker, seemed to be well satisfied. His directors unfortunately were not. With the publication of the first instalment of *Tess* imminent Hardy did not want his short stories to unsettle *The Graphic*. A note of his dated 23 June 1890, reads 'Here's a pretty job! Must smooth down these Directors somehow I suppose.' Accordingly all six stories were bowdlerised and the publication of *Tess* went ahead.

One other consequence of the directors' intervention is worth recalling. At the thought of Angel Clare carrying Tess and the other milkmaids bodily through the floodwater Arthur Locker's nerve failed. Rather than risk a further demonstration of his board's disapproval the editor asked Hardy to have a wheelbarrow at hand, in which the girls could be transported without any suspicion of indecorous handling by Clare; and Hardy, in his mood of grim cynicism, duly introduced the famous wheelbarrow which was to become a symbol of Victorian prudery.

8

Tess 1890 - 1895

Item: She can milk; look you, a sweet virtue in a maid with clean hands

(*Two Gentlemen of Verona*)

The law court facts of Tess's life are easily summarised. Like many girls of her time she was seduced by her employer's son and gave birth to a child which died. Her subsequent marriage is left unconsummated when her husband deserts her after learning of her misfortune. To protect her family from poverty after her father's death she goes back to her seducer, but murders him when her lawful husband returns unexpectedly to seek a reconciliation, whereupon she is arrested and hanged. Baldly put, this is the unremarkable and seemingly rather squalid little story that Hardy lifts, by his art and his compassion, to the exalted level of high tragedy.

In its construction the novel is poised on a couple of slight incidents which at first have only a momentary effect, but accumulate significance as the story develops. The first incident involves Tess's father, John Durbeyfield, a petty 'higgler' or dealer in the village of Marlott, who learns that he is descended from the ancient and noble family of the d'Urbervilles—a discovery that he celebrates by getting drunk. At the same time Tess is taking part in a village ceremony—the traditional club walk at Whitsun—which culminates in openair dancing. The sons of a clergyman are walking through Marlott and one of them, Angel Clare, stops briefly to dance with the girls, who are short of male partners. His choice is casually made: he disregards Tess and chooses another girl. He is not destined to see Tess again until, after the death of her illegitimate child, they find themselves in daily companionship at Talbothays Farm where Clare is studying agriculture and Tess finds employment as a dairymaid. But now, as their hearts kindle to love, it is already too late.

This sense of a lost opportunity, which was to have been stressed in the earlier book title, 'Too Late Beloved', is shown as no mere storyteller's caprice but as a flaw in the natural order of things. Criticising 'the ill-judged execution of the well-judged plan' Hardy observes that 'the call seldom produces the comer, the man to love rarely coincides with the hour for loving'; and he goes on to speculate whether 'at the acme and summit of the human progress these anachronisms will be corrected by a finer intuition, a closer interaction of the social machinery than that which now jolts us round and along'. The whole tragedy of Tess's life, and of Clare's also, might have been averted if he had been endowed with that 'finer intuition' which would have made him fall in love with her at first sight rather than at second.

Instead, what prevails among the events of that Whitsun is the befuddled *folie de grandeur* of Tess's father. 'There's not a man in the county', he proclaims, 'that's got grander and nobler skillentons in his family than I.' He is loyally supported by his wife, Joan, who declares: ''Tis well to be kin to a coach, even if you don't ride in 'en.' What differentiates the parents is that what is for 'Sir' John pure fantasy is turned to practical account by the worldly wisdom of Joan. She recalls that a wealthy woman bearing the name of d'Urberville lives within twenty miles of Marlott, and she is drawn to the idea of sending her very presentable daughter, Tess, to 'claim kin'.

The character of Joan Durbeyfield is one of the finest of Hardy's secondary portraits. Superstitious, sentimental, incompetent and impulsive, she nevertheless has a prudent eye for the main chance. Her secretive and devious realism is the perfect foil to the innocent nobility of Tess. Comparing mother and daughter Hardy writes 'when they were together the Jacobean and the Victorian ages were juxtaposed'. Her modern schooling had largely emancipated Tess from the superstitions which still swayed Mrs Durbeyfield and which—for example—made her keep 'The Compleat Fortune-Teller' in the thatch of the outhouse rather than allow a volume of such potency to remain in the house at night. But for all that, it is the sure instinct of a mother on the make that steers Tess to Trantridge and the home of the d'Urbervilles. When it transpires that the wealthy lady is a blind widow with an unmarried son, Joan is ready enough to risk Tess's chastity on the prospect of a marriage with this rich and eligible 'cousin'. Her strategy is a simple one: 'if he don't marry her aforc he will after'.

Tess by contrast conforms with the cardinal rule of tragedy which stresses her inability to accept those stratagems and compromises and venal deceits that most of us use, with a rueful shrug, to make life endurable. When the worst has happened, and she returns home pregnant, Tess reproaches her mother with these words:

> 'I was a child when I left this house four months ago. Why didn't you tell me there was danger in men-folk? Why didn't you warn me? Ladies know what to fend hands against, because they read novels that tell them of these tricks; but I never had the chance o' learning in that way, and you did not help me.'

To this direct challenge Joan Durbeyfield characteristically offers the excuse that the effect of a warning might only have been to cause Tess to 'be hontish wi' him and lose your chance', and she relapses fatalistically into the acceptance of what is after all, in her judgment, a normal act of Nature and 'what do please God'.

The character of Alec d'Urberville, Tess's seducer, is modelled on similar lines to Troy and Fitzpiers. There is the same panache, the same confident mastery over women, combined with the rootless instability of a spirit searching for a coherent identity. Hardy makes a very effective use of the phoniness of Alec's most conspicuous feature, his family name, which is no true badge of aristocracy but was crudely annexed by his father to the more plebeian name of Stoke. When Mr Simon Stoke, the north-country businessman, retired to Wessex he chose to metamorphose himself and his heirs into the more dignified style of Stoke-d'Urberville. In his description of the son, Hardy significantly records 'touches of barbarism in his contours'. Alec's role is to symbolise the brash new commercial class which is destined to ravish the old-style rural England that can no longer be defended by decaying feudal families. Tess represents those who in the past rode roughshod over the innocent but have since gone 'down, down, down' and now must themselves suffer what they once inflicted on others. When Angel Clare enters the story it is a part of his function to represent the impotence of Christian idealism and progressive moral enlightenment when they have to confront the havoc wrought by Alec. And there is, I believe, a further and deeper significance in Alec as what Blake called 'the Devourer', the element of destruction by which the principle of tragic nobility is purified and made clear. In that sense Alec is the embodiment of Blake's proverb of Hell: 'The roaring of lions, the howling of wolves, the raging of the stormy sea, and the destructive sword, are portions of eternity, too great for the eye of man.' Such a 'portion of eternity' is Alec d'Urberville in his relationship with Tess.

Meanwhile Angel Clare, after that first casual encounter at the Whitsun dance, has faded into the background. Having broken away from the family tradition of the church he has now embarked on a course of training as an agriculturist. It is as a gentleman-pupil that he lodges and works with Dairyman Crick at Talbothays Farm in the Vale of the Great Dairies, and it is to Talbothays that Tess comes to work as a hired hand when she sets out to make a fresh start in life after the death of her baby. Prompting her to a new optimism is her 'unexpended youth, surging up anew after its temporary check, and bringing with it hope, and the invincible instinct towards self-delight'. When she asks herself 'was once lost always lost really true of chastity?' she finds a wistful consolation in the thought that 'she might prove it false if she could veil bygones. The recuperative power which pervaded organic nature was surely not denied to maidenhood alone.' Thus the scene is set for the love that draws her and Angel together.

The Talbothays section of the novel is a tremendous hymn to the fecundity and prodigality of nature in the lush meadows of the Froom valley. The opening words—'On a thyme-scented, bird-hatching morning in May'—establish the mood at once and as spring deepened into summer: 'Rays from the sunrise drew forth the buds and stretched them into long stalks, lifted up sap in noiseless streams, opened petals, and sucked out scents in invisible jets and breathings.'

The young and sappy human beings at Talbothays are all of a piece with this 'leafy time when arborescence seems to be the one thing aimed at out of doors'. In the sleeping chamber that the dairymaids share the air 'seemed to palpitate with the hopeless passion of the girls. They writhed feverishly under the oppressiveness of an emotion thrust on them by cruel Nature's law . . . the torture was almost more than they could endure. The differences which distinguished them as individuals were abstracted by this passion, and each was but portion of one organism called sex.'

Angel could have won any of the four girls but he chooses Tess, impressed by her 'dignified largeness both of disposition and physique, an almost regnant power', and finding in her 'a visionary essence of woman—a whole sex condensed into one typical form'. The months spent at Talbothays, compared with the homelife of his father's rectory, affect Angel 'like throwing off splints and bandages'. He is impatient to marry Tess, who is now under immense pressure to reconcile in some way the forces that pull her in opposite directions.

Her primary resolution had been that she could 'never conscientiously allow any man to marry her'. She even believed that there was 'a certain moral validity' in her previous union, with Alec d'Urberville. In any case she felt obliged to confess her lost maidenhead to Angel before any commitment to marriage could be entertained. This was the coinage in which she reckoned to pay her debt to society and its conventions. But she had also to contend with forces of a different kind.

> The 'appetite for joy' which pervades all creation, that tremendous force which sways humanity to its purpose, as the tide sways the helpless weed, was not to be controlled by vague lucubrations over the social rubric.

Her sudden cry in the night, 'I can't bear to let anybody have him but me!' is a moment of naked jealousy that finds its extenuation in the broader scene that Hardy draws:

> Amid the oozing fatness and warm ferments of the Froom Vale, at a season when the rush of juices could almost be heard below the hiss of fertilisation, it was impossible that the most fanciful love should not grow passionate.

Repeatedly she tries to confide in Angel, only to be thwarted by accident or indecision. Her dilemma infuses the everyday events of the farm with a lurid colour of its own. When the butter is slow to form in the churn the conversation turns to the superstitious belief that such an event can be caused by a guilty or secret love affair in the house. A complaint, at another time, that the milk is tainted with wild garlic leads to a communal search through the sweet herbage of the pasture to eradicate the one evil weed—an expressive symbolism. Dairyman Crick's comic tales of the love life of Jack Dollop give unexpected depth and contrast to the main theme; like pages from a Wessex *Decameron* they imply that the whole tormented business of sex is really a gigantic broad comedy and not the stuff of tragedy at all. And yet, in its grotesque way, Crick's droll anecdote disturbs and alarms Tess by arousing the key question in her mind—should everything be confessed before marriage? 'What was comedy to them', Hardy comments, 'was tragedy to her.' In this he was recalling a note he had written in October 1888: 'If you look beneath the surface of any farce you see a tragedy.'

This interplay of low comedy and high tragedy, the one offsetting and heightening the other, is a crucial element in Hardy's work: to find a parallel to it in English one really needs to look back to Shakespeare, from whom I believe Hardy derived this technique. Indeed what gives such richness of texture to the character of Tess is the complex of native peasant qualities that fuse into her own individual sensibility. She does not emerge as a noble and 'pure' woman from a personal void but from a powerful matrix of superstition and comic guffaws and self-seeking guile—the guile particularly of her mother—who seeks to temper Tess's zeal for truth with those gems of prudence that make her letter to her daughter a classic of its kind:

> I say between ourselves, quite private but very strong, that on no account do you say a word of your Bygone Trouble to him. I did not tell everything to your Father, he being so proud on account of his Respectability, which, perhaps, your Intended is the same. Many a woman—some of the Highest in the Land—have had a Trouble in their time; and why should you trumpet yours when others don't trumpet theirs?

The upshot of it all is that Tess and Angel marry, with the fatal words still unsaid until the moment of mutual confession comes on the wedding night. The weighing of Tess's 'sin' against Angel's admission of 'eight-and-forty hours' dissipation with a stranger' develops into a much-quoted display of the traditional controversy over a 'double-standard' morality. The sympathy that Hardy excited for Tess had an impact on Victorian opinion that is easy to imagine. To give a single example, the Duchess of Abercorn told Hardy that the novel had saved her all future trouble in the assortment of her friends, who had been almost fighting across her dinner table over Tess's character: her plan was to group them as being 'For' or 'Against'.

However, as so often with Hardy in his most imaginative moments, the characters he has created begin to reveal successive layers and depths of meaning. The more profound and elemental forces that move them become momentarily articulate, in sudden flashes of insight. The wedding night scene is more than an argument about the 'social rubric' of the nineteenth century, or even —more widely—about Christian morality in general. Tess and Angel both find themselves in a crisis of identity as they strive to reconcile the Real with the Ideal. To Tess's anguished cry, 'I thought, Angel, that you loved me—me, my very self!', Angel's response is: 'The woman I have been loving is not you.'

With a head full of progressive ideas Angel imagines himself to be liberal, humane and compassionate—as indeed he is in abstract and ideal terms. But in personal contact with the realities of Talbothays Farm he falsifies his experience by the application of romantic arcadian concepts, as if an idyllic purity were the invariable state of Wessex dairymaids. His own admission, 'I thought I should secure rustic innocence as surely as I should secure pink cheeks', closely echoes that other self-deceiving man of principle, Henry Knight, who assumed that, when he embraced the heroine of *A Pair of Blue Eyes*, he would kiss 'untried lips'.

The woman Angel imagined he had been loving was not merely a being other than Tess: she was a figment of his imagination, a private fantasy, no woman at all. But what then was the 'very self' that Tess invited him to love? To simplify her as one of the wronged to whom a second chance has been given is to overlook the uncertainties that prey on her mind: 'She was Mrs. Angel Clare, indeed, but had she any moral right to the name? Was she not more truly Mrs. Alexander d'Urberville?'

It is this aspect of her identity that increasingly troubles Tess as the conflict between Real and Ideal intensifies. In the Ideal world the priestly sacrament of marriage should have sealed her irrevocably as Angel's wife. But when he rejects and abandons her she is increasingly persuaded that her true identity lies outside the periphery of a man-made morality and that in some greater natural order it is the realities of copulation and birth that establish her as the wife, or at any rate the physical mate, of Alec. The ultimate tragedy of Tess is to be torn apart between these two internecine forces. As Hardy observes in a beautifully cool understatement: 'She knew not what was expected of women in such cases; and she had no counsellor.'

In Angel Clare, as in Henry Knight, the fatal defect is a blend of moral daintiness and sexual hesitancy. As a lover Angel is described as 'more spiritual than animal . . . singularly free from grossness. Though not cold-natured, he was rather bright than hot.' It is a description that calls to mind Elfride's perceptive words: 'I almost wish you were of a grosser nature, Harry . . . Ordinary men are not so delicate in their tastes as you.'

At this point in his analysis of human nature Hardy evidently felt himself to be on dangerous ground. It was with notable caution that he commented on Clare obliquely: 'Some might risk the odd paradox that with more animalism he would have been the nobler man. We do not say it. Yet Clare's love was doubtless ethereal to a fault.'

In the last resort it is Tess's readiness to suffer and her lack of artifice which leave Clare impotently held in 'the fury of fastidiousness with which he was possessed', and it is from these uncompromising attitudes that the tragedy now gathers momentum. Angel reacts explosively and flings off to a new life in Brazil. Tess drifts passively into a life of fading hopes and degrading circumstances. We follow her to Flintcomb Ash where she joins one of the Talbothays milkmaids, Marian, to work in the fields on a farm that is as cheerless and hostile as Talbothays had been genial and benign.

In painting this contrast Hardy draws on those poetic qualities which so strikingly enhance his novels. The bitter cold of winter on the exposed uplands of Wessex combines with the harshness of the employer and the strength-sapping monotony of the work. The world of nature now becomes unrelievedly cruel and frightening: its new and terrifying role is symbolised in a breed of birds, drawn from far beyond the realms of ornithology, which haunt the fields where Tess works and which echo melodramatically the hazards of her life. The innocence that sweetened the bucolic

Plate 5 The successful novelist in middle age, as he appeared in an engraving by W. Strang and a photograph

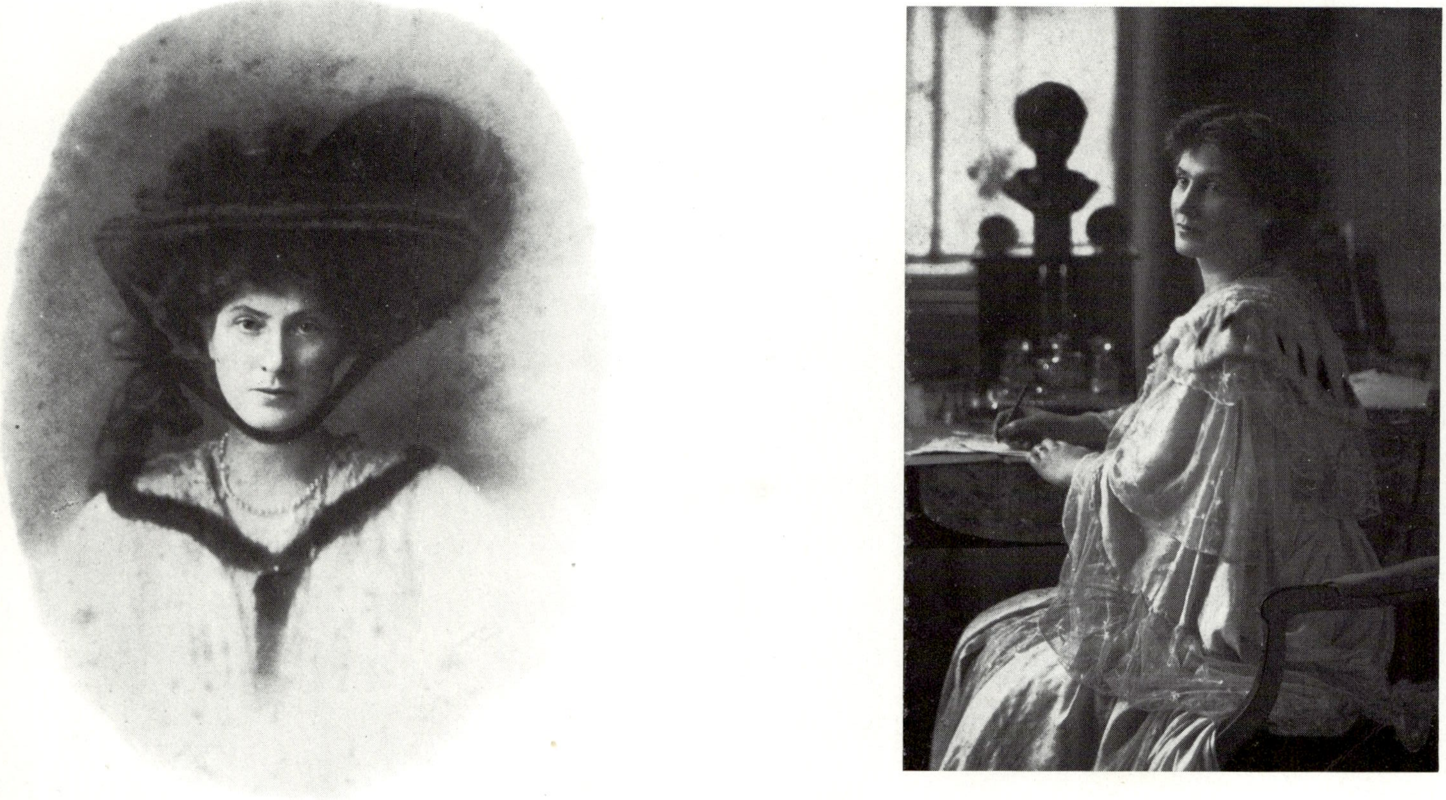

Plate 6 Agnes, Lady Grove, the 'good little pupil' with whom Hardy danced at the Larmer Tree Gardens on a notable occasion

humours of the Froom Valley changes at Flintcomb Ash to the habitual drunkenness of Marian and her ribald jokes about the phallic shapes of the stones she picks up while they work in the fields.

It is in this setting of increasingly brutalised misery that Alec d'Urberville reappears. He too is greatly changed. In a mood of penitence he has become a 'ranter', a self-ordained preacher. He meets Tess by chance, falls under her spell again and tries to form a fresh relationship with her. Hardy's touch is never so sure with Alec as with Angel and the uneven quality of the writing in this section descends at moments to a novelettish dialogue; even so, it operates forcefully at several levels. Intellectually there is the mounting irony of Tess's use of rationalist arguments, learnt from Clare, to demolish Alec's newly adopted Christian doctrines and thus to liberate him from moral restraints that might have protected her. Emotionally Alec is genuinely moved by the knowledge—until now withheld from him—that Tess has given birth to a child of his and once more he is captivated by the sensual power of her beauty. He brings a marriage licence and asks her to marry him, unaware that she is already Clare's wife. When at last the cards are on the table, it is an inward violence of frustration that drives them to that quarrel of elemental savagery, when Tess strikes Alec in the face with a heavy leather glove and exclaims: 'Now, punish me! . . . whip me, crush me . . . I shall not cry out. Once victim, always victim—that's the law!'

It is a law not made by man but belonging to some deeper and imperfectly realised natural order. It is endorsed by Alec with the threat: 'Remember, my lady, I was your master once! I will be your master again. If you are any man's wife you are mine!'

Though the words are Alec's, the thought they echo—indeed the doom they pronounce—comes from the bitter phrase of rejection that Angel used, after Tess's confession, 'he being your husband in nature, and not I'. Step by inevitable step she is drawn into Alec's orbit. Her father dies, her mother is evicted, the younger children face poverty and hunger. While Angel remains silent and self-absorbed in Brazil, Tess has to recognise that it is only Alec who can play a husband's part in such a time of misfortune. Hard pressed by the Real, she sacrifices the Ideal to it. Alec undertakes the responsibility for the family's welfare. Tess consents to live with him as his wife. In her despair 'a consciousness that in a physical sense this man alone was her husband seemed to weigh on her more and more'.

It is in these circumstances that Angel returns to England. He has learnt at last, and too late, the difficult lesson that Hardy condenses in an aphorism 'the defective can be more than the entire'; in other words, an imperfect masterpiece is better than a faultless mediocrity. Determined now to make amends and not doubting that the opportunity still exists, Angel seeks out Tess and finds her in the Southbourne guest house where she is living with Alec. The meeting of Angel and Tess, low-keyed and sombre, crystallises in a single sentence: 'Both seemed to implore something to shelter them from reality.' But the ideal state to which their love might once have raised them is dispelled for ever. From reality they can now escape only for a brief respite and by way of an act of violence. Tess murders Alec and follows Angel. There is a pathetic interlude of fragile tranquillity while the two fugitives hide in the New Forest. When they move inland and come to Stonehenge there can be no further escape from the net that is closing round them.

The choice of Stonehenge for this moment of climax is a reminder that, for all his modernity of thought, Hardy was a true Victorian when it came to the use of bold melodramatic effects. How well Emily Brontë or Berlioz would have understood what Hardy was striving to do! It is a typically Gothic sensibility that sets the immediate tragedy of Tess and Angel against one of the massive Wessex symbols of eternity and mystery. This juxtaposition of our little human perils with the great monuments of unrecorded time is a device that appealed to Hardy. It is what gives peculiar force, for example, to that moment in *A Pair of Blue Eyes* when Henry Knight is clinging to the edge of a cliff in danger of falling to his death and in front of his eyes, in the rock, there is a fossil, a trilobite. It too had once had eyes which, 'dead and turned to stone, were even now regarding him'. In Hardy's writings one is constantly made aware of this confrontation of man with the immense geological perspectives of earth's history, showing us to be no more entitled to self-importance than the ants and weevils under our feet.

So Tess, about to be arrested and tried and hanged, comes to Stonehenge in a mood of total serenity—almost impersonal now, her spirit almost dissolving back into the great flow of life. Like Henchard she suffers defeat in the grand manner. But the Mayor of Casterbridge is the epitome of all that is male, a modern Macbeth, a bull in the arena, going down savagely and bitterly under repeated blows. Tess is the complete contrast, the totally feminine victim, caught in a web of tragedy by her meekness, her tenderness, her generosity. At the end she simply surrenders and withdraws herself into some inner fastness of the spirit where one may believe she at last finds peace. At any rate, in that famous and provocative comment of Hardy's, 'the President of the Immortals, in Aeschylean phrase, had ended his sport with Tess'.

Hardy's skill in the portrayal of women is often praised as one of his particular achievements and there can be little doubt that Tess is in that sense his masterpiece. Like Henchard she is 'on-stage' for almost the entire action. She swiftly accumulates, or has inherent within her, the numinous power that radiates from a figure of impending tragedy. Like Shaw's St Joan or Ibsen's Hedda Gabler she lingers in our minds as one of the great feminine portraits in the modern idiom, as Hardy understood the word 'modern'. To quote his phrase, 'the ache of modernism' is in them.

In a comparison with Hardy's other principal heroines Tess stands apart as having a degree of voluptuousness—unawakened, no doubt, but not absent—which they lack. Bathsheba and Grace Melbury both owe more to Diana than to Venus; even more so does Sue Bridehead; if Eustacia Vye seems to be the exception it is in the fevered romantic style of an overheated imagination. But in Tess, Hardy aimed to present the true life force in eloquent silence, offering and in return requiring what Blake symbolised as 'the lineaments of gratified desire'. In the opinion of Henry James the attempt failed. In a letter to Robert Louis Stevenson, James wrote: 'Oh, yes, dear Louis: *Tess of the d'Urbervilles* is vile. The pretence of sexuality is only equalled by the absence of it.' It was a comment that later drew from Hardy the rarity of a neatly waspish retort, dismissing James and Stevenson as 'The Polonius and the Osric of novelists'.

Be that as it may, what I want to do here is to examine a technical device that Hardy used and to relate it to his studies of real-life women as we see them in his notebooks and poems. In dialogue Tess is consistently modest, innocent and free from any trace of what Hardy signifies as 'animalism' or 'grossness'. By Marian's ribaldry at Flintcomb Ash she is not amused. Even in the sunniest passages of her courtship by Angel Clare there is no spoken indication of that amative exuberance which James looked for in vain. And yet Hardy evidently intends Tess to arouse desire in a more than ordinary degree by the suggestion of a sensual responsiveness which, though veiled and inarticulate, is vivid enough to infatuate first Alec and then Angel. To do this he makes an extraordinary and obsessive use of the mouth as an erotic symbol. It is in the invitation of Tess's mouth that he seeks to express the secret of her appeal—'her mobile peony mouth', 'the pouted-up deep red mouth', 'the red and ivory of her mouth', 'that pretty red mouth', 'her flower-like mouth', 'the unpractised mouth and lips', 'that too tempting mouth', to quote some examples. Alec d'Urberville pleads for 'one little kiss on those holmberry lips' and there is a moment rich in overtones when he tries to press a strawberry into Tess's mouth, and she puts up her hand to stop him: ' "Nonsense!" he insisted; and in a slight distress she parted her lips and took it in.'

When he rediscovers her at Flintcomb Ash Alec's infatuation renews itself in predictable terms. 'I was firm as a man could be', he says, 'till I saw those eyes and that mouth again—surely there never was such a maddening mouth since Eve's.'

It is a sentiment that he shares with Angel Clare, whose contemplation of Tess as she sits milking leads to the realisation that her face has 'nothing ethereal about it; all was real vitality, real warmth, real incarnation. And it was in her mouth that this culminated . . . her mouth he had seen nothing to equal on the face of the earth . . . that little upward lift in the middle of her red top lip was distracting, infatuating, maddening.'

There is a similar moment of 'real incarnation' when, in the heat of a summer afternoon, Tess has just woken—

> She was yawning, and he saw the red interior of her mouth as if it had been a snake's . . . The brim-fulness of her nature breathed from her. It was a moment when a woman's soul is more incarnate than at any other time.

Even Angel's mother, that very prim and proper lady, refers to 'these simple, rosy-mouthed, robust girls of the farm'. 'Rosy-mouthed' is a strange epithet, surely, for her to use. But the most interesting example is the statement that Angel 'had never before seen a woman's lips and teeth which forced upon his mind with such persistent iteration the old Elizabethan simile of roses filled with snow'. What that passage forces on the mind of the more assiduous reader of Hardy's *Life* is the little reminiscence dated 23 July 1889—

> Of the people I have met this summer, the lady whose mouth recalls more fully than any other beauty's the Elizabethan metaphor 'Her lips are roses full of snow' (or is it Lodge's?) is Mrs. Hamo Thornycroft—whom I talked to at Gosse's dinner.

This connoisseurship of beauty appears to have been an increasing preoccupation of Hardy's at this time. A couple of months earlier he noticed a girl 'in the omnibus' who had 'one of those faces of marvellous beauty which are seen casually in the streets but never among one's friends'. He wondered: 'Where do these women come from? Who marries them? Who knows them?'

The following London season, when Hardy celebrated his fiftieth birthday, he 'had a humour for going the rounds of the music-halls', studying the beauties 'whose lustrous eyes and pearly countenances show that they owe their attractions to art'. It is a characteristic that he embodied in Jocelyn Pierston, who frequented music-halls and burlesque theatres and sometimes found that his 'Well-Beloved' had migrated into an exotic dancing girl, like the one he saw at the Royal Moorish Palace of Varieties. To identify an author biographically with any of his fictitious characters is always dangerous and usually ill-advised but it is difficult not to consider that 'The Well-Beloved' is in some measure a fable of one aspect of Hardy's inner life at this time.

The Shelleyan 'one shape of many names' led Pierston into 'beauty-chases' when he dodged and followed like a detective in the wake of some fleeting incarnation of the feminine Ideal. This loved one must always remain a fantasy since a contact with reality brings disillusion. Hardy seems to be offering a plain enough clue to his meaning in her name—'Caro', a most unlikely name to find on the Isle of Slingers. In a letter published at the time Hardy maintained that Caro 'imitated' a local name and was adopted because of its resemblance to the Italian for 'dear'—a not entirely convincing explanation from one who was a good enough Latin scholar to know it as the word for flesh, from which we derive 'carnal' and 'incarnation'. Pierston underlines the point when he says: 'As flesh she dies daily, like the Apostle's corporeal self; because when I grapple with the reality she's no longer in it, so that I cannot stick to one incarnation if I would.'

This seems to be a fairly accurate representation of Hardy's own state of mind at this period. His marriage was drifting into an increasingly irreversible estrangement. His views on the contractual restraints of marriage were growing more bitter and outspoken, and one of the fruits of his success as a writer was to find himself among the tormenting delights of those admiring ladies of fashion, whose beauty and aristocratic style engaged much of his attention during the London season. In his own words 'he found himself continually invited hither and thither to see famous beauties of the time'. Some of them had artistic gifts and literary talents or pretensions. With the Hon Mrs Henniker Hardy collaborated in a story, 'The Spectre of the Real'. For Agnes, Lady Grove he corrected and revised the proofs of *The Social Fetich* and accepted her dedication of the book to him.

His favourite hostess was Mary Jeune, wife of a judge who, after being knighted, became eventually Lord St Helier. Back at Max Gate Emma may have become pardonably impatient of the constant bulletins on Lady Jeune that reached her from London in Hardy's letters. 'I am staying over tonight at Lady Jeune's—she's having a dinner-party at which she wants me to be present... Lady Jeune seems to wish us to be not so far off as South Kensington ... Lady Jeune and all of them extremely kind ... Irving and Ellen Terry are coming to dine with them tomorrow: and I felt I might as well stay on ... This evening I take Lady Jeune's girls to the theatre. They are such dears that it is a pleasure to go with them ... I fear I shall not have time to see about [renting] a house. I am rather tired already. I shall have to come up again about it.' But the next day (Sunday) he wrote 'I am not coming Tuesday after all. Lady Jeune has a dinner, and a big party afterwards, on Wednesday, for which she has asked me to stay.'

By this time Emma's eccentricity may have been marked enough to justify a local opinion that she was 'not quite right in the upper storey' but one cannot withhold one's sympathy from the comment she reportedly made to T. P. O'Connor that Hardy's frailties were inflamed by 'these women that he meets in London society ... They are the poison; I am the antidote.' Hardy's own attitude is an ambivalent one. He evidently took a pride in his ability to move easily 'between the artificial gaieties of a London season and the quaintnesses of a primitive rustic life'. He sometimes deprecated his interest in the former, particularly in *The Life* where he protests that it was a fear that he might be 'driven to society novels' that impelled him to keep a record of his experiences in social life 'though doing it had always been a drudgery to him'. He develops this lofty tone in a somewhat gratuitous reference to Emma's diaries from which *The Life* was embellished with some details of social functions which, at the time, 'Hardy himself did not think worth recording'.

But there was another and more secret factor of resistance, I believe, to that susceptibility to feminine charms which seems to have kept Hardy in a state of incipient flirtatiousness. Like Yeats, Hardy made his poetry from 'the quarrel with himself'. If he wanted at some times to break out of his marriage and find his ideal woman somewhere amid the gaieties of the London season, at other times he perhaps echoed Pierston's cry, 'When was it to end—this curse of his heart not ageing while his frame moved naturally onward?' And is there not some sense of a personal self-examination in this passage from *The Well-Beloved*:

> When he beheld those of his fellows who were defined as buffers and fogeys—imperturbable, matter-of-fact, slightly ridiculous beings, past masters in the art of populating homes, schools and colleges, and present adepts in the science of giving away brides—how he envied them, assuming them to feel as they appeared to feel . . . They had got past the distracting currents of passionateness, and were in the calm waters of middle-aged philosophy. But he, their contemporary, was tossed like a cork hither and thither upon the crest of every fancy.

Fatherhood and a passionless placidity—the consolations of middle-age from which Hardy was excluded, irrespective of whether or not there is an autobiographical element in the writing. The same may be said of the final excerpt I want to make from Hardy's portrait of Pierston:

> Nobody would ever know the truth about him; *what* it was he had sought that had so eluded, tantalised, and escaped him . . . It was not the flesh; he had never knelt low to that. Not a woman in the world had been wrecked by him, though he had been impassioned by so many.

Again the texture of a fiction seems here to be impregnated with traces of a more personal feeling.

The significance of all this in relation to Hardy's writings is two-fold. The mounting scepticism about the institution of marriage, and hostility to it, which we can trace through *The Woodlanders*, *Life's Little Ironies* and *Tess* to a culmination in *Jude* gain much of their force from the correlations with Hardy's own experience. The idealised, platonic, fantasy-relationships that he pursued in consequence—'impassioned' by so many beauties but 'wrecking' none—are the key to some of his more deliberately mysterious poems. Let us here consider one of them, the poem entitled 'A Thunderstorm in Town'. It is so short that I give it in full:

> She wore a new 'terra-cotta' dress,
> And we stayed, because of the pelting storm,
> Within the hansom's dry recess,
> Though the horse had stopped; yea, motionless
> We sat on, snug and warm.
>
> Then the downpour ceased, to my sharp sad pain
> And the glass that had screened our forms before
> Flew up, and out she sprang to her door:
> I should have kissed her if the rain
> Had lasted a minute more.

Two things are immediately obvious. One is that the reference to the 'terra-cotta' dress gives a hidden clue to identity that will not be lost on the lady in the hansom, should she read the poem. The other is that the two closing lines adopt a technique, much used by shy adolescents, for taking a fond liberty at long range after a loss of nerve at close quarters. One suspects that another hour's steady downpour would have made no great difference in such circumstances.

Other poems show similar clues that appear to conceal an identity. There is

> that kiss
> Away from the prancing folk, by the strawberry-tree!

for example in 'Lines to a Movement in Mozart's E flat Symphony'; and the opening two lines of a poem called 'A Kiss'

> By a wall the stranger now calls his,
> Was born of old a particular kiss.

A strawberry-tree is not an absolute rarity but it is uncommon enough to retain specific associations with place and time. Its presence in the poem has a circumstantiality which serves no purpose except to authenticate a recollection. Similarly the precision of 'a wall the stranger now calls his' can only invite the reader to try to interpret the significance of the passing of the wall into some new and impersonal ownership. Does it matter? And if so, why—and to whom?

In many of Hardy's poems these details of private reference leave pockets of obscurity that tantalise the reader. If there is felt to be an intemperate investigation of those more personal areas of Hardy's life in which the student risks losing his way in a morass of gossip and tale-bearing, it must be recognised that Hardy stimulates curiosity by seeming to draw the reader into the mysterious autobiographical contexts that these poems represent. If the poem itself defies discovery he sometimes signals an additional clue by adding a date. In the case of 'A Thunderstorm in Town' Hardy added in later editions the subtitle 'A Reminiscence: 1893'; to the initiated '1893' at once suggests an association with Florence Henniker.

Hardy met Mrs Henniker for probably the first time when he and Emma visited Dublin in May 1893 as the guests of Mrs Henniker's brother, Lord Houghton, who at that time was Lord-Lieutenant of Ireland. 'A charming, *intuitive* woman' was Hardy's first impression of her, and they arranged to meet in London as soon as they both returned there. The attentions of so eminent an author must have been flattering but there is no indication that Florence Henniker's feeling for Hardy was ever more than an affectionate friendship, although she was too intelligent and sensitive a woman not to realise that Hardy was stirred by her to a stronger emotion than friendship. Perhaps she took it as her due and reckoned she could steer a safe course.

Within a few days Hardy was expressing the hope 'to number you all my life among the most valued of my friends'. Before many weeks had passed she had become his 'dear fellow-scribbler' and seemed to him 'a nearer friend—almost a sister'. The kind of 'nearer friend' that he wanted her to be is perhaps defined, in his own words to her, as 'a friend with whom mutual confessions can be made of weaknesses without fear of reproach or contempt'. This was what he offered and it of course implied a confidentiality that she had earlier broken, and thereby drawn a rebuke from him, when she read some of his letters aloud in company. Perhaps it was her reluctance to extend the relationship to a total candour, with the conspiratorial undertones that would be inescapable, that led Hardy to write wistfully in his notebook: 'I often think that women, even those who consider themselves experienced in sexual strategy, do not know how to manage an *honest* man.'

As one reads through the correspondence that they maintained until Mrs Henniker's death in 1923 it is apparent that they soon recognised the limits that circumscribed their relationship. Emotionally there was to be no serious indiscretion: intellectually the conventional views of Mrs Henniker could not be reconciled with Hardy's *avant-garde* attitudes on such acrimony-provoking Victorian themes as evolution, religion and the marriage laws. But within these limits they enjoyed a friendship which, in Frank Pinion's words, 'was based from the first to last on high mutual esteem and genuine sympathy'.

What matters ultimately, however, is that other dimension of their relationship—the elaborately transmuted expression of it that Hardy uttered in his poems. Here, unbridled by circumstance, he could release the imaginative drive of each passing emotion, great or small. Sometimes there is good authority for identifying the woman whose personality flowers in a poem or a single verse; at other times one must accept or reject this conjecture or that. 'In Death Divided' and 'At an Inn' are two of the poems that can probably be associated with Mrs Henniker: more certainly so are 'A Broken Appointment' in which he chides her for not having the compassion 'to soothe a time-torn man', and —best of all—the verse in one of his finest poems, 'Wessex Heights':

> As for one rare fair woman, I am now but a thought of hers,
> I enter her mind and another thought succeeds me that she prefers;
> Yet my love for her in its fulness she herself even did not know;
> Well, time cures hearts of tenderness, and now I can let her go.

Hardy dated the MS of 'Wessex Heights' 1896 and the letters suggest that the fulness of his love was ebbing in 1895, when another emotional graph began a similar though fainter curve. In September 1895 the Hardys went to stay at Rushmore in Cranborne Chase as the guests of General Pitt-Rivers. The General was one of the great pioneer figures in modern archaeology, but he was also a wealthy landowner with an inventive mind and diverse interests. One of his preoccupations was the Larmer Tree Gardens, a pleasure ground which he created and furnished with buildings brought from the Indian Exhibition at Earls Court in 1890. There was also a theatre and each autumn it was the custom to hold a day of festivities which included sports, horse races, a concert, dancing and general merrymaking. The visit of the Hardy's was obviously planned to coincide with this event.

Its effect on Hardy merits a brief consideration. Immediately on his return to Max Gate he wrote to Florence Henniker to tell her that the visit to Rushmore had been 'the most romantic time I have had since I visited you at Dublin'. In all the circumstances those are large words. He apparently preserved a newspaper cutting which contained an account of the Larmer Tree sports: when he came to write his autobiography he quoted verbatim a long passage from the *Dorset County Chronicle*, which included a reference to some country dances which were 'started by the house-party, and led off by the beautiful Mrs Grove, the daughter of General Pitt-Rivers'. Recalling the occasion Hardy remarked that 'this was the last occasion on which he ever trod a measure... at any rate on the greensward'; he claimed that 'It was he who started the country dances, his partner being the above-mentioned Mrs (afterwards Lady) Grove.'

In her diary Agnes Grove made no reference to the dancing. 'Went to Larmer Tree Sports' she wrote, 'met and talked to Thomas Hardy, found him interesting. Dined there.' Next day she started for Paris and Switzerland, but no time was lost in developing this first acquaintance by an exchange of letters. Hardy sent her a copy of *Jude* as soon as it was published—less than two months after the Larmer Tree dance—and she rapidly acquired the status that Mrs Henniker was relinquishing of the favourite literary pupil. After a spell of sickness in the early months of 1896 Agnes Grove travelled to London on 23 March. Two days later she wrote in her diary 'Mr Thomas Hardy came to see me'.

He was now acting regularly as coach and teacher in her first attempts at journalism and considered her a 'good little pupil'. A flurry of references to him during that spring and summer occurs in her diary as they attended each other's tea parties and met at the various social occasions that marked the London season. Sometimes Florence Henniker was also present and the two women developed a friendship.

After 1896 the references to Hardy in Lady Grove's diary become fewer. The relationship settles down to a friendship which persisted—as in the case of Mrs Henniker—until death. With more than twenty years dividing them in age it is perhaps not surprising that Agnes's attitude to Hardy was strongly blended with hero worship: even when she sought some advantage for herself she did so with a placatory submissiveness to his eminence and seniority. She could not have sustained in him the depth of passion that Florence Henniker aroused, but her beauty and undoubted vivacity seized his imagination as they danced in

The Larmer Tree Gardens. That single incident gives us a remarkable insight into the way Hardy's poetic powers gathered in and slowly transformed the finer essences of a 'romantic' moment. To suggest that she inspired the poem 'The Lady of Forebodings' is perhaps to do no more than illustrate the problems that Hardy's poems present. The Larmer Tree Gardens were lit with hundreds of Vauxhall lamps and I seem to discern a reflection of them in the lines:

> The lamps above and round were fair,
> The tables were aglee.

But be that as it may we have a surer and more poignant record in the response of old age to times remembered when, at the age of eighty-six, Hardy heard that 'the beautiful' Lady Grove had died; and he began to write—under the simple title 'Concerning Agnes'—the noble elegy that begins—

> I am stopped from hoping what I have hoped before—
>   Yes, many a time!—
> To dance with that fair woman yet once more
>   As in the prime
> Of August, when the wide-faced moon looked through
> The boughs at the faery lamps of the Larmer Avenue.
> I could not, though I should wish, have over again
>   That old romance,
> And sit apart in the shade as we sat then
>   After the dance
> The while I held her hand, and, to the booms
> Of contrabassos, feet still pulsed from the distant rooms.

9

Jude 1893 - 1896

How good to dwell beyond the reach of pain!
Cithaeron! Why did you accept me?
(*Sophocles: Oedipus the King*)

At about the time when *Tess* was beginning to take shape Hardy was also thinking of suitable themes for short stories. Tillotson's, for whom *Tess* was intended, had already taken three of Hardy's stories and would presumably welcome more. The period 1888–93 represents not only the climax of Hardy's novel writing but also a busy and prolific time in his production of short stories. No doubt the success of *The Woodlanders* in 1887 stimulated the desires of editors to include Hardy among their contributors.

But the idea he sketched in his notebook on 28 April 1888 did not find its way into any of his collections of short stories. As outlined it was intended to be: 'A short story of a young man—"who could not go to Oxford"—His struggles and ultimate failure. Suicide.' Here was the germ of something that, in Hardy's words, 'the world ought to be shown, and I am the one to show it to them'. The idea returned to his mind after the publication of *Tess*, when he was preparing to undertake a new serial for simultaneous publication in Britain and the United States in *Harpers New Monthly Magazine*.

Undeterred by his previous experiences with serialisations Hardy confidently promised 'a tale that could not offend the most fastidious maiden'. The title he originally favoured, *Hearts Insurgent*, has a conventionally romantic sound. If he had at this stage gone back to the original note about the young man rejected by Oxford he was perhaps intending a crusading piece on behalf of the underprivileged—and no 'fastidious maiden' could object to that, provided she were guided by respectable liberal principles.

However, as Hardy worked on the full length version during the autumn and winter of 1893, he came increasingly to recognise that 'the development was carrying him into unexpected fields and he was afraid to predict its future trend'. In April 1894 he requested Harpers to cancel their contract. The original theme of the frustration of a young man's thirst for scholarly knowledge had become entwined with 'the fret and fever, derision and disaster, that may press in the wake of the strongest passion known to humanity'. It was now the marriage laws that served 'in great part as the tragic machinery of the tale'. Although Hardy continued to maintain that he was 'not aware of anything in the handling to which exception can be taken' he was no longer concerned with the special requirements of 'fastidious maidens' when, in the Preface to *Jude the Obscure*, he made it clear that the book was addressed 'to men and women of full age' and would attempt 'to tell, without a mincing of words, of a deadly war waged between flesh and spirit'.

Perhaps the simplest description of the structure of the book is in terms of ballet—as a double *pas de deux* in which the dancers ring the changes on the possible pairings. The first to appear are the two males, the boy Jude Fawley and the schoolmaster, Richard Phillotson, who inspires the boy with a vision of 'Christminster'. Next Arabella captivates Jude and they marry. After their separation Jude finds a new but ill-starred relationship with his cousin, Sue. He leads Sue to Phillotson who marries her. She deserts him and returns to Jude. Arabella now reappears and renounces Jude but puts in his care the child of their wedlock. In jealousy Sue bears children to Jude—and when they are murdered by Arabella's child she returns to Phillotson in a mood of self-mortification. Arabella finally ensnares Jude for the second time. He dies, trying to regain Sue.

What gives significance to these changing partnerships is the

Plate 7 (above) Hardy with his second wife, Florence, at the seaside

(left) a cartoon of Hardy drawn in 1919 by Max Beerbohm as a gift to Florence Hardy

Plate 8 (left) The poet in old age: a study by Francis Dodd

(right) Hardy in his eightieth year: the pencil drawing by W. Strang in the National Portrait Gallery

fact that the two lesser characters, Arabella and Phillotson, represent the more conventional, tolerant, conformist elements in society, while Jude and Sue are correspondingly unconventional, rebellious and critical of the social order. Just as Hardy chose to present Tess as 'a pure woman', so here he invites the reader to regard Jude and Sue as living in sin—or at any rate unworthily—when they are with their legal spouses, but pursuing an ideal when they are living together without the benefit of a marriage ceremony. In effect Hardy is renewing the questions he asked about Tess's relationships with Angel Clare and Alec d'Urberville. What really does constitute a marriage? How do you reconcile the inner subjective forces with social circumstance? Where does the flesh have mastery, and where the spirit?

The book opens with two key statements about the orphan boy, Jude, who lives with his great-aunt Drusilla at Marygreen. The first is that his character is such that he is doomed to 'ache a good deal before the fall of the curtain upon his unnecessary life should signify that all was well with him again'. The second is his vision of 'Christminster' (Oxford) only a score of miles away, to which the village schoolmaster has moved with the ambition eventually to graduate and be ordained. As he says to Jude: 'By going to live at Christminster, or near it, I shall be at headquarters, so to speak.' This concept of a holy city, a mecca of learning, is developed into one of the most commanding passages in any of Hardy's novels—seen first through the boy's eyes and then in a parallel account in dialect by an unnamed carter, who certainly ranks with Jan Coggan, John Upjohn, Michael Mail and the rest as a master of the Wessex vernacular. The sequence ends with one of those plain, austere, low-keyed yet eloquent passages in the vein of Bunyan and Defoe, of which Hardy was a superb exponent—and in which the whole Westcountry tradition of puritan dissent seems to be made articulate. The tightly disciplined understatement with which Jude closes this majestic meditation on Christminster could not be simpler nor—in its context—more moving: 'It would just suit me.'

To equip himself to follow in Phillotson's footsteps, Jude learns Greek and Latin. To support himself at Christminster he becomes a stone-mason, reckoning that 'that ecclesiastical romance in stone' would always have employment to offer him. For a moment it seems that his dream might prosper—until, that is, he encounters 'the strongest passion known to humanity', embodied in Arabella Donn. She is a buxom, lusty, rather coarse and worldly-wise daughter of a pig farmer. With her, to feel is to act; and her feelings are unequivocal and direct: 'I want him to have me—to marry me! I must have him. I can't do without him. He's the sort of man I long for. I shall go mad if I can't give myself to him altogether!'

In short, Arabella is Hardy's symbol of the Flesh. In his drawing of her he stresses her animalism, her big-breasted fecundity, her blind assertion of the life force pursuing its biological goal. Wanting to hatch a valuable hen's egg she follows an old custom in secreting it between her breasts, saying: 'I suppose it is natural for a woman to want to bring live things into the world.' In its turn the egg becomes a trophy for the adventurous male to snatch. Her whole personality radiates 'the unvoiced call of woman to man'. Under her spell Jude is impelled 'towards the embrace of a woman for whom he had no respect, and whose life had nothing in common with his own except locality'. Against his better judgment Jude imagines he is 'living for the first time' and convinces himself that it is 'better to love a woman than to be a graduate, or a parson; ay, or a pope!'

By a pretence of pregnancy Arabella 'entraps' Jude into marriage. Her essentially easygoing and flexible nature assumes that: 'He'll shake down, bless 'ee—men always do. What can 'em do otherwise? Married is married.' Her confidence is well founded in the knowledge that hers is the way of the world: she is in tune with the community in which she lives.

But Jude is not. He is—and will continue to be—an outsider. There is no prospect of his 'shaking down' with Arabella and they part. The vehemence with which Jude rails against his misfortune is hardly justified by what might appear to be the more practical factors in his new situation. He is restored as nearly as possible to his bachelor state with no continuing responsibilities or obligations for Arabella, who emigrates to Australia and later proposes a divorce which cancels their marriage. Nevertheless he considers their lives to be ruined, and he blames social convention for compelling him to abandon 'well-formed schemes involving years of thought and labour' and to surrender his one opportunity of 'showing himself superior to the lower animals . . . because of a momentary surprise by a new and transitory instinct'.

What is notable here is an element of special pleading which persists through the book and in my view weakens it. The economic consequences of marriage need not have cancelled his 'well-formed schemes'. For example, the assertion that 'his wife was absolutely useless in a town-lodging' is manifestly absurd as she has previously been employed as a barmaid. The early married life of William Cobbett offers a useful comparison. Again, Jude's superiority to 'the lower animals' must rest on his powers of reflective reasoning and discrimination; but it was the failure of these powers which left him so vulnerable to the 'momentary surprise of a new and transitory instinct'. In his self-pity he appears to be wishing, as we may all at some time wish, that our social institutions could achieve the impossible task of protecting the fool from his folly.

In a calmer moment Jude comes nearer to the truth when he recognises that the crucial fault in his marriage was that it was based on 'a temporary feeling which had no necessary connection with affinities that alone render a life-long comradeship tolerable'. In that context, 'tolerable' is a significantly grudging concession. Here, as in the later episodes of his life, Jude exhibits a pronounced bias towards failure and a recriminatory self-pity. His misfortunes are no less pitiable than those of Henchard or Tess but he is the more willing accomplice in his own downfall.

With Arabella gone, Jude makes a fresh attempt to realise his dream of a scholar's life at Christminster. For the second time he is distracted by a woman—but on this occasion it is a nature the very opposite of Arabella's that captivates him. His cousin, Sue Bridehead, is intellectually unorthodox, anticlerical, contemptuous of conventions and stylishly brilliant in a way that dazzles Jude. She declares that: 'We have had enough of Jerusalem . . . nothing first-rate about the place . . . as there was about Athens, Rome, Alexandria.' On an occasion when Jude suggests that they should sit in the Cathedral at Melchester, Sue says 'I'd rather sit in the railway station . . . That's the centre of the town life now. The Cathedral has had its day.' And when Jude exclaims 'How modern you are!' She replics 'I am not modern, either. I am more ancient than mediaevalism, if you only knew.' This identification with the pagan world of 'Greek joyousness' is a recurring element in Sue's character, a latent symbolism that Hardy stresses at times.

There is another aspect of Jude's relationship with Sue that must be mentioned here. When his marriage with Arabella collapsed, his great-aunt Drusilla warned him that he comes of a stock that is ill-suited to marriage—'sommat in our blood that won't take kindly to the notion of being bound'. Sue equally (her mother being a Fawley) is subject to this doom of 'not being made for wedlock'. From Drusilla therefore came the later warning to Jude to avoid Sue if he should chance to meet her in Christminster. The response of Jude to this 'doom' is in the classic Greek tradition. Just as Oedipus was miraculously preserved from death on the slopes of Cithaeron, so Jude fails in his attempt to end his life; in Hardy's words: 'Peaceful death abhorred him as a subject, and would not take him.' In consequence, just as Oedipus goes inexorably to meet and kill his father and then to wed his mother, as his destiny required, so Jude is drawn to Sue at the fatal rendezvous in Christminster to which Drusilla has unwittingly directed him.

In correspondence with Edmund Gosse Hardy wrote: 'Sue is a type of woman which has always had an attraction for me, but the difficulty of drawing the type has kept me from attempting it till now.' He had in mind particularly an extreme sexual fastidiousness which makes her withhold herself from even those men to whom she is keenly attracted. 'I have never yielded myself to any lover', she tells Jude, 'I have remained as I began.' She takes some pride in her ability to mix with men 'almost as one of their own sex'. Her very name—Bridehead—comes to seem like a typically Hardyesque playing round the theme of 'maidenhead' and an impending but not yet realised bridal night. In her disclosure to Jude of her earlier life—so unlike Tess's confession to Angel!—she describes how she lived with a Christminster undergraduate in London for fifteen months of 'friendly intimacy', refusing to become his mistress because she was not 'in love' with him. When he died she suffered remorse 'for my cruelty—though I hope he died of consumption and not of me entirely!'

The vulgarity of feeling in that sort of remark, which falls often enough from Sue's lips, has to be reconciled with Hardy's insistence that it is a common trick with her to put on flippancy 'to hide real feeling'. Guidance of that kind from an author makes a helpful stage direction to an actress, but it leaves partially unresolved the problem in a novel of interpreting dialogue which, as print, lacks the colour of a precise tone of voice. The reader is put on his guard against taking Sue's words at face value, but an impression of shallowness remains; it is reinforced when she speaks of 'my curiosity to hunt up a new sensation'—something which she does as 'an epicure in emotions'. Whatever one may discount as a protective flippancy it is difficult not to recognise in Sue an element of coquetry, a pleasure in teasing and provoking and evading her frustrated lovers, to the verge of a more specifically sadistic delight in their humiliation.

One can well understand Hardy's sense of the difficulty of presenting so unusual and complex a character, where every slight nuance has to be just right. He was moreover carried into forbidden areas of speculation, where the Victorian fiction reading public was concerned. Today most readers of this page will be visited by the thought that Sue's 'fastidiousness' was a sign of a lesbian tendency, whether acknowledged or suppressed. To this Hardy must have felt he could make no reference in the book, although he expressed his view plainly enough in the correspondence with Gosse:

> There is nothing perverted or depraved in Sue's nature. The abnormalism consists in disproportion, not in inversion, her sexual instinct being healthy as far as it goes, but unusually weak and fastidious. Her sensibilities remain painfully alert notwithstanding, as they do in nature with such women.

When they first meet, Jude is still married to the absent Arabella. Sue works and lives with Miss Fontover at a shop selling ecclesiastical furnishings—'fal-lals' in Sue's estimation. Miss Fontover's customers include Phillotson, who is now a schoolmaster at the nearby village of Lumsden; he has abandoned the ambitions that he originally confided in Jude. With the aim of helping Sue to train as a teacher Jude introduces her to Phillotson, who engages her as an assistant and swiftly finds himself thinking of her 'in a novel way which somehow seemed strange to him as preceptor'. Although he is much older she agrees to marry him in two years' time after she has had the necessary training to qualify her to take charge of the feminine half of a large double school in partnership with him. As a first step she goes to a training college at Melchester.

Jude meanwhile has been rebuffed in his attempts to find acceptance as an undergraduate. He is now 'deprived of the objects of both intellect and emotion' and he plunges into drunkenness and despair. When he recovers he responds to the thought of lowering his sights and entering the church through a theological college as a licentiate. 'A man could preach', he tells himself, 'and do good to his fellow-creatures without taking double-firsts in the schools of Christminster.' He is not unaware of the happy coincidence that Melchester has the facilities for training curates as well as school-teachers; he can again be near Sue. As a first step he finds employment as a stone-mason in

Melchester and redirects his private studies from the classics to theology.

The scene is now set for the mutual recognition that they can hardly postpone any further. Their indiscreet behaviour leads to Sue's rustication from the college. By spending a night in Jude's lodgings she is 'compromised' by him; and although she tells him, 'You mustn't love me. You are to like me—that's all', she soon relents and begins to play with the idea of marrying him instead of Phillotson. He is at last impelled to tell her of his marriage to Arabella. His confession shatters the relationship of confidence that he has enjoyed with Sue: 'She was his comrade, friend, unconscious sweetheart no longer.' A return to their earlier friendship is impossible. Sue recalls that she is still engaged to Phillotson, and people would not believe it possible for her to have an 'innocent' friendship with Jude since 'their philosophy only recognises relations based on animal desire. The wide field of strong attachment where desire plays, at least, only a secondary part, is ignored by them.'

With notable speed Sue hastens to marry Phillotson, who has shown himself to be sensitive in understanding and magnanimous in judgment. He is also so ill-advised as to agree that the relative giving her away at the altar should be Jude, in whose lodgings she must stay for a short period as she is no longer resident in Melchester. With her flair for 'tempting Providence at critical times' Sue takes Jude into the church, before Phillotson arrives for the ceremony, and walks through a macabre sort of rehearsal with him. The latent cruelty in Sue's actions is recognised by herself and by Jude: it is perhaps an essential part of the bond between them. Jude ponders on her behaviour in these terms:

> Was Sue simply so perverse that she wilfully gave herself and him pain for the odd and mournful luxury of practising long-suffering in her own person, and of being touched with tender pity for him? . . . Possibly she would go on inflicting such pains again and again, and grieving for the sufferer again and again, in all her colossal inconsistency.

The marriage with Phillotson is a disaster from the outset. Sue tells Jude that she had 'never thought out fully what marriage meant', and that 'it is a torture to me to—live with him as a husband' because of 'a physical objection—a fastidiousness . . . a repugnance on my part, for a reason I cannot disclose'. To Phillotson she says bluntly: 'For a man and woman to live on intimate terms when one feels as I do is adultery, in any circumstances, however legal.'

This paradox is echoed by Jude, who chances to meet Arabella —returned from Australia and bigamously married there. Ostensibly to talk things over, they spend a night in a hotel together. The obvious satire on their legal status as man and wife suggests a second adultery of the spirit, matching Sue's with Phillotson. When Sue leaves Phillotson and joins Jude she is steered by a gruesome coincidence into the same hotel bedroom where Jude had slept with Arabella and is now recognised accordingly by the chambermaid.

Not that Sue has come with any intention of sharing her bed with Jude. 'My liking for you is not as some women's perhaps', she tells him, adding 'I resolved to trust you to set my wishes above your gratification.' There are moments when Jude tries to make a case for himself—'You concede nothing to me and I have to concede everything to you'—but it is his willingness to suffer that prevails. 'Crucify me, if you will!' is his cry as he acquiesces in passive adoration of the woman he praises as 'You spirit, you disembodied creature, you dear, sweet, tantalizing phantom—hardly flesh at all.' And when he asks forgiveness for 'being gross, as you call it!' she has a little Shelleyan transport and gives him permission to 'kiss me just once there—not very long'. It is the unmistakable accent of Fancy Day, flirting prettily in *Under the Greenwood Tree*. In this context it sets one's teeth on edge.

Although they are both married to other partners at this stage, Jude and Sue are soon liberated by divorce. Arabella wishes to legalise her bigamous union with Mr Cartlett, and Phillotson—in his sympathetic and unselfish way—decides that he ought to make it possible for Sue to marry Jude. Welcome as this new situation is to Jude, it is certainly no part of Sue's plan to replace one husband with another. 'I would much rather', she says, 'go on living always as lovers, as we are living now, and only meeting by day. It is so much sweeter—for the woman at least.'

As she is not apparently troubled in Jude by the personally physical aversion that Phillotson aroused she changes the ground of her objection to a more general opposition to the sense of bondage and servitude that marriage suggests to her, arguing that: 'I think I should begin to be afraid of you, Jude, the moment you had contracted to cherish me under a Government stamp, and I was licensed to be loved on the premises by you.' Whatever the true causes of her 'pruderies', as she calls them, Sue is determined to subject Jude to the same tormenting 'friendly intimacy' that her undergraduate comrade endured for fifteen months before he died from a blend of tuberculosis and frustration. There is all the time the suggestion that it is nobler to give or withhold as the spirit moves rather than as the law dictates—but in the event Sue is never moved that far by the spirit. A cynic might be pardoned for suggesting that she aimed to replace the register office with the clip joint.

What breaks the deadlock is the unexpected reappearance of Arabella. Her plan to marry Cartlett now she is divorced is in danger, and she turns to Jude for help in her difficulties. Jude's goodnatured readiness to respond so excites Sue's jealousy that she at last surrenders herself sexually and agrees to marry Jude, as the price of asserting her ascendancy over him and preventing any possibility of a reunion with Arabella. It is a climax that Hardy deliberately veils in obscurity, hinting rather than stating, and surrounding their intended marriage with uncertainty as Jude and Sue change their minds about it and repeatedly advance towards it only to retire again, still unwed and with Sue still keeping to her separate bedroom and clinging to the pleasure of having Jude kiss her 'as a lover, incorporeally' instead of as a husband exercising rights over her that she fears.

All seems to be well enough when Arabella and Cartlett are reconciled and wedded. But it now transpires that Arabella was pregnant with Jude's child when she first emigrated to Australia, and her parents—who have until now reared the boy—are no longer able to do so. Arabella knows that Cartlett would have no welcome to offer a stepchild so she sends the lad to Jude. Not having been christened he is known by his nickname as 'Little Father Time' because of his aged countenance—a fact that prompts Sue to comment that 'these preternaturally old boys almost always come from new countries'.

The sudden acquisition of the child, added to their continuing reluctance to marry, reinforces in Jude and Sue the sense of being outside the bounds of conventional society. Each rebuff strengthens their inclination to see themselves as desert island people, increasingly anxious not to be traced or identified. For two and a half years they 'follow a shifting, almost nomadic life, which was not without its pleasantness for a time'. Sue gives birth to two children and becomes pregnant with a third, but her maternity occasions only the most perfunctory references. What Jude's response may have been is not indicated: even the names of the children are withheld, and there is no sense of the expanding and diversified family life that might be expected to accompany an increase in numbers from two to five. Instead Hardy concentrates our attention on the inner collapse that impels Jude to make a last return to Christminster.

He has of course long since abandoned any hope of an academic or ecclesiastical career, but Christminster is still 'the centre of the universe to me, because of my early dream'. He loves the place and wants to die there although, he says: 'I know how it hates all men like me—the so-called Self-Taught.' With Sue and the children he returns on 'Remembrance Day', which he re-names 'Humiliation Day', and which Father Time observes in his sinister fashion 'do seem like the Judgment Day!' Excited by the occasion and by the crowds of bystanders, some of whom recognise him as the 'Tutor of St. Slums', Jude launches into an impassioned address which represents his final apologia. With the dignity and courage of a rare spirit facing inevitable and overwhelming defeat Jude makes his testament as 'a sick and poor man . . . in a chaos of principles—groping in the dark'. The 'neat stock of fixed opinions' with which he first came to Christminster have 'dropped away one by one; and the further I get the less sure I am'.

It is an emotionally searing scene, from the very nakedness of suffering with which it is charged. There can be no escape now from the tragic forces that are gathering round Jude and Sue, and this oppressive sense of doom becomes so potent that the literal machinery—the not very convincing circumstantial detail which triggers events—is of no great consequence. Little Father Time kills the two younger children and destroys himself. Sue miscarries in consequence and her baby is stillborn.

Whatever their temerities, this may seem retribution enough; but Jude and Sue still live, and for them a further pitiless degradation lies ahead. Having staked everything on the total self-sufficiency of their union, they must now be torn apart. In her grief Sue exclaims 'O my comrade, our perfect union—our two-in-oneness—is now stained with blood!' and she recognises 'something external' which crushes their hopes and aspirations one by one. She continues:

> We went about loving each other too much—indulging ourselves to utter selfishness with each other! . . . I said it was Nature's intention, Nature's law and *raison d'être* that we should be joyful in what instincts She afforded us—instincts which civilisation had taken upon itself to thwart . . . And now Fate has given us this stab in the back for being such fools as to take Nature at her word!

From there it is no great step to her decision, 'We must conform . . . It is no use fighting against God!' Even when she recognises that she is becoming 'as superstitious as a savage', she still confesses 'I am cowed into submission . . . I am beaten, beaten!' She begins to speak of the 'solemnity' of their original marriages and entertains the thought that she is still Phillotson's wife. Her aim now is 'self-renunciation—that's everything! I cannot humiliate myself too much.'

A faint odour of incense clinging to Sue's person reveals to Jude how completely their roles are being reversed—he now the agnostic, she the church worshipper. When Jude urges 'surely we are man and wife, if ever two people were in this world. Nature's own marriage it is, unquestionably!' Sue replies, 'But not Heaven's. Another was made for me there.' It can be only a question of time, and of Phillotson's concurrence, before she leaves Jude and expunges her divorce by a remarriage. The act of Arabella's child in killing hers comes to symbolise for Sue 'the right slaying the wrong'.

And so the horror mounts in the closing scenes. Reunited with Phillotson Sue 'brightens a little' when he says 'I shan't expect to intrude upon your personal privacy any more than I did before'. Arabella, conveniently widowed, has no great difficulty in manoeuvring a drunken and apathetic Jude back into her bed and a second marriage ceremony—for which he is commended by Sue when he goes, knowing himself to be dying, to pay her a farewell visit. The intellectual gulf that separates them is now enormous. While she is proud of saying 'I have nearly brought my body into complete subjection', he sees her as the 'dear, sad, soft, most melancholy wreck of a promising human intellect that it has ever been my lot to behold!'

Their mutual reproaches lead to a sudden and passionate outburst of a love that can no longer be restrained. Jude tries to win her back but she rejects him although she is 'even now unsubdued by her fetters'. To make amends for her momentary surrender to 'the flesh—the terrible flesh—the curse of Adam!' she determines to make her ultimate sacrifice 'on the altar of duty'. Knocking on Phillotson's bedroom door she says 'I supplicate you, Richard, to whom I belong, and whom I wish to honour and obey, as I vowed, to let me in'. He replies: 'Think it over well. You know what it means.'

She is determined, in her own words, to 'drink my cup to the dregs'. In the face of Phillotson's repeated cautioning she persists, standing nervously like a child attending at the headmaster's door to be summoned in for a thrashing. 'A quick look of aversion passed over her face, but clenching her teeth she uttered no cry.' After that moment, the death of Jude merely draws a line of finality beneath the complete extinction of everything they had stood for. All that remains is the sad-toned memory of Jude's words:

> Perhaps the world is not illuminated enough for such experiments as ours! Who were we, to think we could act as pioneers!

10

Novelist into Poet 1896 - 1907

Poetry. Perhaps I can express more fully in verse ideas and emotions which run counter to the inert crystallized opinion—hard as rock—which the vast body of men have vested interests in supporting.

(*Hardy's notebook entry, 17 October 1896*)

In a letter to Shelley, Byron laid it down that 'in the career of writing, a man should calculate upon his powers of *resistance* before he goes into the arena'. It was this calculation that Hardy had increasingly to make in the 1890s—the more so as his powers of resistance were far less robust than Byron's. No reader of *The Life* can fail to recognise sympathetically the acuteness of Hardy's sensitivity to adverse criticism. After reading a 'smart and amusing' review of *Tess* in *The Quarterly*, Hardy wrote 'if this sort of thing continues no more novel-writing for me. A man must be a fool to deliberately stand up to be shot at.' Though his books might excite controversy he neither sought it nor enjoyed it. He was no polemicist, and he liked to stress his view of the novel as 'an impression, not an argument'.

The vehement hostility from some quarters that greeted *Jude* undoubtedly wounded Hardy and reinforced his growing distaste for novel writing in such an atmosphere of public reproach and acrimony. He came to feel that his intention to abandon fiction sooner or later and instead to concentrate on verse had reached the stage when any further delay would impair his own self-respect. By the time the uproar occasioned by *Jude* had died down he was, in his own phrase, 'completely cured', of further interest in novel writing.

If we are to look for other factors that would have influenced his decision to write no more fiction we might recall that he had worked unremittingly through about a quarter of a century to publish fourteen novels and three collections of stories. He had considered serial writing first and foremost as a means of livelihood, which obliged him to endure the irksome business of bowdlerisation or submission to editorial timidities that bordered at times on the grotesque; by 1896 he was financially secure. *Jude* sold twenty thousand copies within a few months, thus consolidating the wider popularity that *The Woodlanders* and *Tess* had earned. Moreover, as Carl Weber pointed out, Hardy was one of the first English authors to profit from new copyright legislation in the United States—a benefit reflected in his estate after death which amounted to about £90,000. In the context of the period, that must be considered a substantial fortune for an author to have earned. His early anxieties about the wisdom of giving up the safe income of an architectural draughtsman for the hazardous rewards of authorship must have seemed agreeably misplaced in later years.

To hypothesise about the stories that, in other circumstances, might have followed *Jude* is pointless, but the possibility should not be overlooked that Hardy had worked out all that was worth having in his own particular vein of material. The primary narrative theme in all his novels—except *The Mayor of Casterbridge*, so often the odd man out—is the conventional romantic one of young lovers striving to reach the goal of a happy union. Put crudely and simply, his main characters tend to be in their twenties and to be much occupied with affairs of the heart, as young people often are and as magazine editors have traditionally wished them to be. It was in this mould that Hardy cast the serials which satisfied his ambition to 'live by the pen'. Older characters appear only in supporting roles or to trigger off some necessary action, and they are introduced sparingly. I have not counted the number of Hardy's leading characters who fail to reach the age of twenty-five without losing one parent, or both, but it would be an impressive figure.

The requirements of this limiting and normally stereotyped convention must always have been frustrating to Hardy, with his predilection for social satire and ironical *bouleversements* and his progressive probing and questioning of the sexual *mores* and marriage laws which had somehow to be reconciled with idealised romance. To measure his dilemma one has only to examine his heroines. Of the earliest ones Cytherea Graye, Fancy Day and Anne Garland conform devoutly to accepted romantic notions and are presented as a sort of luscious fruit or sweetmeat, a treat for a lucky young man. Bathsheba and Eustacia start in the same style but are rapidly transformed by Hardy's first developments of tragedy. Paula and Viviette and Ethelberta take their colouring from Hardy's radical ideas and his taste for satire. Elfride stands apart, enigmatically foreshadowing Tess before a spasm of black comedy carries her off.

With these portraits completed Hardy had no new variation to offer on the conventional theme. Instead he departed from the idiom of romantic love to concentrate on his unique portrayal of a middle-aged man at full length in *The Mayor of Casterbridge*. When he subsequently returned to his habitual mould he strained it to breaking point with the transitional Grace Melbury, and then with Tess and Sue. After them, one wonders, what was there left for Hardy to use in any unborn heroine who might tempt his pen? Taken together, Tess and Sue form a very comprehensive and final statement on the theme of young women in love within the romantic conventions of Victorian literature. *The Mayor* may seem to point to another line of development, but there can have been no real chance that Hardy, after *Jude*, would embark on a totally different course from the one he had pursued so long and successfully. The breaking of fresh ground was a task for a new generation. 1895, the year of *Jude*'s publication, also saw the debut of Joseph Conrad and H. G. Wells. From the climate of

Wessex it was an abrupt change to the worlds of Almayer and the Time Machine.

Most conclusive of all, however, is the conviction, from which Hardy never wavered, that poetry and not fiction was the 'form of literary art . . . which had always been more instinctive with him'. He had now made up his mind not to be deflected by thoughts of the fortune he could make by taking advantage of his popularity and 'ringing changes upon the novels he had already written'. Instead he prepared his first volume of verse, *Wessex Poems*, published in 1898—two years before his sixtieth birthday. The volume contained fifty-one poems of which exactly one-third were written in the 1860s and were mostly set bravely in the van of this first display of his talents. To reach the best of the poems the reader had to digest or put aside uneven and derivative examples of Hardy's fledgling skills—lines like 'Then high handiwork will I make my life-deed', which seems to come straight from *Everyman*, for example; or the clumsiness which rounds off a sonnet with

> Believe me, Lost One, Love is lovelier
> The more it shapes its moan in selfish-wise.

The composition of the collection is interesting in what it omits as well as what it includes. The remarkable group of poems associated with his bachelor days in Weymouth is not represented in this volume, nor indeed in its successor. They may conceivably have been contained in a notebook that Hardy did not discover until later, or he may have preferred to withhold them. He did include one poem that is customarily associated with Florence Henniker, 'At an Inn'; and he closed the volume with the elegant economy and neat structure of 'I Look into my Glass', in which he took that lament of Pierston's in *The Well-Beloved* that, while his body aged, his heart remained young and romantic, and transposed it into an indictment of Time, which 'shakes this fragile frame at eve/With throbbings of noon-tide'.

With these two poems I find myself wishing to group another

ten as representing Hardy at his best—'The Dance at the Phoenix', 'A Meeting with Despair', 'Unknowing', 'Thoughts of Phena', 'Middle-Age Enthusiasms', 'In a Wood', 'The Slow Nature', 'In a Eweleaze near Weatherbury' and 'Heiress and Architect'. A further eleven poems have strong claims for a place in any balanced selection from Hardy's entire output. The remaining twenty-eight seem to me inferior to poems of a similar type published later, or of only a specialised interest to critical students of Hardy's technique, or plainly expendable.

In mentioning this personal way of categorising the poems I have in mind the rather forbidding massiveness of Hardy's verse in bulk. Nearly nine hundred poems compressed into the single volume of the collected edition can be daunting at the first approach; some readers may find it helpful, as I did, to formulate their own system of grouping and evaluation as the ground plan for an imaginary volume of about three hundred poems which would epitomise all that the individual reader comes gradually to recognise and cherish as the permanently valuable core of Hardy's work. I stress the personal element here because of the remarkable diversity of the responses that Hardy's poetry excites. As Frank Pinion has justly observed: 'The problem of reaching a reliable critical judgement of Hardy's poetry is confirmed by most selections. What is most evident about them is not the degree of concurrence but their wide range of variation and some astonishing omissions.'

In *Wessex Poems* there are half a dozen poems devoted to Napoleonic themes and a similar number that can be regarded as little more than technical exercises. The three main groups are: (a) Narratives and characterisations drawn from Wessex life—of which there are nine examples; (b) Poems in a satirical vein or emphasising the ironies of life, of which there are seventeen; (c) Poems of personal feeling and experience, usually charged with some romantic emotion, of which there are twelve. Some poems of course fall into more than one of such broad categories as these. Taken together they offer a foretaste of the principal ways in which Hardy's poetry developed, and two of them may be singled out here to show the versatility of Hardy's technique. 'The Slow Nature' is one of those bitter-sweet anecdotes—short stories in embryo—that Hardy loved to versify in a plain, ballad style, but with a deceptively sure control of the implicit sentiment, culminating in a reflective silence, during which the whole texture of the poem is suffused with a gradual and retrospective irony. How mawkish it could have been in other hands!

By contrast 'Heiress and Architect', written more than twenty-five years earlier, shows how well Hardy had learnt to elaborate a conceit and ornament it with a fluent virtuosity. The progress from dream house to coffin—a theme to arouse the gloomiest expectation—is in fact enchantingly light and entertaining.

His second collection, published three years later, brought together nearly twice as many poems. *Poems of the Past and the Present*, appearing in 1901, contains only three which can be positively ascribed to the 1860s; in general the volume suggests more clearly the style and character of the phoenix-poet who was rising from the ashes of the novelist. His personal responses to the world he lived in during the eighties and nineties are reflected here in poems about his literary pilgrimages in Europe, about the Diamond Jubilee and the Boer War. The 'occasional' poem engaged his interest at this time and he developed a serviceable technique for it. A more general interest in technique, particularly in metrical forms, is another feature of *Poems of the Past and the Present*.

Theological/philosophical poems occupy a more prominent place than in *Wessex Poems*: there are twelve in addition to the three which share the title 'In Tenebris'. By contrast the poet's Napoleonic interest almost vanishes and his pleasure in Wessex life has only a meagre four examples. Satire and irony are no less abundant than before, but what is most striking is the broadening of Hardy's range in the class of poem which crystallises a mood or a thought. Not specifically related to Wessex or to his struggles with God and the Immanent Will, not particularly ironical or

plain, ballad but controlled

anecdotal, these mood poems emerge increasingly as one of the finest elements in Hardy's poetry. Good examples in this collection are 'The Seasons of Her Year', 'The August Midnight', 'A Commonplace Day', 'To an Unborn Pauper Child' and 'The Well-Beloved'. Reflective pieces of this type are happily suited to his characteristic genius.

As a whole the collection is uneven, at times preserving what are probably early examples of stylistic uncertainty in such lines as

> Man's mountings of mindsight I checked not

and

> Yet her primal doom pursues her, faultful, fatal is she ever.

However the best of the poems include a few that Hardy never excelled. In 'To Lizbie Browne' Hardy used his neat, short-lined, closely textured verse to magical effect. And the same economy, paring away inessentials, is found in what might be a Tudor miniature—'The Seasons of Her Year', which seems to recapture the spirit and flair of Campion. Among the Boer War poems two stand out with a surprisingly modern accent that already anticipates Sassoon and Owen. 'The Souls of the Slain' is a majestic visionary piece which exploits Hardy's fine control of a compassionate irony. 'Drummer Hodge' sets out a plain and luminous statement that invalidates in advance Rupert Brooke's 'Corner of a foreign field/That is for ever England'. Killed under 'foreign constellations' in South Africa Hodge's fate is to be for ever 'portion of that unknown plain'. The poem concludes:

> His homely Northern breast and brain
> Grow to some Southern tree,
> And strange-eyed constellations reign
> His stars eternally.

Finally 'The Darkling Thrush' consciously marks the passing of the nineteenth century, in tones of a grave simplicity that reaches back to Wordsworth. Setting aside for a moment his own

Reflective

Darkling Thrush
tone—grave simplicity
(Wordsworthian)

sense of 'the growing gloom' Hardy takes from the bird a cautious portent of hope in the heralding of a new age. With so much of his poetry still to come this dignified backward look at the turn of the century has an added significance. Who could have foretold what lay ahead?

At sixty Hardy must have seemed to many of his contemporaries to be ripe to enter into a semi-retirement which might produce a little more poetry but would not alter the belief that his major work was all completed. He had no urgent compulsion to write, as in the days of his serialisations, and there were times when the creative drive was lacking. To Mrs Henniker, in July 1900, he admitted that he had had 'no energy of late to write anything'.

Energy for cycling was a different matter. Hardy's bicycle was for many years a great source of pleasure to him and was the means by which he gained much of his intimate knowledge of the Wessex countryside. Often Emma accompanied him; sometimes his literary and artistic friends did so. In the letter just quoted he refers to a ride to Weymouth with the sculptor, Hamo Thornycroft. At other times a cyclist in Wessex in the 1890s might have been startled to see Thomas Hardy and Rudyard Kipling pedalling abreast towards him—surely a sight to be treasured in the memory.

Hardy's idea of a good day's run was forty or fifty miles—not excessively athletic but daunting enough to many a middle-aged man. He liked to tour by this means and at least one such expedition had a dangerous episode. Riding into Bristol he skidded on a wet road and landed inelegantly in the mud; a coal heaver picked him up, surveyed his muddy appearance and rubbed him down with a sack.

The death of Queen Victoria seemed to emphasise the closing of the century which she had regally dominated, and Hardy took up his pen to record how

> Her waxing seasons bloomed with deeds well done,
> And the world's heart was won . . .

death of Queen Victoria

The poem 'V.R. 1819–1901: a reverie' was an appropriate one to set at the front of *Poems of the Past and the Present*. But while he was preparing that collection of poems for delivery to his publishers Hardy was also engaged in writing verse of a very different kind—a project far more ambitious than any he had yet attempted. To write in dramatic form had been an early aim of his, in those far-off London days in the 1860s when his attempts at poetry met only with rejection. He made no headway then as a playwright but the idea of an epic drama remained in his thoughts. In 1875 he and Emma spent the sixtieth anniversary of Waterloo at Chelsea Hospital talking to pensioners who had taken part in the battle, and in the same month Hardy was considering 'an Iliad of Europe from 1789 to 1815' which would include 'a Ballad of the Hundred Days' and others dealing with the retreat from Moscow etc. In *The Life* Hardy describes this note as the first mention of what was to become *The Dynasts*, but there is in fact an even earlier note that he overlooked: on 13 March 1874 he made this entry in his notebook: 'Let Europe be the stage and have scenes continually shifting.'

Hardy's keen and enduring interest in Napoleon springs naturally from his childhood days in the middle of the nineteenth century, when the great victories over the French were still vivid in the memories of his elders. It was a preoccupation to which he must have felt he had done less than justice in the flummery of *The Trumpet-Major* and a handful of mediocre poems like 'San Sebastian' and 'Leipzig'. Only a few months after the publication of *The Trumpet-Major* he was noting 'A Homeric Ballad, in which Napoleon is a sort of Achilles, to be written'. Throughout the 1880s the thought recurs, whether he is on pilgrimage in Italy or in the Reading Room of the British Museum. In 1887 he recorded another outline scheme in which Napoleon was to be haunted by an Evil Genius or Familiar; and when this was abandoned he considered a Napoleon endowed with necromantic powers by which he could see the thoughts of opposing generals. By 1889 he was feeling the need for a 'larger canvas' and a 'spectral tone' in carrying out 'that idea of Napoleon, the Empress, Pitt, Fox etc'. In 1892 he was considering 'methods for the Napoleon drama'.

With *Jude* completed Hardy and Emma went to Brussels in the autumn of 1896 and, as they had done twenty years before, explored the scenes associated with Napoleon's defeat at Waterloo. But now the long period of gestation was ending: Hardy was ready to start work on 'Europe in Throes. Three Parts. Five Acts each.' What he now began to outline as a working plan was 'a play intended simply for mental performance, and not for the stage', which would show 'The rulers of Europe in their desperate struggle to maintain their dynasties rather than to benefit their peoples.'

No reader of *The Dynasts* can fail to recognise the antiquarian zeal with which Hardy accumulated authentic detail. One must be grateful—if only with a muted gratitude—for the devoted research that informs such lines as

> Jarred now by Reille's fierce foot-divisions three,
> Flanked on their left by Piré's cavalry—
> The fourfold corps of d'Erlon, spread at length,
> Compose the right, east of the famed chaussée—

But Hardy had always been acutely conscious that the work he contemplated was not to be merely or primarily an historical chronicle. To retell the Napoleonic story, with no matter how much loving attention to detail, was not enough. To make a metaphor from comparable examples, he was undertaking simultaneously his *War and Peace* and his *Paradise Lost*. *The Dynasts* was to be his biggest work, physically and in literary stature—a majestic narrative combining dramatic force with a philosophy interpreting human motive and action.

Writing to Edward Wright in 1907 Hardy claimed no more for the supernatural apparatus of *The Dynasts* than that 'some philosophy of life was necessary, and I went on using that which I had denoted in my previous volumes of verse (and to some extent prose) as being a generalized form of what the thinking world had gradually come to adopt'. This is deceptively disarming: it does scant justice to the inventiveness of 'the Overworld' in *The Dynasts*, or to the staunch tenacity of Hardy's personal struggle to formulate a coherent credo of his own. To the end of his days Hardy protested that he had 'no harmonious philosophy' to offer and that his writings on philosophical themes were merely impressions, speculations, responses to a given mood; but it is possible nevertheless to formulate a few propositions that he appeared to hold persistently and to validate in his writings. One was the view he claimed to share with Spinoza and Einstein that 'neither Chance nor Purpose governs the universe, but Necessity'. Another was the belief that the Prime Cause or Immanent Will, in essence an unconscious force, was beginning to become conscious of itself and might eventually be modified by a concept of compassion. But until then human emotion remained a sort of disastrous epiphenomenon, an accidental development to which the Immanent Will was by definition indifferent. A notebook entry in 1889 expresses it thus: 'the human race is too extremely developed for its corporeal conditions, the nerves being evolved to an activity abnormal in such an environment . . . this planet does not supply the materials for happiness to higher existences.'

There is no need here to labour the logical untidiness. These are the main threads of Hardy's thought that he was trying to bring together in a coherent pattern. The fact that the first three speeches in *The Dynasts* are given to characters designated 'Shade of the Earth', 'Spirit of the Years' and 'Chorus of the Pities' is neither a suddenly adopted innovation nor a pious revival of the Greek chorus. It is a bold attempt to give an expressive literary form to ideas that Hardy had lived with for many years. In one of his earliest notes on 'a historical Drama' he wrote that Action should be mostly automatic and 'not the result of what is called *motive*, though always ostensibly so, even to the actors' own consciousness'. The idea that an apparently individual will was really acting only as part of a larger group will attracted Hardy early in his career. In *Far from the Madding Crowd* he makes a diversion to describe some approaching farmworkers in this unexpectedly zoological way:

> The whole string of trailing individuals advanced in the completest balance of intention, like the remarkable creatures known as Chain Salpae, which, distinctly organised in other respects, have one will common to a whole family.

Similarly in *The Woodlanders* the isolation and self-containment of Marty and Giles are said to form 'no detached design at all, but were part of the pattern in the great web of human doings then weaving in both hemispheres from the White Sea to Cape Horn'.

This 'web' image is developed in *The Dynasts* into a visionary transparency which reveals every interconnection of the weaving pattern. In the words of a stage-direction:

> The Scene becomes anatomised and the living masses of humanity transparent. The controlling Immanent Will appears therein, as a brain-like network of currents and ejections, twitching, interpenetrating, entangling, and thrusting hither and thither the humans.

This is further refined in the contemplation of Wellington at Waterloo, when again

> the ubiquitous urging of the Immanent Will becomes visualised. The web connecting all the apparently separate shapes includes Wellington in its tissue with the rest, and shows him, like them, as acting while discovering his intention to act.

That simultaneity of the One with the All makes an illusion of individual will and profoundly influences the whole form and style of *The Dynasts*. The character analysis of the protagonists, which is so peculiarly the province of the novelist, becomes irrelevant if they are to be reduced to little more than puppetry. It is a contingency that Hardy had certainly foreseen in 1887 when he was busily at work on *The Woodlanders* but found time to jot down this remarkable note:

> Novel-writing as an art cannot go backward. Having reached the analytic stage it must transcend it by going still further in the same direction. Why not by rendering as visible essences, spectres, etc., the abstract thoughts of the analytic school? . . . The human race to be shown as one great network or tissue which quivers in every part when one point is shaken, like a spider's web . . . The Realities to be the true realities of life, hitherto called abstractions. The old material realities to be placed behind the former, as shadowy accessories.

Fox, Pitt, Wellington, Nelson, Napoleon himself, are shadowy accessories to the true realities of Hardy's epic drama. In their portrayals there are few of the personalising and revealing touches that their author might have given them. They appear to serve his purpose best as wooden figures arranged in a sequence of tableaux. To compare Napoleon with Henchard, or Josephine with Tess, is as irrelevant as to attempt a comparison—because both are mobile—between a tractor and a racehorse.

Hardy then had his grand design—the Napoleonic Wars set in a philosophical macrocosm of abstract realities. For this play within a play he set the scene in The Overworld, which he peopled with the Ancient Spirit and Chorus of the Pities, the Shade of the Earth, the Spirits Sinister and Ironic with their Choruses, Rumours, Spirit-Messengers and Recording Angels. Of these it is 'Years' and 'Pities'—if I may so abbreviate them—that carry the central argument. 'Years' is the dispassionate witness, insisting that: 'Our scope is but to register and watch.' It is 'Pities' who voices the human question: 'Why doth It so and so, and ever so,/This viewless, voiceless Turner of the Wheel?' and again it is 'Years' who answers with an unemotional objectivity:

> The Will has woven with an absent heed
> Since life first was; and ever will so weave.

When Hardy turned from prose to poetry he intended to formulate his philosophical preoccupations more explicitly than he felt he had been permitted to do by the fiction reading public. At the first opportunity, in *Wessex Poems*, he posed bluntly the thoughts that haunted him:

Has some Vast Imbecility,
Mighty to build and blend,
But impotent to tend,
Framed us in jest, and left us now to hazardry?

Or come we of an Automaton
Unconscious of our pains? . . .
Or are we live remains
Of Godhead dying downwards, brain and eye now gone?

To these questions Hardy's immediate response was 'no answerer I', and this disclaimer of personal certainties was often repeated. What he achieved in the metaphysical framework of *The Dynasts* was not the pronouncement of a consistent answer to the riddle of the universe, but a poet's way of embodying and dramatising those emotional and intellectual forces which informed the human dilemmas of his time; of these probably the most potent sprang from the prodigious expansion of geological time and interstellar space to which the Victorians had to adjust as they digested the implications of evolution and modern astronomy. The agony of religious doubt is certainly not peculiar to the nineteenth century, but when else could it have been expressed in these stark and wide ranging terms:

A local cult, called Christianity
Which the wild dramas of the wheeling spheres
Include, with divers other such, in dim
Pathetical and brief parentheses
Beyond whose span, uninfluenced, unconcerned,
The systems of the suns go sweeping on
With all their many-mortaled planet train
in mathematic roll unceasingly.

This is the summation of that visionary account of the heavens by Swithin St Cleeve in *Two on a Tower* when he reveals to Viviette the 'monsters of magnitude without known shape' and warns 'if you are cheerful, and wish to remain so, leave the study of astronomy alone'. In *The Dynasts* when 'Pities' exclaims 'Something within me aches to pray/To some Great Heart', the Chorus Ironic retorts:

'Ha-ha! That's good. Thou'lt pray to It:—
    But where do its compassions sit?
    Yea, where abides the heart of It?

Is it where sky-fires flame and flit,
Or solar craters spew and spit,
Or ultra-stellar night-webs knit?

What is Its shape? Man's counterfeit?'

As the play develops it is this dialectic between 'Pities' and the other spirits which begins to adumbrate some form of amelioration of the harsh predetermined automatism that the forces of reason support so immovably. To suggest that Hardy took a mournful pleasure in 'pessimism' is to miss the point of his belief, expressed in 'In Tenebris', that 'if way to the Better there be, it exacts a full look at the Worst'. A retreat from Christian values, if it meant the abandonment of individual responsibility, of compassion, of conscious choice, was not a goal to be striven for but a fate to be endured and if possible transformed. The progressive withering of a personal faith, which tormented so many of his contemporaries, was not to Hardy an emblem of triumphant rationalism. It was, whatever its necessity, a privation and one keenly felt in such lines as:

O, doth a bird deprived of wings
Go earth-bound wilfully!

If we are to look anywhere in *The Dynasts* for an authentic expression of Hardy's own personal values it is probably to be found in the Chorus of the Pities proposing to 'Earth' a new ideal:

We would establish those of kindlier build,
In fair Compassions skilled,
Men of deep art in life-development.

This, hopefully, is to replace the false dawn that Napoleon represented, when he at first seemed to come to 'level dynasts down to journeymen' but later revealed his aim as 'but to win/The golden seats that other bums have warmed'.

The plan of the work, then, is this interaction between historical characters and 'phantom intelligences'. In nineteen acts, comprising over 130 scenes, the drama ranges across Europe during the ten years from Trafalgar to Waterloo. Whatever reservations one may have about its literary merits it must be recognised as a *tour de force* on a monumental scale. Those who recall Charles Lefeaux's impressive radio production in 1967 for the British Broadcasting Corporation, which took seven hours to transmit, may not realise that this was still a severely abridged version; the work as written would probably require twice as long for a complete performance.

To sustain such a weight of material Hardy introduced as much variety as he could. Some incidents are presented in dumb show, some in distant panoramic perspectives, and some in the rustic vernacular of Wessex. Freed from the conventions of the theatre Hardy was able to anticipate visual cinematic techniques, moving as he pleased from intimate close-up to long-range panning shots; and equally to anticipate the aural techniques of radio, with its mobility of imagination and its emphasis on the inherent values of the spoken word divorced from visualisations. His lifelong interest in metrical innovation and variation found valuable scope here as another method of avoiding the monotony that must always threaten a work of such duration.

In all these ways Hardy strove to escape from the straitjacket of the long narrative poem or the unrelieved dialogue drama. Even so, he had to find a style, a language and a metre that could carry the main burden of the action—a norm from which his variations could offer relief. He succumbed to the temptation to revive the iambic pentameter and breathe new life into it—a temptation which has undone many another poet. To English ears the mighty line of Marlowe and Shakespeare at once suggests the dignity and eloquence of high tragedy, and was to that extent an apt choice for Hardy's purpose, but it is a form most difficult to separate from the 'costume' of its time. In the modern dress of later generations it turns all too readily into a windy self-parody or a banal flatness. Sometimes Hardy produced a straightforward Elizabethan pastiche:

> And thus their deeds incautiously disclose
> Their cloaked intention and most secret aim!

or this:

> He who is with himself dissatisfied,
> Though all the world find satisfaction in him,
> Is like a rainbow-coloured bird gone blind,
> That gives delight it shares not.

Such lines—and, alas, there are many of them—might as easily have come from the contemporary pen of Stephen Phillips, who seemed at the time to be leading a revival of poetic drama in the Edwardian theatre. Where Hardy reasserts his individuality is in the superabundance of the vocabulary from which he draws and to which he inventively adds. His fondness for the prefix 'un' (as for the suffix 'ness') is given full rein: 'His projects they unknow, his grin unsee!' He unashamedly introduces such archaisms as 'yclept' and 'wots not of', and he ornaments the Phantoms with weird linguistic gargoyles, such as 'You cannot swerve the pulsion of the Byss', for example, or:

> so may ye judge Earth's jackaclocks to be
> Not fugled by one Will, but function-free.

Like Browning, Hardy was a restless collector and coiner of words which he sometimes failed to bring into the discipline of a personal diction. How unnecessarily choked and uncouth, for example, is this statement made by the verbal portentousness of its last two lines:

> Should the corvette return
> With the anxious Scotch colonel,
> Escape would be frustrate,
> Retention eternal.

In a work of such magnitude it is of course unfairly easy to pick out moments when the poet's powers flag or his critical vigilance is relaxed. Such captiousness must not obscure those occasions when Hardy's gifts are displayed to their best advantage. There are sharp, clearly lined images, such as the sniper at Trafalgar falling from the rigging 'like an old rook, smack from his perch, stone dead'. There is—again at Trafalgar—that grimly humorous cameo of a French 'captain's woman' jumping from a burning vessel and swimming like a mermaid 'her great breasts bulging on the brine'. There are memorable turns of eloquent phrasing, as in Napoleon's final speech:

> Great men are meteors that consume themselves
> To light the earth. This is my burnt-out hour.

There is the sudden contemplative beauty of the Chorus of the Years, which reveals the sub-world of mole, lark, earthworm and butterfly on the battlefield of Waterloo, where nature itself is broken and degraded by war:

> Trodden and bruised to a miry tomb
> Are ears that have greened but will never be gold,
> And flowers in the bud that will never bloom.

There are passages too where the reader may rest affectionately in the familiar Wessex scene that Hardy can call up at will with a long-perfected technique—the burning of Boney's effigy on Durnover Green, for example, or the racy gossip of the bystanders at the Weymouth Review:

> 'They say that a cannon-ball knocked poor Jim Popple's maw right up into the futtock-shrouds at the Nile, where 'a hung like a nightcap out to dry. Much good to him his obeying his old mother's wish and refusing his allowance o' rum!'

It is precisely those deft little touches of genius, to which Hardy has so accustomed us in the novels, that we vainly look for in his portrayals of the famous figures that he invites to step out of the galleries of history. If the intention is to key them down to a subordinate level as puppet figures, the result is a victory for the ideologist over the artist. What else are we to make of a Napoleon talking such banalities as:

I have no remarks to make on that just now.
I'll think the matter over. You shall know
By noon tomorrow my definitive.

How should we respond to a battlefield scene of Wellington with his troops, which reads:

Wellington (to the nearest Square): Hard pounding this,
my men! I truly trust
You'll pound the longest!
Square: Hip-hip-hip-hurrah!

Hardy finished his draft of the third and final part of *The Dynasts* in the spring of 1907, when he entered in his notebook the reflection that: 'To have the strength to roll a stone weighing a hundredweight to the top of the mount is a success, and to have the strength to roll a stone of ten hundredweight only halfway up that mount is a failure. But the latter is two or three times as strong a deed.' *The Dynasts* is, in those terms, an extremely large and heavy stone: if Hardy failed to roll it to the very top there is nevertheless no question but that he performed a 'strong deed' of lasting renown.

To his juniors in the 1920s, to poets like Siegfried Sassoon, *The Dynasts* seemed to tower above all the rest of Hardy's works. If there has since been a diminution of this esteem it may be accounted for in several ways. The metaphysical scenario has inevitably lost some of its pristine impact. The historical glamour that surrounds a Pitt or a Nelson tends to fade as the perspective lengthens and other wars intervene, and the more these separate elements give up some of their potency, the more does each new generation concentrate on the intrinsic literary qualities of the work. If our judgment suggests that Hardy's shorter poems have more to offer to us than the bulk of the verse in *The Dynasts*, we may still view with awe and respect this stupendous creation and accord it a unique place in our literature.

11

Widower and Lover 1908 - 1914

He loved the woman dead and inaccessible as he had never loved her in life

(*The Well-Beloved*)

With the MS of Part One of *The Dynasts* Hardy enclosed a letter to his publishers saying 'though I hope to finish the two remaining parts at an early date it is not indispensable that I should do so'. Bearing in mind that this first part ends with Austerlitz and the death of Pitt it is inconceivable that Hardy could ever have been content to regard the work as concluded there. Understandably he valued the opportunity to test public reaction to such an unusual and ambitious project before proceeding further with it but, in a letter to Edward Clodd a few months after Part One appeared, he made it clear that he originally intended to delay publication until he could issue the completed work as a whole. What had changed his mind was 'a sudden feeling that I should never carry the thing any further, so off it went'.

The impulse may have sprung from sheer fatigue after a long spell of concentrated effort, or conceivably from a recognition that increasing age might deprive him of the health and vigour that so great a task demanded. The colossal scale of the work must have been exhausting, and the pages of *The Life* that deal with the years 1902–7 suggest a gradual dying down of energy. By 1908, when *The Dynasts* was at last off his hands, it might have seemed that his career was coming to a close. He was now engaged in gathering together poems that had appeared individually in periodicals and 'hunting up quite old ones' left in manuscript since the 'sixties, in order to fill a new volume—the third of his collected poems. While he prepared *Time's Laughingstocks* for the press he had to mourn the passing in quick succession of Swinburne and Meredith, leaving to him the seniority of Victorian poets. When the book was published his own seventieth birthday was only six months away and the new poets issuing their first volumes that year included Ezra Pound. The stage was set—apparently—for a farewell performance.

So much for appearances. In fact *Time's Laughingstocks* does not represent even a halfway point in Hardy's output of poems, for there were no less than five more volumes to come after it. It can now be seen as the volume which signalled not his departure, but in a sense his arrival. *Wessex Poems* was to some extent Hardy the novelist testing the temperature of the water. *Poems of the Past and the Present* did something to consolidate his new, second reputation but it is *Time's Laughingstocks* which demonstrated incontrovertibly the stature he was to achieve as a poet. Of the ninety-four poems in this volume more than half can stand with his best work.

There are marked differences from the earlier collections. Poems of self-consciously technical experiment are few: the interest in responding to national occasions has died away; there are no Napoleonic themes; God and the universe seldom occupy Hardy's thoughts explicitly although about a quarter of the poems are reflective in mood or conscious of the ironies of life. The main emphasis is laid on two kinds of poem which between them account for nearly half the total. One is the poem which draws on Hardy's intimate sense of Wessex life and character. There were only four such in the previous volume: here there are more than two dozen. They include the vigorous narrative of 'A Trampwoman's Tragedy' and the lyrical tenderness of the group 'At Casterbridge Fair'. In them the earlier promise of *Wessex Poems* comes to fulfilment and shows one of the most distinctive aspects of Hardy's genius at its best.

The other large group is the personal/romantic poems, charged with powerfully felt emotion and shadowed with mystery. The section entitled 'More Love Lyrics' brings to light an important body of verse, connected with Hardy's early years in Weymouth. Altogether there are a dozen poems dated prior to 1872 in this volume—an unexpectedly high proportion when more than half the collection is undated.

To single out individual poems for quotation is an invidious task, but if one verse must exemplify the technical assurance and fluent ease of this volume there could hardly be a better than this from 'The Farm-woman's Winter', with its alternating feminine endings and its lightly emphasised alliterations:

> If seasons all were summers,
> And leaves would never fall,
> And hopping casement-comers
> Were foodless not at all,
> And fragile folk might be here
> That white winds bid depart;
> Then one I used to see here
> Would warm my wasted heart!

For an example of that bitter-sweet blending of nostalgia with melancholy, which is so characteristic of Hardy's later poetry, consider this:

> Brush not the bough for midnight scents
> That come forth lingeringly,
> And wake the same sweet sentiments
> They breathed to you and me
> When living seemed a laugh, and love
> All it was said to be.

That verse comes from a poem written in 1904, 'Shut out that Moon', which ends with the lines:

> Too fragrant was life's early bloom,
> Too tart the fruit it bore.

It is very much the mood of those Edwardian years when the estrangement from Emma was no longer a matter for either regret or hope but was simply an accepted fact which nothing could change. They appeared together in public at Emma's garden parties at Max Gate or at the first night of the operatic version of *Tess* at Covent Garden, but they were living in different worlds. In a letter of 1911 Emma sent one of her cousins a supply of 'beautiful little booklets' intended to make 'the clear atmosphere of pure Protestantism in the land to revive'. Scattering these about was one of her campaigning enthusiasms. She was also a stout defender of animals against cruel handling and she had marched with the suffragettes in 1907, but it was her religious evangelism that increasingly preoccupied her. 'An Unseen Power of great benevolence directs my ways', she wrote in 1911 at the end of the chronicle of her personal recollections that she had been committing to paper. She is said to have feared that the French might invade England to enforce papist doctrines, and to have a bag ready packed for such an emergency.

Her strange behaviour seems eventually to have exceeded anything that could be described as harmless eccentricity. She withdrew into the attics at Max Gate and had her meals carried up to her there. Hardy's younger sister, Kate, is reported by Irene Cooper Willis to have said that Hardy spoke to her of the possibility that he might go to live with her. No doubt there were alternations of better and worse phases, periods of greater or less tension, but the general condition must have been sad indeed for both husband and wife.

For his part Hardy seems to have put behind him the emotional turbulence of the 1890s. He continued to take an active interest in the literary careers of Florence Henniker and Agnes Grove, being ready with counsel and practical advice whenever his pupils looked to him. His pursuit of romantic fantasies found expression in familiar ways in his poetry. Of these perhaps the most interesting and well documented concerns Helen Paterson, who had illustrated *Far from the Madding Crowd* when it first appeared. Hardy met her, apparently for the first time, in May 1874 at a dinner party in London. He shortly afterwards returned to Dorset to hurry on with the last chapters which were 'done at a gallop' in order to have the work completed before his wedding, and is therefore unlikely to have met her again.

A few weeks before Hardy married Emma, Helen Paterson married the poet, William Allingham. She at once gave up book illustration to concentrate on portrait painting, for which she had a genuine talent. Tennyson sat for her, and Carlyle considered that she was the only painter who had made a successful portrait of him—a view endorsed by Ruskin. One of her works—a portrait of her husband—is in the National Portrait Gallery, in London. She re-entered Hardy's life in 1906 when she was a widow of fifty-eight. At that time Edmund Gosse wanted some information about the illustrator of *Madding Crowd* so he directed his enquiry to Hardy who replied that she 'began as a charming young lady, Miss Helen Paterson, and ended as a married woman—charms unknown'.

In spite of the fact that he had 'never set eyes on her' since that first slight acquaintance in 1874, Gosse's enquiry made Hardy 'feel "quite romantical" about her (as they say here)'. He urged Gosse to 'hunt her up in London' and let him know 'what she looks like as an elderly widow woman'. If he succeeded in tracing her—and that could not have been difficult as she had published a book the year before—Gosse was instructed to give her Hardy's kind regards, 'but you must not add that those two almost simultaneous weddings would have been one but for a stupid blunder of God Almighty'—a thought which disposes of Emma Gifford and William Allingham in a somewhat abrupt and cavalier fashion!

The rather facetious man-to-man tone of Hardy's letter to Gosse does not conceal the germination of yet another of those imaginative relationships that Hardy liked to explore in a 'quite romantical' way; the poem 'The Opportunity' was the outcome. After recalling the casualness of that one meeting long ago, which to both seemed so unimportant, the poet reflects:

Had we mused a little space
At that critical date in the Maytime:
One life had been ours, one place,
Perhaps, till our long cold claytime.

The sense of regret that people fail to recognise the opportunities that chance puts in their way is a familiar one with Hardy. Here, with Helen Paterson, he is enacting privately the first meeting of Angel Clare with Tess at the club dance where he missed the opportunity to pick the 'right' girl as his partner. 'Too late beloved'—the words seem to murmur again and again in the romantical fantasies that Hardy liked to versify. How close he is in spirit at such times to Donne, who described his poems as 'the strict Map of my misery' and wrote:

I thought, if I could draw my pains
Through rhymes' vexation, I should them allay.

To 'The Opportunity' Hardy gave the rare public distinction of a personal dedication, inscribing it 'For H.P.'—her maiden initials, significantly. It was published in 1922 so that—unless he sent her a copy of it earlier—she had four years in which to come across it before her 'claytime'. I wonder what she made of it.

At about the same time Hardy made a more practical and far-reaching move in the direction of the sympathetic feminine companionship that he needed. In 1904 he made the acquaintance of a *protégée* of Florence Henniker's—a young reviewer and authoress of children's books, Florence Dugdale. Before long Miss Dugdale was quietly making herself available—and later indispensable—as research assistant, typist and discreet organiser of domestic arrangements. Hardy first met Miss Dugdale in 1904. The poem 'On the Departure Platform' in *Time's Laughingstocks* records an occasion of parting from one 'who was more than my life to me' and whom Professor Purdy identifies as this new, shy, unobtrusive element in Hardy's life—a sort of Avice the Third unexpectedly materialising. In a letter to Mrs Henniker in 1911 Hardy mentioned that Florence had just gone to Weymouth 'for a week or two's change', adding: 'I am going to run down this afternoon to see how she is getting on.' By the spring of 1912 he was referring to her as 'dear F.D.'

And then, on 27 November 1912 Emma died, suddenly and without warning, though a strange premonition had earlier prompted her to sit at her piano playing all her favourite pieces with the expressed conviction that she would never play again—a weird event that Hardy later versified in 'The Last Performance'. In the hour of Emma's death Miss Dugdale was travelling to Weymouth, intending to stay there but to go over to Dorchester to see *The Trumpet-Major* played by a local amateur dramatic group, the Wessex Players. A telegram from Hardy was awaiting her. She returned to London without seeing the play, but within two or three weeks she joined Emma's niece at Max Gate and helped Hardy to pick up the threads of everyday life. They married fifteen months later, when she was thirty-five and her bridegroom seventy-three; and Hardy was soon able to write gratefully of himself, that during his life 'two bright-souled women clave to him'.

It would be unrealistic to affect surprise that Hardy was not inconsolable at the loss of a wife who had been virtually dead to him in spirit for so long before she perished in the flesh. But what may be true of Hardy the man was certainly not true of Hardy the poet. In *The Life* there is a sentence of chilling ordinariness which reads: 'In the muddle of Hardy's unmistressed housekeeping animal pets of his late wife died, strayed, or were killed, much to Hardy's regret.' This comes from the same hand that wrote Mother Cuxsom's lamentation over the dead Susan Henchard: 'All her shining keys will be took from her, and her cupboards opened; and little things 'a didn't wish seen, anybody will see; and her wishes and ways will all be as nothing.'

It was with the inner vision that could inspire such a psalm of grief that Hardy read through the pathetic legacy of Emma's writings during the following winter and brooded over the ties that, in spite of everything, had held them together for more than forty years. With the approach of spring he set off on a personal pilgrimage to St Juliot and thence to Emma's native city of Plymouth: there he arranged for a memorial tablet of his own design to be set up in the church where, in her young days, she had been the organist. On 7 March, the very date on which he had first set eyes on Emma, he was at Beeny Cliff and the other familiar scenes of their courtship which he had not once revisited since their wedding, although—in a poem composed a month before he made the journey—he had written 'much of my life claims the spot as its key'.

What it now unlocked was an upsurge of poetry that, of its kind, has no parallel in our literature. In poem after poem he poured out the grief of his bereavement in an eloquent and moving lamentation—'woman much missed, how you call to me, call to me'. But it is more than an elegy for a lost love: it is a re-living, a further experiencing and digesting, of the whole emotional gamut of his courtship and marriage. In his own eyes it was 'an expiation'. The journey to St Juliot was so painful that, in a letter, he exclaimed: 'What possessed me to do it!' It was certainly not the sweetness of memory only that occupied the mind of the solitary figure, now in his seventies, who—on the cliffs near Boscastle—

> Comes and stands
> In a careworn craze,
> And looks at the sands
> And the seaward haze
> With moveless hands
> And face and gaze,
> Then turns to go . . .
> And what does he see when he gazes so?

The 'ghost-girl-rider' of his inner vision is the young Emma of 1870, an exciting figure on horseback when they first met—'the woman riding high above with bright hair flapping free'. This image of the carefree, venturesome rider, galloping intrepidly with her hair flying in the breeze, is the happiest expression for

Hardy of the bride he courted. His image of her in later years retains this endearing relish and insouciance and capacity for enjoyment:

> How she would have loved
> A party today!—
> Bright-hatted and gloved,
> With table and tray
> And chairs on the lawn
> Her smiles would have shone
> With welcomings . . .

To the charm of fond memories the poems add the haunting fears of mental aberration in Emma, the self-accusations of a temperamental coldness in Hardy, the ache of division and estrangement. If he designed the tablet for the Plymouth church and the headstone for Stinsford with a conventional reverence, it was with a contrastingly awesome candour that he created this unique mausoleum of verse for the dead Emma. In 'An Upbraiding' he imagines her watching him in his new guise as the bereaved lover, and murmuring to herself:

> Ah, what would I have given alive
> To win such tenderness!

And then she poses the terrifying question of their next and final state: will the change in him endure, or does it depend on her being removed and inaccessible?

> When you are dead, and stand to me
> Not differenced, as now,
> But like again, will you be cold
> As when we lived, or how?

Through all the Emma poems there is a peculiar poignancy which springs from the realisation that, in even the happiest of recollected scenes, there is a tragic 'presence', a germ of foreboding, an ill omen. It shows nowhere more clearly than in 'The Interloper' with its opening sketch of St Juliot in the 1870s:

There are three folk driving in a quaint old chaise,
And the cliff-side track looks green and fair:
I view them talking in quiet glee
As they drop down towards the puffins' lair
By the roughest of ways;
But another with the three rides on, I see,
Who I like not to be there!

This spectral interloper, who continues to haunt them, is revealed to be not death nor a benevolent spirit but 'that under which best lives corrode'. The inference that Hardy used the phrase to signify madness is confirmed by Vere Collins's record of his conversation about the poem with Hardy, who first used the word 'madness' and then added: 'Write down "Insanity"; that is a better word.'

In a letter to Emma's cousin, Kate, Hardy wrote: 'In later years an unfortunate mental aberration for which she was not responsible altered her much . . . but this was contrary to her real nature, and I myself quite disregard it in thinking of her. She was, as you know, most childlike and trusting formerly.'

To these qualities Hardy elsewhere added a vivid sense of 'living' as a special part of Emma's appeal to him. Spontaneity and naivety are valuable qualities in such a relationship where a contemplative spirit like Hardy's makes much of its contact with life indirectly, through the mediation of a companion with more instant and 'childlike' responses. Emma could throw off some artless remark which for Hardy had a special plangency; if it may seem an inexplicable process it is nonetheless characteristic of the creative imagination at work. A striking example, which repays study in detail for the light it throws on Hardy's way of working, is the sentence 'It never looks like summer', which stems from an incident in 1870 when Hardy sketched Emma while they were sitting on Beeny Cliff near the rectory of St Juliot during Hardy's second visit. Although it was raining Hardy completed his drawing and inscribed it with the words 'Beeny Cliff, in the rain—Aug 22, 1870. "It never looks like summer." E.L.G. (on

Beeny).' Presumably there was some humorous comment between them about the portrayal of Emma sitting in the rain, and she made the observation that Hardy jotted down.

The incident gave rise to three poems. Two of them, 'The Figure in the Scene' and 'Why Did I Sketch?' were included in *Moments of Vision*, published in 1917, but were not individually dated. The third, also in *Moments of Vision*, is dated 8 March 1913, and the first of its two verses reads:

'It never looks like summer here
On Beeny by the sea'.
But though she saw its look as drear,
Summer it seemed to me.

The remembered words now took on a new meaning, transformed—like everything else—by her death. More than forty years later they ring for the poet with their early brightness of tone still, but with a deepening significance.

Nor is this all. There is another context, little known or possibly unremarked, where Hardy used those words of Emma's that so tenaciously seized his attention. In *Desperate Remedies* he described a landscape near Tolchurch as 'a wild hill that had no name, beside a barren down where it never looked like summer'. Precisely when he wrote that is something of a mystery, and no MS has survived to suggest an answer. Hardy states in *The Life* that, of the book's twenty-one chapters, all but the last three or four were completed by March 1870, the remainder being added in the autumn of that year—and the passage I have quoted is in chapter 15. It is just conceivable therefore that in August Emma was not coining the phrase but quoting it after reading Hardy's MS. However, during May Tinsley had suggested alterations based on his reader's report, and Hardy would still have been working on the MS, revising and adding to it. In the autumn Emma started to write out the fair copy of the finished work, which reached the publishers in December; it therefore seems probable that Hardy introduced Emma's words within a matter of days only of their utterance.

Even more mysterious is the association in the Tolchurch description of the words 'it never looked like summer' with 'a wild hill that had no name'. When Hardy wrote *A Pair of Blue Eyes* two years later he wished to prevent too close an identification of the setting with the scenes of his courtship, so he suppressed the name of Beeny and called it 'the Cliff without a Name'. Was he consciously repeating a phrase from *Desperate Remedies* or had he forgotten it? Was the hill at Tolchurch—which is assumed to be Tolpuddle—an imaginary Beeny that he planted in Dorset under the enchantment of that first year's encounters with Emma? Was it, in effect, a prototype in his first novel of the true Beeny that he was to describe so fully and dramatically in his third?

In August 1912, Hardy was engaged in the preparation of a new edition of *Desperate Remedies* for which he wrote a fresh preface. Did those words lodge again in some recess of his mind, only seven months before he was to find himself standing once more on Beeny, tormented with memories that stretched back forty-three years, a timetorn man for whom:

> It never looks like summer now
> Whatever weather's there;
> But ah, it cannot anyhow,
> On Beeny or elsewhere!

The ability to intensify his experiences was perhaps the most precious gift that Emma brought to Hardy. For him she symbolised the romantic wildness and headlong splendour of the towering Cornish cliffs where he found her. She earned his gratitude—and ours—for the staunch and potentially self-sacrificing way in which she counselled and supported his first uncertain steps to make authorship his livelihood. In later life she might, in other circumstances, have passed her days contentedly enough, unremarked as the wife of a country parson or a small town professional man. The scale and nature of Hardy's fame may have imposed intolerable strains but it did at the last give to her memory the tenderness and the dignity that, as a bride, she had sought from him. If a single verse from any one of the poems can bear adequate witness it is the opening of 'Beeny Cliff, March 1870–March 1913':

> O the opal and the sapphire of that wandering western sea,
> And the woman riding high above with bright hair flapping free—
> The woman whom I loved so, and who loyally loved me.

12

The Poet's Way 1911 - 1928

I cannot help feeling that his is rather an imaginative and poetical mind than a reasoner's

(*Hardy, in a letter, commenting on Bergson*)

The first group of 'Emma' poems appeared in 1914 as part of the volume entitled *Satires of Circumstance*. A second major group was included in *Moments of Vision*, published in 1917. The satires of circumstance which provided the overall title for the earlier volume had originally appeared in 1911 as a self-contained unit of wryly sketched tales of deceit and error, of masks falling to reveal an attempted chicanery or a pretence of some kind. The idea, incidentally, originated in *The Hand of Ethelberta*, in a reference to Christopher Julian:

> Unable, like many other people, to enjoy being satirised in words because of the irritation it caused him as aimed-at victim, he sometimes had philosophy enough to appreciate a satire of circumstance, because nobody intended it.

As a title it is inappropriate to a collection which includes what Hardy described as 'some of the tenderest and least satirical verse that ever came from his pen'. Not only are there the poems mourning the dead Emma but a number of other poems which rank among his best: 'Wessex Heights', for example, and the mysterious intensities of 'The Place on the Map'. The finest of his occasional poems is here—'The Convergence of the Twain', commemorating the loss of the *Titanic*. And for its technical elegance and assurance, with a rhyming pattern that makes for lightness and neatness—and indeed for speaking aloud—'Ah, are you digging on my grave?' is as good a specimen as any of Hardy's wistfully humorous irony.

Moments of Vision followed three years later. The store of early poems was by now largely exhausted; the majority of poems are still undated but a large proportion—about a third—can be definitely ascribed to the years 1911–17. Setting aside the 'Emma' poems it is the group of about fifty reflective/contemplative poems of mood and thought that characterise this collection—poems that Hardy intended to 'mortify the human sense of self-importance by showing, or suggesting, that human beings are of no matter or appreciable value in this nonchalant universe'.

His lightness of touch is still in evidence in such poems as 'The Pink Frock' and the ebulliently zestful 'Great Things', but these belong to earlier days before The Great War brought a depressing grimness to the world in which Hardy lived and wrote. Perhaps *Satires of Circumstance* was after all no bad title for a book published in 1914—a year of valediction to so much that had prompted his writings. *The Dynasts* had ended with a suggestion of hopefulness that was now to be extinguished in Hardy's mind as the war destroyed his belief in 'the gradual ennoblement of man'. Who could have foreseen that the hundred years from Waterloo would culminate in a cloud of poisonous gas at Ypres?

At such times writers are not immune to the general moods and passions of the hour. Hardy was invited to contribute his skill and reputation to those forms of war effort that were appropriate and—as in the Boer War—he found subjects for his verse. One of the most popular of his 'Poems of War and Patriotism' was the song of the soldiers entitled 'Men who March Away'. Today it reads as a typical specimen of those wartime *ephemerae* by many writers of repute that are best forgotten, but in that sense it is not typical of Hardy. His particular qualities of detachment and emotional honesty retain a sort of negative decency in even the least admirable of his efforts. Instinctively the core of the old poet was in tune with that young generation of soldier poets who, like Sassoon and Blunden, never lost their respect for Hardy among their seniors. But the Great War drew from him nothing to match 'Drummer Hodge' and 'The Souls of the Slain'. Possibly the vast scale of the tragedy—in comparison with the South African War—was to some extent beyond the imaginative compass of an old man living through it and almost overwhelmed by 'the silent bleed of a world decaying/The moan of multitudes in woe'.

In the ten postwar years that remained to him Hardy's close application to his versemaking showed no sign of faltering. With what must be an unprecedented prodigality he produced three further volumes after his eightieth birthday—*Late Lyrics and Earlier* in 1922; *Human Shows* in 1925; and *Winter Words*, published in the year of his death, 1928. It is impossible to comment adequately on so copious a variety. There are many more Emma poems; Wessex narratives; churchyard reveries; humorous anecdotes; strange and charming vignettes, full of inventiveness; deflations of human vanity and pomp; and of course the weird and barbarous locutions in which the old man seems to take a wicked and unrepentant delight. He invents English-style words as a foreigner might—'absentness' instead of 'absence'. He lapses into such vapid poetic jargon as 'that arched fane of leafage', and—in search of a rhyme—he translates 'she sang to him' into 'her warble flung its woo/In his ear.'

But these Gothic irregularities are an essential part of Hardy's texture. They give an individual personality to his work. When he wants to achieve a purity of diction he does so in masterly fashion: 'Waiting Both', for instance, is like a fine carving in ivory, cut entirely in monosyllables except for the one word 'degree'. To the last he retained a zest for the sensations and the ideas of the world around him—this swift impression of a car at night, for example, in 1924:

A car comes up, with lamps full-glare,
That flash upon a tree:
It has nothing to do with me,

And whangs along in a world of its own,
Leaving a blacker air;
And mute by the gate I stand again alone,
And nobody pulls up there.

and this amusing note on relativity:

And now comes Einstein with a notion—
Not yet quite clear
To many here—
That there's no time, no space, no motion
Nor rathe nor late,
Nor square nor straight,
But just a sort of bending-ocean.

There seems to have been no circumstance, grave or gay, that Hardy could not take as the subject for a poem in which he crystallised some distinctive aspect of himself. In all his poetry he is simply a man speaking to others, with an unforced and unpretending candour to which one instinctively responds. And if one leaves it at that, it is for the good reason that Ezra Pound gave in *Culture*:

> When a writer's matter is stated with such entirety and with such clarity there is no place left for the explaining critic. When the matter is of so stark a nature and so clamped to reality, the eulogist looks an ass . . . When we come to estimate the 'poetry of the period', against Hardy's 600 pages we will put what?

In the 'Apology' which prefaces *Late Lyrics and Earlier* Hardy stated that 'poetry and religion touch each other, or rather modulate into each other'; he described them as 'the visible signs of mental and emotional life'. If we follow the direction that this clue suggests we may come to recognise that, in his finest work, Hardy was making articulate and 'visible' some of the deepest tides of mental and emotional life in his contemporary situation; and was doing so in, as he says, 'a series of fugitive impressions which I have never tried to co-ordinate', rather than in a logically inter-related and buttressed system of consistent propositions.

He was, in short, in the prophetic tradition of English poets—in a literary sense the child of Shelley and the father of D. H. Lawrence. In *Lady Chatterley's Lover*, Lawrence put forward his often quoted *dictum*:

> It is the way our sympathy flows and recoils that really determines our lives. And here lies the vast importance of the novel, properly handled. It can inform and lead into new places the flow of our sympathetic consciousness, and it can lead our sympathy away in recoil from things gone dead.

In this he was merely developing and consolidating a view expressed more diffidently by Hardy in the 1892 preface to *Tess*, where he writes:

> So densely is the world thronged that any shifting of positions, even the best warranted advance, galls somebody's kibe. Such shiftings often begin in sentiment, and such sentiment sometimes begins in a novel.

If we now look back to the novels—through the later body of poetry and *The Dynasts*—we can recognise how closely the prose narratives and the verse are all-of-a-piece. In the novels Hardy was constantly and increasingly striving to break through the literal surfaces of life, using satire and tragedy as the two techniques most apt for his purpose. For all his early admiration of Defoe as a model, Hardy was far from being a realist in the sense of writing naturalistically; and nothing could be more ill-judged than the affinity with Zola that some of his contemporaries affected to see. It so happens that Hardy himself has provided, as if by accident, the perfect example of the distance between a specimen of life in the raw and a similar incident projected through his imagination. In a note made in April 1893 Hardy wrote:

> Am told that Nat C—'s good-for-nothing grandson has 'turned ranter' —i.e. street-preacher—and, meeting a girl he used to carry on with, the following dialogue ensued:
>
> HE: 'Do you read your Bible for your spiritual good?'
> SHE: 'Ho-ho! Git along wi thee!'

HE: 'But do you, my dear young woman?'
SHE: 'Haw-haw! Not this morning!'
HE: 'Do you read your Bible, I implore?'
SHE: (tongue out) 'No, nor you neither. Come, you can't act in that show, Natty! You haven't the guts to carry it off!'

The discussion was ended by their going off to Came Plantation.

To put this beside Chapters 45 and 46 of *Tess* is to recognise how powerfully Hardy lifts not only the level of the action but the quality of the language in which it is expressed. To achieve the grandeur of tragedy he moves as far as possible from literal verisimilitudes and accepts the risks of melodramatic rodomontade and self-parody. Time and again one detects an impatience to bend the story and make it yield the kind of situation in which he can give dramatic 'visibility' to the insights of a poetic vision.

It is this impatience which lies at the root of so much of the criticism of Hardy's craftsmanship as a novelist. The so numerous coincidences, the convenient but implausible eavesdroppings, the confused timescales, the plain contradictions and carelessnesses—all these may be partly ascribed to the exigencies of serial writing under pressure. But only partly so; of more consequence is Hardy's evident indifference to the mechanics of the storyteller's trade and his preoccupation instead with the progress of the mental and emotional life of whichever character has seized his attention. When he needs an event to trigger the next scene he summons it in a manner which is sometimes arbitrary and clumsily contrived.

It would be as tiresome for the reader, as it would be easy, to present here a lengthy catalogue of the technical faults and weaknesses in the novels. 'To scrutinize the tool-marks and be blind to the building' is an occupational ailment of those 'junior reviewers' to whom Hardy addressed a magisterial rebuke in his 'Apology'. A single instance may therefore suffice.

In *The Mayor of Casterbridge* one of the mainsprings of the action is the return of Newson, the sailor to whom Henchard twenty years earlier sold his wife. His intervention in the story is heralded in suitably dramatic terms when he appears as an anonymous figure, lost in the darkness on Durnover Moor and calling 'Ahoy—is this the way to Casterbridge?' In conversation at the *Peter's Finger* tavern, where the skimmington is being planned, he reveals his intention to stay for two or three weeks and contributes money towards the cost of the skimmington, which Jopp is planning with the other habitués. No more is heard of Newson for about a fortnight, although his purpose is to find Henchard, who is at that time lodging with Jopp. He eventually calls on Jopp at some time on the day of the skimmington—possibly after it is ended—and Jopp later tells Henchard that 'Somebody has called for you . . . a kind of traveller, or sea-captain of some sort.'

The following morning Newson confronts Henchard and gives this extraordinary account of his movements: 'I've been looking for 'ee this fortnight past. I landed at Havenpool and went through Casterbridge on my way to Falmouth, and when I got there, they told me you had some years before been living at Casterbridge. Back came I again, and by long and by late I got here by coach, ten minutes ago. "He lives down by the mill", says they. So here I am.' And very shortly he departs by the same coach.

At a later stage, talking to Farfrae, Newson repeats this account of a journey westward to Falmouth which took him through Casterbridge, whither he returned to speak to Henchard and then departed, 'without lying in the town half-an-hour'. The truth is that Hardy is not much interested in Newson: the idea of holding him in the background as a possible spectator of the skimmington is probably what prompted the dialogue in the *Peter's Finger*. The visit to Jopp's cottage where Henchard has 'a couple of rooms' (although three are described at various times) is again a momentary touch of suspense that any novelist might introduce. But when the time comes to present the moment of confrontation Hardy simply abandons these earlier notions, apparently to concentrate on a return to Falmouth as necessary to establish the mysterious 'they' who steer Newson in the right direction. And by bringing Newson directly to Henchard from the coach he makes it easier for Henchard to bluff the sailor into believing that Elizabeth-Jane is dead. All that Hardy wants from Newson is a credulity 'so simple as to be almost sublime'. Maybe that is what he also wants from his readers at this point.

It would be no great exaggeration to say that Hardy's construction often consists of a series of *tableaux vivants* or set pieces which obey their own internal rules but are linked together with tenuous, obscure and sometimes irrational connecting passages. From that first wildly emotional scene between Miss Aldclyffe and Cytherea in *Desperate Remedies* to the final duets of anguish between Jude and Sue, Hardy's genius shows at its finest in those situations where he can probe and test to the utmost the moral fabric of his characters. The contrivances that in life precipitate such situations do not interest him greatly and become irksome when they seem to demand a more detailed and careful attention than they merit. As with his primary masters, the Greeks and the Elizabethans, it is the big scenes that count—the explanations must make shift as best they can. Who cares how many children Lady Macbeth had?

If we accept Hardy on these terms we more readily appreciate the way in which each detail in the theatre of his imagination is designed, first and foremost, to harmonise with and to intensify the central action, rather than to conform to literal probabilities. He is an unabashed exploiter of the pathetic fallacy in his setting of a scene, impregnating every inanimate object with mood and sentiment. In *Tess*, for example, after her 'confession' to Angel:

> . . . the complexion even of external things seemed to suffer transmutation as her announcement progressed. The fire in the grate looked impish—demoniacally funny, as if it did not care in the least about her strait. The fender grinned idly, as if it too did not care. The light from the water-bottle was merely engaged in a chromatic problem. All material objects around announced their irresponsibility with terrible iteration.

It is this interplay between the human and the nonhuman which gives to Hardy's writing its enormous changes of perspective, its sudden dramatic detachment, its ability to change scale with the freedom of a camera-zoom—a technique developed supremely in *The Dynasts*, of course, but also much in evidence in the novels. In his 'Study of Thomas Hardy', published posthumously in *Phoenix*, D. H. Lawrence seized particularly on this feature:

> This is a constant revelation in Hardy's novels: that there exists a great background, vital and vivid, which matters more than the people who move upon it. Against the background of dark, passionate Egdon, of the leafy, sappy passion and sentiment of the woodlands, of the unfathomed stars, is drawn the lesser scheme of lives . . . The vast unexplored morality of life itself surrounds us in its eternal incomprehensibility, and in its midst goes on the little human morality play . . . seriously, portentously, till some one of the protagonists chances to look into the wilderness raging round. Then he is lost, his little drama falls to pieces, but the stupendous theatre outside goes on enacting its own incomprehensible drama, untouched. There is this quality in almost all Hardy's work, and this is the magnificent irony it all contains . . . this is the quality Hardy shares with the great writers, Shakespeare or Sophocles or Tolstoi, this setting behind the small actions of his protagonists the terrific action of unfathomed nature.

13

The Man of Wessex

citizens dream of the south and west,
And so do I.

(*Weathers*)

When Hardy died, in January 1928, his ashes were buried in Westminster Abbey, at Poet's Corner, with a spadeful of Dorset earth sprinkled on the casket. His heart was buried in Emma's grave among the Hardy tombs at Stinsford. His national prestige and his regional loyalty were both affirmed in these symbolical acts.

The importance of Hardy's 'regionalism' can hardly be exaggerated although he is too big a figure to be contained in any valid definition of a purely regional author. Any attempt to detach him from 'Wessex' is unthinkable. The highest flights of his imagination prove their authenticity by the touchstones of native realism. What critic can retain his customary habits of disbelief in the presence of Tranter Reuben and Jan Coggan and Dairyman Crick? Real life is never more real than they!

The invention of 'Wessex' was described by Hardy in the preface to *Far from the Madding Crowd* where he first reintroduced the old word to give territorial definition and unity of scene to his novels, for which 'the area of a single county did not afford a canvas large enough'. In its ultimate form Wessex acquired a uniform seriousness in its nomenclature, but in his younger days Hardy was apt to bring a touch or two of jokiness into the way he presented to sophisticated readers the endearing quaintness of his rustic scenes. It was in his role of satirical humorist that Hardy invented the village of Tantrum Clangley and the characters of Farmer Kex and Miss Vashti Sniff in *Under the Greenwood Tree*, or 'Puddle-sub-Mixen' in *Two on a Tower*. But by degrees Wessex developed a dynamism and nature of its own until it became, as Hardy says, 'a utilitarian region which people can go to, take a house in, and write to the papers from'.

Geographically Hardy's Wessex is the Westcountry of England, lying south of the Thames and the Bristol Channel. In this south-western peninsula, extending from Southampton down-Channel to the Atlantic, the heartland of Hardy's writing is Dorset and the adjoining areas of Somerset, Wiltshire and Hampshire. It is a landscape of chalk and limestone downland, of low moors and acid heaths, of alluvial valleys, of the New Forest of the Norman Kings and the old cleared forests on heavy clay soils like the Vale of Blackmoor where in Hardy's view 'superstitions linger longest'. To the visitor's eye Wessex is in many ways the classic embodiment of so much of England's history—enshrined here in Stonehenge and Glastonbury, in the long barrows of Cranborne Chase, in Roman Dorchester and Saxon Winchester, in the ports of the Tudor sea-captains and venturers, in the elegance of eighteenth-century Bath, in the wealth of domestic and ecclesiastical architecture that so many Wessex towns and villages can show—from the church towers of Somerset to the splendours of Longleat and Wilton and Stourhead. And to Hardy's contemporaries it served as a symbol for the feudal tradition, for a vestigial 'Merrie England' which had been left behind by the Industrial Revolution in the Midlands and the North, and which was inhabited by aristocratic landowners and their faithful servant, 'Hodge', in his oldfashioned labourer's smock.

From these ingredients Hardy drew out the folk identity that permeates and enriches his 'imperfect dramas of country life and passions'. His own antiquarian zeal brought to hand a wealth of customs, superstitions, crafts and reminiscences. His family's musical tradition in hymn and folk dance, psalm and ballad, fused together the two strains of musicmaking in which the Westcountry excels—in one mood devoutly and robustly Wesleyan, in the other cheerfully bawdy and lyrical in ways that attracted the collecting talents of Cecil Sharp and Vaughan Williams. By his own quick ear and general observation Hardy captured the essential qualities of dialect speech, and to these regional elements he added two of the centrally formative influences in English literature and English speech—the language of Shakespeare and of the Bible.

In the 1896 preface to *Under the Greenwood Tree* Hardy described the manuscript music books of the old musicians, which had their church music in the front of the book; and then, starting from the back page, an assortment of jigs, reels, hornpipes, ballads and songs, some of which exhibited 'that ancient and broad humour which our grandfathers, and possibly grandmothers, took delight in, and is in these days unquotable'. Through this traditional singing—which lingered in some remote villages into the 1930s or later—Hardy had a direct connection with an unbowdlerised England of which Baring Gould and the rest could not deprive him. From it he derived that occasional 'coarse touch' which the tranter so truly observed 'do always prove a story to be true'. It certainly safeguarded him from the arcadian purity of sentiment with which other rural authors emasculated and deodorised their romantic shepherds and shepherdesses.

Hardy's unremitting struggle with the English language—seeking always, as a writer must, to perfect the tools he needs for his particular task—is most familiar and obvious in his verse, and pre-eminently in *The Dynasts.* But the same inventiveness and experimentation, the same alternations of success and failure, can be found in his prose. Here is a specimen of his barrackroom-lawyer style at its worst: 'Their condition of domiciliary comradeship put her, as the woman, to such disadvantage by its enforced intercourse, that he felt it unfair to her to exercise any pressure of blandishment.'

That, believe it or not, comes from *Tess*. This next example concludes Elizabeth-Jane's dismissal of Henchard at the end of *The Mayor of Casterbridge*: 'Then, before she could collect her thoughts, Henchard went out from her rooms, and departed from the house by the back way as he had come; and she saw him no more.'

The strong Biblical cadences and the high proportion of monosyllables make this typical of Hardy's prose when he refines it down to its extreme simplicity and purity of tone. And when he combines it with the idiomatic phrasing of dialect he achieves those uniquely lyrical passages of which he is the supreme master: such, for example, as Marty South's elegy on Giles Winterborne:

> 'Whenever I get up I'll think of 'ee, and whenever I lie down I'll think of 'ee again. Whenever I plant the young larches I'll think that none can plant as you planted; and whenever I split a gad, and whenever I turn the cider wring, I'll say none could do it like you. If ever I forgot your name let me forget home and heaven! . . . But no, no, my love, I never can forget 'ee; for you was a good man, and did good things!'

An interest in regional accent and dialect was a pronounced feature of the nineteenth century, and Hardy in a sense grew up in the shadow of one of the acknowledged masters of dialect poetry, William Barnes, and was indeed influenced by him. But Hardy never found much reward in quasi-phonetic systems which sought to reproduce vernacular sounds accurately: he was more concerned to devise a few simple and easily recognisable conventions which would suggest the style and flavour of Wessex speech, without labouring greatly over it. When he wants to give a touch of the Devonshire accent to the dialogue in *The Romantic Adventures of a Milkmaid* he concentrates solely on the characteristic Devon 'u', writing 'to' as 'tew', 'do' as 'dew' etc. Similarly he makes the difference between 'med' and 'mid' (for 'might') serve to separate Berkshire speech from Dorset. When he moved outside Wessex he tended to adopt uncritically the conventions of the time for rendering Scottish, Irish, cockney etc. His presentation of Farfrae's way of speaking is perfunctory and lacklustre.

What Hardy perfected in the dialogue of his rustic chorus was not primarily the utterance of a distinctive grammar and vocabulary and mode of pronunciation, but a kind of folk poetry in which alone was it possible to express certain nuances of thought and feeling and humour. What is said is as important as the way of saying it, and the two things are inseparable; whereas in the following passage one admires the sensitive fidelity to Wessex speech, but only as the ornamentation of something intrinsically commonplace:

> 'This throwing o' stones ought to be put down. Why, I once heard grandfather tell, that when he were a chile in petticoats, young John Toop het he upon the head wi' a stone, and knocked un down all of a crump wi' his little lags under un; and Mrs. Toop, looking over that very hedge, gived herself such a turn to see the blood, that that was how 'twas wold Isaac Toop walked bow-legged to the day of his death.'

That comes from *Gentleman Upcott's Daughter* (1893) by Walter Raymond, whose public recitations of Barnes's poetry were considered by Hardy to be 'excellent'. For comparison it is interesting to set beside it a passage from *Far from the Madding Crowd*, in which an authentically rustic speech is suggested with the minimum of departures from 'standard' English:

> 'Do anybody know of a crooked man, or a lame, or any second-hand fellow at all that would do for poor me?' said Maryann. 'A perfect one I don't expect to get at my time of life. If I could hear of such a thing 'twould do me more good than toast and ale.'

There it is not a quaintness in its forms of speech that strikes the reader but the way in which imagery and rhythm are blended to give the words a clear personality, firmly secured in time and place. It springs from the art which conceals art—a skill that Hardy gradually mastered in dialect writing, but occasionally set aside for the sake of experiments. At times he tried laying it on thick as in Creedle's 'This is a bruckle het, maister, I'm much afeard' or tranter Reuben's 'If thou beestn't as mad as a cappel-faced bull let me smile no more.' With Grammer Oliver in *The Woodlanders* he showed his familiarity with deep Saxon dialect forms like 'ich woll'. But in the main he shunned a literary peasantry of the greasepaint-and-glossary kind.

Equally he rejected the music-hall lampoon of 'Hodge'. When Mr Bellston refers, in 'The Waiting Supper', to 'simple peasants', Christine is quick to warn him not to be 'too sure about that word "simple"! You little think what they see and meditate! Their reasonings and emotions are as complicated as ours.' And Angel Clare had the same lesson to learn when he went to live at Talbothays Farm and was surprised by the 'real delight' he found in the companionship of humble stockmen and dairymaids: 'The conventional farm-folk of his imagination—personified in the newspaper-press by the pitiable dummy known as Hodge—were obliterated after a few days' residence. At close quarters no Hodge was to be seen.'

As for the way they spoke, Hardy came increasingly to defend the countryman's use of dialect words—'those terrible marks of the beast to the truly genteel', as he observed sarcastically. For him this other language provided wonderful opportunities that he could never have found in the more restrained and often impoverished idiom of polite society. It is a poet's delight in the power of words that gives such vivacity and richness of colour to, for example, Jan Coggan's defence of the Church of England:

> 'There's this to be said for the Church, a man can belong to the Church and bide in his cheerful old inn, and never trouble or worry his mind about doctrines at all. But to be a meetinger you must go to chapel in all winds and weathers, and make yerself as frantic as a skit. Not but that chapel-members be clever chaps enough in their way. They can lift up beautiful prayers out of their own heads, all about their families and shipwracks in the newspaper . . . We know very well that if anybody do go to heaven, they will. They've worked hard for it, and they deserve to have it, such as 'tis. I bain't such a fool as to pretend that we who stick to the church have the same chance as they, because we know we have not. But I hate a feller who'll change his old ancient doctrines for the sake of

getting to heaven . . . No, I'll stick to my side; and if we be in the wrong, so be it; I'll fall with the fallen!

The laodicean spirit, the wry humour, the self-satire, the ruthless practicality, the silent communion of kindred souls—these are the qualities that rule the low horizon of the Wessex rustics. They have somehow achieved an enduring if slightly uneasy truce with adversity. 'We are bruckle folk here', says Christopher Coney, 'the best o' us hardly honest sometimes, what with hard winters, and so many mouths to fill, and God-a'mighty sending his little taties so terrible small to fill 'un with.' For all the charm of the verbal cadenza, the accent is unmistakably an anti-romantic one. The role of the rustics is to bear witness to the tragedies that are played out in their midst, to 'hold the ring', to add the resonance of their endorsement as the high themes echo back from them. Where the noble spirits of Tess, of Henchard, of Jude are finally broken and beaten down, it is by forces which sweep well above the heads of the Mellstock Quire.

What Hardy celebrates, in his chorus of rustic characters, is that force which is the dialectical opposite of tragedy and yet its ultimate support—the enduring, persistent, indestructible life that the peasant knows, and learns to take with a droll humour, because it will not get very much better and it cannot get very much worse; but nor will it fail and come to an end. Theirs is the gift of bending to the storm without sacrifice of principle or loss of human dignity. For them as good a spokesman as any is Nat Chapman in *Two on a Tower*, allaying Hamoss's fear that the comet they are watching portends a famine:

'Famine—no!' said Nat Chapman. 'That only touches such as we, and the Lord only concerns himself with born gentlemen. It isn't to be supposed that a strange fiery lantern like that would be lighted up for folks with ten or a dozen shillings a week and their gristing, and a load o' thorn faggots when we can get 'em.'

Not for them are noble aspiration and high tragedy. Portentous comets have no place in the peasant's world. They are reserved for 'born gentlemen'—for the aristocrats of feeling, the passionate and vulnerable souls who challenge human destiny, the pioneers who break the mould of convention and pursue their own individual quest. The rustic mood is something shared with Eliot's *Prufrock*:

> No! I am not Prince Hamlet, nor was meant to be;
> Am an attendant lord, one that will do
> To swell a progress, start a scene or two.

In that sense the Wessex worthies are the ballast in Hardy's keel, and it rides less securely whenever he discards them. But they are also a more positive factor in their own right, soaring above the requirements of the story to a level where we delight in them for their own sake. For sheer comic exuberance and richness of invention they are in a class shared only by Shakespeare's bucolics and Dickens's cockneys.

Among those who have the good fortune to know Wessex at firsthand there must always be a special affection for this fusing of the most distinctive and intimate elements of Wessex speech and Wessex life into a unique literary idiom; but when every feeling of regional pride has been discounted it remains true that Hardy and Wessex are still—in the larger sense—inseparable. From Fielding to Thackeray the English novel had been largely a novel of society: its arena was contained within the existing social order, which was conceived as a field for comedy or satire or moral indignation. It was ill-fitted to accommodate the spirit of tragedy or the loneliness of the individual soul. It belonged, as it were, indoors and among company. What Hardy's Wessex introduced was a landscape which could dwarf the human figures that moved upon it, a landscape where solitude and the immensities of spiritual travail could be a normal condition—in story or in poem.

For in spite of his earlier ambitions as a satirist the whole bias of Hardy's visionary imagination is by its nature rightly and inevitably disposed towards tragic themes and occasions. His greatest novels—and many of his poems—are graphs of suffering and of the pity that suffering inspires in a generous mind. Really everything is subordinate to that, everything is bent to uncover and irradiate those moments when human pride and stubborn hope break under the strain of what Hardy called 'the plight of being alive'.

Whether or not one calls this 'gloom' is a matter of personal taste. To my mind Hardy had a surer grasp of the elements of tragedy than any other English novelist of the last century. He never weakened into pathos, he was not perverted into cruelty. By the happy circumstance of his origins he drew his inspiration from a tradition which gave him the ingredients of tragic drama already tinged with the instinctive poetry of the ballad. The folk art and dialect speech of the countryside formed a sort of reservoir of strong natural passions and lyrical expression which had been very little used—except in terms of burlesque—since the Elizabethans. The literature of polite society, even in its transpontine moments, had no direct need for such things. Hardy by contrast is closely and patently rooted in the speech and song of the peasantry. The glamour of the nomadic redcoat, the pervasive image of the county jail and the small stark tragedies of dairymaids are as familiar to him as the flavoursome humours of taproom speech. His lifetime spanned the decline and break-up of that strong rural tradition which had conserved so much of our cultural heritage and it is he who has given that tradition its fullest expression.

Therein lies the key to his achievement. He created a coherent and distinctive world out of the latent and imperfectly formulated feelings that surrounded him. He constructed in words an image of the Wessex landscape, of its people and its atmosphere, its speech and its legends, informed with an order and a permanence that did not before exist. And upon that world of his creation he concentrated a contemplative genius of rare sensitivity. His way of seeing is not the orthodox novelist's way of seeing and it often translates clumsily into terms of fiction, but it is a unique and prophetic vision. Stayed with his intuitive power, Bathsheba and Tess and Henchard rise up and possess our minds as great symbols of human passion and tragic ruin. Fleeting minor figures of village girls, betrayed in love or cast aside—Marty South and Fanny Robin—are touched with an unforgettable and moving dignity. The streets of Casterbridge, the waste of Egdon, the woodlands of the Hintocks become arenas of the human spirit, suddenly charged with great elemental issues. The murmuring voices of little groups of local country folk infuse the atmosphere with an instinctive lyrical feeling. The whole scene is impregnated through and through with the perceptive sensibility of a poet who speaks for those 'into whose souls the iron has entered'. It is perhaps appropriate, then, that the poet rather than the novelist should have the last word:

> So I am found on Ingpen Beacon, or on Wylls-Neck to the west,
> Or else on homely Bulbarrow, or little Pilsdon Crest,
> Where men have never cared to haunt, nor women have walked with me,
> And ghosts then keep their distance; and I know some liberty.

Appendix I

Synopses

Assuming that very few readers are likely to have the whole of Hardy's fiction freshly in mind, these synopses are added in the hope that they will provide an aid to memory and an occasional key to the quotations and references.

Desperate Remedies

Published 1871. Principal characters: Cytherea Graye; her brother, Owen; her hero-suitor and ultimate husband, Edward Springrove; her employer, Miss Aldclyffe; Clerk Crickett, a Wessex prototype; and the villain of the piece, Aeneas Manston. An involved 'novel of ingenuity' with a melodramatic secret allying Manston to the wealthy landowner, Miss Aldclyffe. A night fire, murder and dark plotting lead to a happy conclusion. Interesting sketches of Weymouth and the life of a young architect. Worth reading for some fine passages which survive the absurdities of the plot—notably the fire, some of Manston's portrayal, a boat trip in Weymouth Bay, the rustic characters, and a night scene between Cytherea and Miss Aldclyffe.

Under the Greenwood Tree

Published 1872. Principal characters: tranter Reuben and the Mellstock worthies; the two lovers, Fancy Day and Dick Dewy; Parson Maybold. The most endearing of Hardy's pictures of Wessex village life. The plot is a very slight and not particularly satisfactory romance, but the detail of rustic speech and character is finely observed. Rightly cherished as the dawn chorus of Hardy's Wessex worthies.

A Pair of Blue Eyes

Published 1873. Principal characters Elfride Swancourt and her father; their servant, William Worm; her rival suitors, Stephen Smith and Henry Knight; her eventual husband, Lord Luxellian; and a local fury who pursues her with a doomful countenance, Mrs Jethway. Origin of the psychological elements in Hardy's novels—Stephen, the humble Wessex architect's assistant who betrays his kindred for the sake of 'London ideas'; Elfride, who deceives her lover about her past and loses him by doing so. Henry Knight could be described as a descendant of Sir Charles Grandison and Mr Knightley, and a forerunner of Angel Clare. This is Hardy's first expedition into the real jungle-country of sex and marriage.

Far from the Madding Crowd

Published 1874. His first great achievement. Principal characters: Bathsheba Everdene; her neighbour, Farmer Boldwood; her bailiff, suitor and ultimate husband, Gabriel Oak; her unhappy destiny and first husband, Sergeant Troy; Troy's subsidiary victim, Fanny Robin; Bathsheba's maid, Liddy; and not forgetting the rustic chorus, Joseph Poorgrass, the Maltster, Laban Tall, Jan Coggan and the rest. Bathsheba is a well-to-do farmer. Gabriel Oak becomes her bailiff, proves himself sturdy and reliant but lacks the audacity to win her. Because of a silly prank she feels obliged to accept the attention of Boldwood, a rigid, honest, worthy but unlovable character. Troy, a dashing soldier without substance or principles, sweeps Bathsheba off her feet and marries her—in spite of his promise to Fanny Robin, whom he has seduced. As a husband Troy soon runs amok, the death of Fanny brings her revenge, and a very powerful climax leaves Gabriel as the only survivor of Bathsheba's three lovers.

The Hand of Ethelberta

Published 1876. The silliest and most interesting of Hardy's failures. Principal characters: Ethelberta Chickerel, a spirited Wessex girl, who is 'disloyal to her class and kin' for the unselfish reason that she wants to help her family financially and therefore poses as a 'lady' and succeeds in hoaxing London society; Picotee, her sister, and a horde of brothers and other sisters; her humble and unsuccessful suitor, Christopher Julian; and her eventual husband, Lord Mountclere. Hardy seems to have convinced himself that a successful novelist ought to find his subjects in fashionable society. He was avowedly seeking to escape the 'rustic' label when he wrote this, and adopted what he considered an appropriate style for the occasion. Characters appear with Restoration names—Neigh, Ladywell, Mrs Menlove—and there are witticisms, social satire and disquisitions on the art of fiction. An extraordinary medley.

The Return of the Native

Published 1878. Principal characters: Mrs Yeobright and her son, Clym, a modern idealist who marries Eustacia Vye, who has a secret amour with Damon Wildeve, who in turn has married—at the second attempt—Clym's cousin, Thomasin. And, to round off these romances, Thomasin finally marries the travelling reddleman, Diggory Venn, after Wildeve has been drowned with Eustacia. The plot is probably as weak as it sounds, but the book is memorable for other reasons—for Hardy's personal ideas about Clym, for the poetic insight of some individual scenes, for the rustic chorus—Granfer Cantle, Christian, Timothy Fairway—and, above all, for the magnificent evocation of Egdon Heath.

The Trumpet-Major

Published 1880. An historical romance of the Napoleonic War. Principal characters: John Loveday, the trumpet-major; Bob

Loveday, his sailor brother; Miller Loveday, their father; Anne Garland, the girl the two brothers love; Festus Merriman, a boorish rival; Matilda Johnson, an inconvenient actress from Bob's past. A pleasant reconstruction of Weymouth when George III paid a visit and Bonaparte was across the Channel. A few vivid scenes, some good humour, and a magazine plot.

A Laodicean

Published 1881. Hardy's worst effort. Paula Power, the heroine, having inherited the ancient mansion of the De Stancy's from her wealthy engineer father, lives there with her friend, Charlotte De Stancy, poor descendant of the venerable family. Paula has building plans, so along comes the familiar young architect hero, George Somerset. To confuse the course of true love Hardy produces some of the dreariest villains ever known—Havill, a jealous and envious architect, Captain William De Stancy (Charlotte's brother), who hopes to marry Paula and recover the ancestral mansion, and an oddity called Dare who turns out to be De Stancy's bastard son. Some melodramatic moments over an architectural competition between Havill and Somerset are followed by a wearisome European tour, during which Hardy demonstrates his familiarity with the Continent, and Dare pops in and out with forged telegrams and faked photographs like a character in an Aldwych farce.

Two on a Tower

Published 1882. Principal characters: Lady Viviette Constantine; Swithin St Cleeve; Tabitha Lark; Mr Torkingham; and some rustics, Sammy Blore, Hamoss, etc.

A protracted love-duel between the aristocrat, Viviette, and the humble self-trained young astronomer, Swithin. Hardy's first novel, unpublished and later destroyed, was entitled *The Poor Man and the Lady*. The theme obviously attracted him as it appears in several of his novels, notably in this one. Viviette finances Swithin's astronomy and, believing herself a widow, marries him secretly. Some confusion over the date of her husband's death—he is in darkest Africa—cancels the marriage. Viviette recovers her self-possession, decides not to marry Swithin again but discovers herself to be pregnant and—to appease convention—turns to her other suitor, the pompous Bishop of Melchester, for a respectable second marriage. The book falls away in its later stages but it certainly offers a first glimpse of promising country: one is aware that much more is at stake between Viviette and Swithin than Hardy is yet able to discover.

The Mayor of Casterbridge

Published 1886. Principal characters: Michael Henchard, Mayor of Casterbridge; his wife, Susan; their daughter, Elizabeth-Jane; Donald Farfrae, manager of Henchard's business and later his successful competitor; Lucetta Templeman, an old 'flame' of Henchard's; Mother Cuxsom, Christopher Coney, Abel Whittle and the other cronies of the *Three Mariners*; Joshua Jopp, a man with a grudge against Henchard.

The most successfully elaborate of Hardy's plots. Having sold his wife and baby to a sailor, Newson, in a drunken fit at Weyhill Fair (an act based on a true story) Henchard takes the pledge and twenty years later becomes the Mayor of Casterbridge. He owes marriage to Lucetta and is considering it when wife and daughter return. He goes through another form of marriage with his wife who then conveniently dies and leaves behind the inconvenient knowledge that the daughter, Elizabeth-Jane, is not the original baby but the child of the man who paid Henchard for his wife at the Fair. Henchard quarrels meanwhile with Farfrae, who has been courting Elizabeth-Jane, and Farfrae starts in business on his own account. Lucetta, inheriting wealth, moves to Casterbridge in order to accomplish her marriage with Henchard, but soon transfers her attention to Farfrae. Henchard's prosperity and ease of mind are steadily crumbling away as Farfrae rises, and the exposure of his misdeed at Weyhill Fair accelerates his ruin. The inexorable beating down of Henchard, until he is like a great shattered castle eroded by time and the elements, is one of Hardy's supreme achievements.

The Woodlanders

Published 1887. Principal characters: Grace Melbury; her father; her husband, Fitzpiers; Suke Damson, a mistress of Fitzpiers; Giles Winterborne; Marty South; Creedle, Giles's servant; Farmer Cawtree; Mrs Charmond, a wealthy and attractive widow.

The plot is a variant of *Far from the Madding Crowd*, with Grace in the place of Bathsheba and Giles as another Gabriel Oak. Instead of marrying the solid golden-hearted countryman, Grace chooses Fitzpiers. And Fitzpiers is first carelessly unfaithful with the jolly wanton, Suke, and then develops a consuming passion of the grander sort for Mrs Charmond. Giles's death robs Grace of any second thoughts and puts an end to the dumb hope of poor Marty.

Grace is on a smaller scale than Bathsheba, but the woodland scene is beautifully animated and rich, and Hardy's views on marriage notably expressive.

Wessex Tales

Published 1888. Short stories. One or two powerfully dramatic pieces and an unusual story, *Fellow Townsmen*, that might have been the first sketch for a novel.

A Group of Noble Dames

Published 1891. A related group of short stories of small merit—a collection of plot formulas of varying ingenuity, reflecting

Hardy's antiquarian interest in the family histories of Wessex grandees.

Tess of the d'Urbervilles

Published 1891. Principal characters: Tess; Angel Clare; Alec d'Urberville. Tess is seduced by Alec, and omits to mention the fact to Angel until their wedding night. Angel goes abroad and fails to make his intentions clear to Tess, who again becomes involved with Alec. Angel returns and discovers them together. Tess murders Alec, flees with Angel, is arrested and hanged.

The Well-Beloved

Published (in serial form) 1892. Principal characters: Jocelyn Pierston; Nichola Pine-Avon; Marcia Bencomb; Avice Caro. The weird adventures in the 'love-world' of a sculptor, born on the isle of Portland, who finds his ideal love successively in three generations of a neighbouring Portland family. One of the curiosities of English literature.

Life's Little Ironies

Published 1894. Could more accurately have been entitled 'Marriage's Little Ironies'. This astringent collection of cautionary tales includes two of Hardy's best efforts, 'On the Western Circuit' and 'The Fiddler of the Reels'. There are some amusing episodes of rustic humour among the anecdotes linked together in 'A Few Crusted Characters'.

Jude the Obscure

Published 1896. Principal characters: Jude Fawley; Sue Bridehead; Arabella; Phillotson; Mr Cartlett; Little Father Time.

Jude, carnally attracted to Arabella, marries her and regrets doing so. Sue, a platonic lover, inspires his idealism, but she marries Phillotson, a middle-aged schoolmaster who is not unreasonably bewildered by her frigidity. She deserts Phillotson for a sexless union with Jude, but Jude fails to live up to this exacting standard. He persuades Sue into a normal union and is also unable to resist the old appeal of Arabella when she reappears. His ideals of scholarly wisdom and emotional high-mindedness are torn from his grasp by his own frailties, and the spark of original spirit in him is crushed and extinguished. This is Hardy's bitterest and most controversial book, and a summary of its ostensible plot does little to convey its character.

A Changed Man

Published 1913. Short stories. Described by Hardy as 'a dozen minor novels', some of them painfully minor, none worth recalling individually. One or two of the earlier and better ones would have fitted harmoniously into *Life's Little Ironies* and were perhaps a rejected surplus from that group.

Appendix 2

Dramatisations

I am not aware that anyone has compiled a check list of the principal adaptations that have been made of Hardy's works for dramatic production in the various media—theatre, cinema, radio and television. I offer the following as a first attempt which others may care to supplement or amend. Without wishing to attach an undue importance to these secondary artforms for which, as a practitioner, I admittedly have an affection, I may perhaps usefully suggest that they can tell us something by the particular relationship that develops between the original work and the dramatic medium. The bias imposed by new technical dimensions tends to set the work in a different light from what we are accustomed to as readers; if in consequence some important features are shadowed or obscured, others may be emphasised with an unusual clarity. In particular we can hardly fail to notice the strength of the purely dramatic element in those stories which, over the years, have beckoned most insistently to producers in the various media. Of the novels *Madding Crowd*, *Tess* and *The Mayor* show the most powerful appeal, while among the short stories it is perhaps *The Withered Arm*, *The Three Strangers* and *The Distracted Preacher* which have been most in demand.

If I refer only briefly to theatrical productions during Hardy's lifetime it is because they are already documented in substantial detail in three works:

Thomas Hardy, a bibliographical study, R. L. Purdy
Hardy of Wessex, Carl J. Weber
Tess in the Theatre, Marguerite Roberts

1879. The Mistress of the Farm. Hardy's interest in playwriting in the late 1860s produced no drafted attempts that have survived. It was the success of *Madding Crowd* that revived his interest in the theatre and encouraged him to adapt his own story for the stage as *The Mistress of the Farm.* The same idea occurred to a dramatic critic, J. Comyns Carr, who proposed himself to Hardy as an adaptor. Recognising perhaps that Carr, as a man of the theatre, could develop the work he had begun, Hardy established a collaboration; Carr offered the play to the St James's management of Hare and Kendal. Some unscrupulous behaviour by Mrs Kendal led to the rejection of the Hardy-Carr adaptation and the immediate commissioning of Arthur Pinero to write *The Squire*, a suspiciously similar play for the same management. The plagiarism was detected, although Pinero himself had acted innocently in accepting the outline of the story from Mrs Kendal.

Carr now made a further extensive revision of the original script, renamed it with the title of the novel, and was successful in having a production mounted in Liverpool at the Prince of Wales theatre in February 1882, with Marion Terry as Bathsheba. Hardy and Emma travelled to Liverpool for the opening performance. Subsequently the production came into London, though with a different Bathsheba, and had a useful run at the Globe. As Mrs Kendal was appearing in *The Squire* at the same time Londoners could compare the two versions.

1886. The Mayor of Casterbridge. Hardy's first practical acquaintance with the professional theatre was scarcely endearing and he was in no hurry to renew it; nor were the stories he wrote in the period following *Madding Crowd* of such great appeal dramatically. But with the publication of *The Mayor* he had again created a powerful story with a strong central character. Quick to recognise the book's possibilities, Robert Louis Stevenson wrote to ask if Hardy would let him try to dramatise it. Hardy must have agreed as he recorded his disappointment that nothing came of the project. It was in fact left for John Drinkwater many years later to take up the task that Stevenson laid aside.

1889. The Woodlanders. Another abortive project worth mentioning is a proposal to adapt this novel made by J. T. Grein. Hardy was not unwilling but Grein's failure to proceed drew from Hardy the interesting comment that 'no English manager at this date would venture to defy the formalities to such an extent as was required by the novel, in which some of the situations were approximately of the kind afterwards introduced to English playgoers by translations from Ibsen'.

1893. The Three Wayfarers. The 1890s represent a peak in Hardy's personal interest in dramatisation for the theatre. The friendly reception of *The Three Wayfarers*—his own dramatisation of *The Three Strangers*—in a mixed bill of short plays at Terry's theatre must have encouraged him. His frequent visits to theatres at this period and his personal contacts with leading players like Irving, Ellen Terry and Mrs Patrick Campbell would also have stimulated his desire to score a success of his own in the theatre commensurate with his reputation outside it.

1894/5. Tess. In the summer of 1894 Hardy visited the Adelphi to see a melodrama that, in his words, was 'said to be based without acknowledgement on *Tess*'. The experience may have added to the pressure he was under to prepare a dramatisation himself. He had many requests to do so and they included expressions of interest from the leading actresses of the day. Hardy therefore made a stage version which he evidently hoped to see played by 'Mrs Pat' and Forbes Robertson. One of the factors influencing his choice of a London residence in 1895 was the desirability of being near Mrs Patrick Campbell (Weber, *op cit*).

The failure of the scheme was ascribed by Hardy to the 'notorious timidity' of London's actor-managers. The hostility that greeted *Jude* was an additionally discouraging factor, as Purdy points out (*op cit*). There is the further point that the tremendous opportunity offered by the part of Tess to a tragedienne was not matched by the role of Angel Clare for a leading man. It is significant that 'Mrs Pat' spent some time in Dorchester trying vainly to persuade Hardy to meet Forbes Robertson's request for changes in the script.

While any thought of a London production had to be abandoned, in the United States matters progressed more smoothly, probably because Hardy withdrew the stipulation that his text must be inviolate. Lorimer Stoddard was given a free hand with the script by the New York manager, Harrison Grey Fiske, and in March 1897 at the Fifth Avenue Theatre Mrs Fiske enjoyed the triumph that had been denied to Mrs Pat, Ellen Terry, Duse and Bernhardt. At this time the nearest London got to seeing a stage *Tess* was in 1900 at the Coronet Theatre in Notting Hill, where an unauthorised version by H. A. Kennedy, a dramatic critic, was produced and promptly repudiated by Hardy.

1906. The *Tess* opera. The first suggestion for an opera came from an American librettist, Charlotte Pendleton, who approached Hardy in 1900. The composer working with her was Walter Damrosch's assistant, Gilbert Schenk. She seems to have been inspired by the Fiske production as Hardy warned her to work direct from the novel and not to risk Mr Fiske's disapproval of a misuse of the New York script.

The next proposal came from Baron Frederic d'Erlanger, a composer of repute who saw in *Tess* 'a wonderful book for an opera' in which he had interested the Italian librettist, Illica—the author of *Boheme* and *Tosca* among others. At one stage Hardy considered having his name given as part-author, but this idea was dropped as he could not read Italian and an English translation of Illica's work was not available until much later. The premiere took place in 1906 at San Carlo, Naples, with Rina Giachetti as Tess. Unfortunately the performance was disturbed by an eruption of Mount Vesuvius which obliged the authorities to close the theatre. For d'Erlanger it was a calamity, but Hardy commented philosophically 'the volcano was all of a piece with Tess's catastrophic career!'

In 1908 a new production was mounted at the Teatro dal

Verme, Milan, with Tullio Serafin conducting and Tina Desana in the role of Tess. Despite a musicians' strike the opera did well enough to win acceptance for Covent Garden the following year, with the added advantage of Emmy Destinn in the title role—Destinn who, four years earlier had introduced Puccini's *Butterfly* to London, and was to be acclaimed again for her performance as Tess. Further performances took place during the following season, 1910, but the death of Edward VII had inevitably a depressing effect on London theatregoing. Hardy considered d'Erlanger's music 'very haunting' and thought the Covent Garden management should have kept *Tess* in the repertoire.

In 1974 Leo d'Erlanger, the composer's nephew, lodged Hardy's side of the correspondence in the Hardy Memorial Collection at the Dorset County Museum, Dorchester, where d'Erlanger's letters to Hardy were already preserved. For fuller information see Marguerite Roberts (*op cit*) and Desmond Hawkins, *Contemporary Review*, London, July 1974.

1908. The Hardy Players. Members of the Dorchester Debating and Dramatic Society started in 1908 a tradition—as it became—of local amateur performance of dramatisations of Hardy's works, commencing with *The Trumpet-Major*, and continuing until 1924. The company became known as the Hardy Players and their work attracted a good deal of attention. A full account of their activities is given in an appendix by Purdy (*op cit*) and also by Roberts (*op cit*). Their version of *Madding Crowd* (1909) adapted by A. H. Evans was judged by Hardy to be 'a neater achievement than the London version of 1882'.

1913/15. This was an interesting period which saw the first entry of a movie camera into Hardy's world, and a brave attempt by Granville-Barker to get some essence of *The Dynasts* inside a proscenium arch. In December 1913 the son of Sir Hubert Herkomer, who had illustrated *Tess*, hired the Dorchester 'picturedrome' in order to show some of his father's films to Hardy. Sir Hubert was 'doing films of *Far from the Madding Crowd* for the picture palaces' and his son was seeking out the correct settings and props, and generally acquiring local colour. The scenario was prepared by Larry Trimble, who also directed the film for Turner Films Ltd. Its trade show took place in November 1915; the souvenir programme prepared for the occasion included a synopsis contributed by Hardy. The film was released in February 1916.

The stage production of *The Dynasts* opened at the Kingsway Theatre in November 1914 and ran for 72 performances. Although he had described his work as 'intended simply for mental performance' Hardy accepted Harley Granville-Barker's invitation to prepare a suitable version of selected scenes.

1920. In the early twenties the cinema took on a new importance in Hardy's mind. A film of *Tess*, made in 1919 (Roberts *op cit*) was discussed by Vere Collins in his *Talks with Thomas Hardy at Max Gate*, when he mentioned to Hardy that *Tess* was at that time (April 1920) being shown 'on the films'. Surprisingly he quotes Hardy as saying 'I was present at a rehearsal of it in the United States' which is of course impossible as Hardy never crossed the Atlantic. Describing his own cinemagoing as 'unfortunate' Hardy went on to express surprise that people cared for *Tess* in this film version as he thought it was 'mainly young people who go to see the cinematograph'.

In July 1921 another company of 'film actors' arrived in Dorchester to make a production of *The Mayor*. Hardy took an interest in them and accompanied them to Maiden Castle. These new activities in an untraditional medium impressed Hardy sufficiently for him to say that 'perhaps the cinematograph will take the place of fiction, and novels will die out, leaving only poetry' (Vere Collins, *op cit*).

1923. The Queen of Cornwall. Described by Hardy as a new version of the Iseult legend 'arranged as a play for mummers in one act', this romantic verse play was at first intended for a local production by the Hardy Players and not for publication (Purdy, *op cit*). It attracted the interest of Rutland Boughton, composer of *The Immortal Hour*, who set Hardy's play to music for a professional production in the Glastonbury Festival, which Hardy attended, in 1924.

1924. Tess. After their struggles with the blank verse of *The Queen of Cornwall* in the previous year the Hardy Players were now allowed to perform Hardy's own original version of *Tess*. A contributory cause of this change of heart may have been the grotesque new film of *Tess* made by Goldwyn, with Blanche Sweet as Tess and Conrad Nagel as Clare. With Tess meeting Alec in a night club, and a total disregard of place and period, this film seems to have been the typical bad joke for which Hollywood was to become infamous. Critical protests were loud and unanswerable, and it would indeed have been droll if Hardy had continued to suppress his own dramatisation and leave the field to such commercialised rubbish. The Goldwyn film seems to have appeared in October 1924. The Hardy Players presented Hardy's version at the end of November, and their efforts were so successful that London managements were at once interested: a professional production by A. E. Filmer was presented, first at the Barnes Theatre and subsequently at the Garrick.

There had earlier been abortive discussions with the Haymarket management for a production in which Tess would have been played by one of the Hardy Players, Gertrude Bugler, who had performed the role locally to Hardy's satisfaction. The manner in which Florence Hardy apparently chose to thwart this plan is described in Weber (*op cit*) and in Mrs Bugler's own account (*Personal Recollections of Thomas Hardy*). The title role in Filmer's production was played by Gwen Frangcon-Davies, with Ion Swinley as Angel Clare and Austin Trevor as Alec. Miss Frangcon-Davies had a preliminary discussion at Max Gate where Hardy showed her the Herkomer 'portrait' of Tess, on which she modelled her appearance. She had heard of Hardy's wish that Gertrude Bugler should have the part so she tried, at this first encounter, to create an impression as unlike that of a professional actress as she could.

The Life contains a graphic account of a performance given privately to Hardy at Max Gate by the London company. The Press was firmly excluded from this very private occasion, but one or two journalists bluffed their way into the house by pretending to belong to the company as stagehands. The combined run at the two theatres reached 100 performances but the play never really settled down at the Garrick and must be considered a disappointment. It is significant that Miss Frangcon-Davies and Mr Trevor both independently used the word 'stilted' in their recollections of the dialogue (*in litt*).

After the death of Hardy there was renewed interest in a fresh London production; and in the summer of 1929 Florence Hardy invited Mrs Bugler to play Tess—as a kind of amends possibly—in a revival at the Duke of York's. This she did, and the production was subsequently seen at the King's, Hammersmith and at Margate.

1926. The Mayor of Casterbridge. The Barnes Theatre had its second Hardy production in September 1926, when John Drinkwater's dramatisation of *The Mayor* was presented. For Hardy's benefit the company put on a 'flying matinee' in Weymouth at the Pavilion. Hardy's presence there was accompanied with great popular acclaim but he seems not to have found much pleasure in the performance, considering the 'scene outside the theatre finer than within'. This must have been his last visit to a theatre, but his interest in drama persisted in thoughts of a possible dramatisation of *Jude*. To the friend who proposed this—St John Ervine—he revealed that he had sketched several outlines in bygone years of suitable treatments of *Jude*, and he recommended as the most feasible his '4th Scheme'—an interesting sidelight on the preparatory work that Hardy regularly accumulated in readiness for the propitious moment.

1928. The Mayor of Casterbridge. The Drinkwater version that Hardy had seen at Weymouth was re-adapted for radio and produced by Howard Rose for the BBC. This was not quite the first broadcast of a Hardy story, as the Hardy Players had twice been heard from the local BBC studio at Bournemouth, station 6BM, in 1923 and 1926. On the first occasion they performed two short items that had been combined with *The Queen of Cornwall* in their theatre production of 1923—one was the mummers' St George play, the other a traditional piece that Hardy had prepared for them, entitled 'O Jan! O Jan! O Jan!' On the second occasion they gave *The Three Wayfarers*. If Hardy heard either of these broadcasts he did not record the fact. He certainly had a wireless-receiver in 1925, if not earlier.

Howard Rose's production of *The Mayor* was however the first major presentation of a Hardy story with a professional cast to a nationwide audience. Many more were to follow and in noting them here I shall limit myself to what could be described as full-scale dramatic productions, using the following abbreviations to save space and unnecessary repetition—'dram' for 'dramatised by'; 'prod' for 'produced' or 'directed by'; 'BBC' for 'British Broadcasting Corporation'; 'ITV' for the group of commercial companies which collectively form the Independent Television Network in Britain. Dates given are for the first broadcast of each production (usually from London or Bristol) though in many cases the productions would have been heard subsequently in other English-speaking countries.

1930s. I can trace no theatre or cinema productions in this decade. There were two in radio:

The Dynasts, Part One, dram & prod Alan Wade, 1933 (BBC radio)

Tess, dram Barbara Couper & Howard Rose, prod Howard Rose, 1937 (*Ibid*)

1940s.

The Dynasts, dram & prod Barbara Burnham, 1940 (*Ibid*)

A Tragedy of Two Ambitions, dram Hugh Stewart, prod Lance Sieveking, 1941 (BBC radio)

Madding Crowd, dram Sybil Clarke, prod Howard Rose, 1942 (*Ibid*)

Greenwood Tree, dram Sybil Clarke, prod Hugh Stewart, 1943 (*Ibid*)

The Dynasts, dram Muriel Pratt & Dallas Bower, prod Val Gielgud, 1943 (BBC radio)

The Three Strangers, dram Ann Stephenson, prod Barbara Burnham, 1945 (BBC radio)

Tess. In 1946 a new stage version by Ronald Gow was produced by Hugh Hunt for the Bristol Old Vic at the Theatre Royal, Bristol, transferring subsequently to the New Theatre, London. Wendy Hiller played Tess, with William Devlin as Angel Clare. This production was revived in the following year for a provincial tour and also for a London season at the Piccadilly. In 1948 the Gow dramatisation was adapted for radio and produced by Owen Reed from Bristol, with Aileen Mills as Tess (BBC radio)

The Withered Arm, dram Aileen Mills, prod Owen Reed, 1949 (BBC radio)

Madding Crowd, dram Desmond Hawkins, prod Owen Reed, 1949 (*Ibid*)

Greenwood Tree, dram Kenneth Owen, prod Owen Reed, 1949 (*Ibid*)

1950s.

The Mayor of Casterbridge, dram Desmond Hawkins, prod Owen Reed, with Hedley Goodall as Henchard. The music specially commissioned for this production was composed by Ralph Vaughan Williams, 10 episodes, 1951 (BBC radio)

The Dynasts, dram in 6 parts by Henry Reed, prod E. A. Harding and Douglas Cleverdon, 1951 (BBC radio)

Tess. A new production of the Gow version was arranged in 1952 at the Theatre Royal, Bristol, with Barbara Jefford as Tess, for transmission as a television 'outside-broadcast' directed by Owen Reed. This was the equivalent of a single 'gala' performance, arranged to mark the inauguration of the BBC's television service in the west region, 19 August 1952. It can claim the distinction of being the first presentation of a Hardy story by means of television.

The Woodlanders, dram Desmond Hawkins, prod Owen Reed, 1955 (BBC radio)

The Queen of Cornwall, prod Charles Lefeaux, 1956 (*Ibid*)

1960s.

Tess. The Gow version was given a TV studio production by Michael Currer-Briggs, with Geraldine McEwen as Tess in July 1960 (ITV)

England's Harrowing, adapted from *The Dynasts* by Frederick Bradnum, prod R. D. Smith, 1960 (BBC radio)

The Return of the Native, dram Frederick Bradnum, prod Brandon Acton-Bond, 1960 (BBC radio)

Madding Crowd, a feature film, dram Frederic Raphael, prod John Schlesinger, with Julie Christie as Bathsheba, 1967

The Dynasts, in 6 parts, dram & prod Charles Lefeaux, 1967 (BBC radio)

The Mayor, new production of the 1951 version, dram Desmond Hawkins, prod Brian Miller, 1968 (BBC radio)

Fellow Townsmen, dram Patrick Simpson, prod Brian Miller, 1969 (BBC radio)

Greenwood Tree, dram Denis Constanduros, prod Brian Miller, 1969 (BBC radio)

The Distracted Preacher, dram John Hale, prod Brandon Acton-Bond, 1969 (BBC TV)

1970s.

The Woodlanders, dram Harry Green, prod Martin Lisemore, 1970 (BBC TV)

The Withered Arm, a new production of the 1949 version by Aileen Mills, prod Brian Miller, 1970 (BBC radio)

Tess, a new serial dramatisation by Desmond Hawkins, prod Brian Miller, 1971 (BBC radio)

Jude, dram Harry Green, prod Martin Lisemore, 1971 (BBC TV)

The Day after the Fair (based on 'On the Western Circuit'), dram Frank Harvey, prod Frith Banbury at the Lyric Theatre, London, October 1972, with Deborah Kerr as Edith Harnham: published Samuel French, London 1973

Wessex Tales, collective title for a TV series of six Hardy stories: *The Withered Arm*, dram Rhys Adrian, prod Desmond Davis;

Fellow Townsmen, dram Douglas Livingstone, prod Barry Davis; *A Tragedy of Two Ambitions*, dram Dennis Potter, prod Michael Tuchner; *An Imaginative Woman*, dram William Trevor, prod Gavin Millar; *The Melancholy Hussar*, dram Ken Taylor, prod Mike Newell; and *Barbara of the House of Grebe*, dram David Mercer, prod David Jones. November/December 1973 (BBC TV)

Madding Crowd, a new and revised centenary production of the 1949 version, dram Desmond Hawkins, prod Brian Miller, November 1974 (BBC radio)

In the preparation of this list I have had the assistance of Kathleen Hutchings, the play librarian in the BBC's radio drama department, Pamela Stone of BBC, Bristol, Owen Reed, and Ronald Gow. To them all I express my gratitude.

Sources and Bibliography

For biographical material I have drawn mainly from two sources:
The Life of Thomas Hardy, Florence Emily Hardy (London 1962). Originally published in two volumes as *The Early Life of Thomas Hardy* (1928) and *The Later Years of Thomas Hardy* (1930)
Thomas Hardy, a bibliographical study, Richard Little Purdy (Oxford 1954)

I am indebted particularly to Professor Purdy's work for information about Hardy's relations with Tinsley, the publisher, and later with Tillotson's, and for the episode with Edmund Gosse concerning Helen Paterson, as well as for those items which supplement or correct a detail given in *The Life*. That I make no reference here to Robert Gittings's *Young Thomas Hardy* (an obvious source of biographical material) is due solely to the fact that it was not published until just after my text had gone to press.

For quick reference on many points I have constantly referred to:
A Hardy Companion, F. B. Pinion (London & New York 1968)

Among general biographical narratives I found points of interest in:
Thomas Hardy, a critical biography, Evelyn Hardy (London 1954)
Hardy of Wessex, Carl J. Weber (Columbia Univ Press & London 1940, revised 1965)

For more specialised biographical subjects I have drawn on:
Dearest Emmie. Thomas Hardy's letters to his first wife, ed Carl J. Weber (London 1963)

One Rare Fair Woman, Thomas Hardy's letters to Florence Henniker, ed by Evelyn Hardy & F. B. Pinion (London 1972)
Some Recollections, Emma Hardy. Edited by Evelyn Hardy & Robert Gittings (Oxford 1961)
Rebekah Owen and Thomas Hardy, Carl J. Weber (Colby College Library, Maine, 1939)
Talks with Thomas Hardy at Max Gate, 1920–22, Vere H. Collins (London 1928, reprinted Guernsey 1971)
Thomas Hardy's Notebooks, ed Evelyn Hardy (London 1955)
Personal Recollections of Thomas Hardy, Gertrude Bugler (Dorset Nat Hist & Arch Soc 1962)
Memories of Fifty Years, Lady St Helier (Mary Jeune) (London 1909)
Thomas Hardy, Irene Cooper Willis (Colby Library Quarterly, Maine)
Thomas Hardy and Emma, Henry Gifford. Essays & Studies. (1966)

I have also consulted the collection of Hardy papers and associated material at the Dorset County Museum, Dorchester: and rate-books and other contemporary material at Weymouth library.

The topography of Hardy's Wessex tends to become a subject for study in its own right and is begetting a specialised literature —starting with:

The Wessex of Thomas Hardy, Bertram C. A. Windle, with illustrations by Edmund H. New (London & New York 1902)

This was followed in 1913 by:

Thomas Hardy's Wessex, Hermann Lea (London, reprinted Guernsey 1969)
Hardy's Wessex Re-appraised, Denys Kay-Robinson (Newton Abbot 1972). This has the advantage of incorporating an updated description of the places listed—many of which have of course been greatly changed since Hardy described them. Also worth noting are the inexpensive tour pamphlets issued by the

Thomas Hardy Society, which give a map and an itinerary for each of the principal novels. I should perhaps emphasise that I am referring to the English 'Thomas Hardy Society' of Dorchester, Dorset, which was founded in 1967—and is therefore something of a parvenu in comparison with the Thomas Hardy Society of Japan, which led the way ten years earlier.

Critical appraisals of Hardy came at first mainly from fellow-poets:

The Art of Thomas Hardy, Lionel Johnson (London 1894. New ed 1923)
Thomas Hardy, Lascelles Abercrombie (London 1912)
Thomas Hardy, Edmund Blunden (London 1942)
Study of Thomas Hardy, D. H. Lawrence (written 1914, published posthumously in *Phoenix*, London 1936)

In the last twenty-five years scholarly and analytical studies of many kinds, and with increasing specialisation, have multiplied to such a degree that it would be an affectation to pretend that I am competent even to list them all. Some are addressed primarily to fellow-scholars, some to the more general reader, and some again to readers with specific interests. I append details of those which seem to me particularly to merit attention, or which happen to have come my way and aroused my interest:

Thomas Hardy's Personal Writings, Harold Orel (Kansas 1966. London 1967). A very useful collection of Hardy's articles, prefaces, etc
Thomas Hardy and his Readers, L. Lerner & J. Holmstrom (London 1968). A selection of contemporary reviews of his novels
Thomas Hardy, W. R. Rutland (Oxford 1938)
Hardy the Novelist, David Cecil (London 1943)
Thomas Hardy, the Novels & Stories, Albert J. Guerard (Harvard & Oxford 1949)
The Poetry of Thomas Hardy, J. O. Bailey (Oxford 1970)
Young Thomas Hardy, Robert Gittings (London 1975)

Thomas Hardy & the Modern World, ed F. B. Pinion (Dorchester 1974). A symposium of lectures given at the Thomas Hardy Society's summer school at Weymouth, 1973
Thomas Hardy, the poetic structure, Jean Brooks (London 1971)
Thomas Hardy and Rural England, Merryn Williams (London 1972)
Thomas Hardy and British Poetry, Donald Davie (London 1973)
The World of Thomas Hardy, Tetsuwo Maekawa (Kyoto 1974)
The Poems of Thomas Hardy, Kenneth Marsden (London 1969)
Thomas Hardy, his Career as a Novelist, Michael Millgate (London 1971)
Thomas Hardy, J. I. M. Stewart (London 1971)
Thomas Hardy, Douglas Brown (London 1951)
Tess in the Theatre, Marguerite Roberts (Toronto 1950)
Thomas Hardy, his Life and Work, F. E. Halliday (Bath 1972)
Providence and Mr Hardy, Lois Deacon & Terry Coleman (London 1968)
Hardy's Vision of Man, F. R. Southerington (London 1971)

Index

Numbers shown in italics refer to the synopsis of the work in question